HIGH STREET

Bath has a number of large scale retail developments but it's the independent retailers that attract visitors to the town.

HIGH STREET

HOW OUR TOWN CENTRES CAN BOUNCE BACK FROM THE RETAIL CRISIS

David Rudlin, Vicky Payne and Lucy Montague

RIBA Publishing

© RIBA Publishing, 2023

Published by RIBA Publishing, 66 Portland Place, London, W1B 1AD

ISBN 9781914124303

The rights of Authors David Rudlin, Vicky Payne and Lucy Montague
to be identified as the Authors of this Work have been asserted
in accordance with the Copyright, Designs and Patents Act 1988
sections 77 and 78.

British Library Cataloguing-in-Publication Data
A catalogue record for this book is available from the British Library.

Commissioning Editor: Alex White
Production: Jane Rogers
Designed and typeset by Fakenham Prepress Solutions
Printed and bound by Page Bros, Norwich
Cover image: David Rudlin, Vicky Payne and Lucy Montague.

www.ribapublishing.com

All illustrations are original and copyright of David Rudlin, Vicky
Payne and Lucy Montague.

FSC
www.fsc.org

MIX
Paper from
responsible sources
FSC® C023114

CONTENTS

ABOUT THE AUTHORS

David Rudlin is a leading urbanist and author of the book *Climax City*, winner of Urban Design Group Book of the Year in 2020. He was a director of URBED for more than 30 years and is now Director of Urbanism at BDP. He is also a past Chair of the Academy of Urbanism and in 2014 he won the Wolfson Economics Prize. Together with Vicky Payne he has recently completed the National Model Design Code for the Government.

Vicky Payne is Strategy, Research and Engagement Lead at the Quality of Life Foundation and Chair of the RTPI Urban Design Network. She co-authored the National Model Design Code with former colleagues and national government.

Dr Lucy Montague is Senior Lecturer at Manchester School of Architecture and Programme Leader of the MA Architecture & Urbanism. She researches widely across urban design and has particular expertise in research with, for and through practice. In 2019, Lucy founded the innovative URBED+ for research, advocacy and public engagement in urban design. She has previously held positions at UCL, Huddersfield and Edinburgh, and worked internationally for consultancies in masterplanning, regeneration, retail and residential.

PREFACE

The Great Exhibition, held in the Crystal Palace in Hyde Park in 1851, was a celebrated success. Not only was it widely popular, it also made a huge financial surplus. The money generated was invested in the Albert Hall, The Natural History, Science and V&A Museums, Imperial College and the Royal Colleges of Art and Music. The commission that organised the exhibition exists to this day, investing its income in supporting these institutions and funding research in science, engineering, the built environment and design. Every two years it awards a Built Environment Fellowship and this book is the result of the 2019 fellowship which focussed on the crisis on the high street.

The aim of the fellowship has been to understand a little more about the high street crisis that was already raging in 2019, with weekly news stories about the collapse of major retailers. Prophets of doom were proclaiming the high street could not survive the onslaught of online retailing and this was before COVID forced all non-essential retailers to close their doors, or indeed the cost of living crisis. Within months of us starting the work, lockdown was imposed, everyone was working from home and high streets were deserted. By the end of the year, two of the UK's largest retailers, Debenhams and Arcadia Group (owner of Topshop and many other brands), had collapsed, forcing the closure of all their stores and the acquisition of their brands by online retailers. The Centre for Retail Research has documented more than 75,000 store closures since the beginning of 2018 (up to the end of 2022) and the loss of almost 700,000 jobs.[1] It was hard to imagine that anything would ever be the same again.

Surveying the landscape of high streets' research and initiatives, there was no shortage of suggestions about what should be done. The government had allocated £1 billion to the Future High Streets Fund and local authorities were busy preparing bids to spend this money on their town centres. Strategies included environmental improvements, transport infrastructure, land assembly and capital works to diversify town centres, reuse of vacant shops and the promotion of markets and events. Nothing wrong with any of that, but was it enough given the scale of the crisis?

Our contention is that, before we prescribe the medicine, we should be sure of our diagnosis. Yes, we need to understand what is happening on high streets across the country and the socio-economic forces they are having to contend with, and yes, we need to understand previous crises that have beset the high street and how it recovered. But most of all we need to understand the diversity of high streets. We always talk about the 'high street' as if it is just one generic place, but Oxford Street in London has little in common with the high streets in Dundee, Derry or Doncaster, or with the Metrocentre in Gateshead for that matter (except, of course, that they all have a branch of Boots!). Even places that may seem similar can face radically different issues and pursue very different strategies. Sometimes the differences come down to one individual or group, who took the initiative and made things happen (or in some cases stopped things from happening).

None of these backstories are captured in national data on high streets. So we called the project Tales from the High Street, with a plan to tell the stories of 100 high streets. Working with Experian we acquired the data for the high streets covered by their town centre reports and supplemented it with interviews, site visits, local news stories and the retail assessment reports commissioned by councils every few years. We were looking for stories rather than trying to write a comprehensive case study of every place; some run to many pages while others are quick sketches. They are available online and provide far more detail than we have been able to include in this book. [2]

Our 100 case studies use a loose definition of what we mean by a high street. In addition to the 87 places shown on the map we include four general tales: IKEA, the big four supermarkets, retail parks and Aldi. We also include nine online 'high streets': Amazon, eBay, Spotify, Ocado, Boohoo, Alibaba, Etsy, Gumtree and Deliveroo.

The choice of places sought to achieve a good geographical spread and range of types of place. They include 11 large cities and regional centres, 12 smaller cities and larger towns, 35 towns, 10 smaller towns and villages, 13 high streets and suburban centres and 6 out-of-town centres. The list includes 9 coastal towns, 21 industrial towns, 24 historic towns, 7 new towns or modernist centres and 17 commuter towns, with some places ticking a number of boxes. The categorisations are useful in looking at trends in different places but are not definitive. Norwich, for example, we have in the city category because it is a regional centre whereas Bradford, which is larger, is in the small cities category because it is in the shadow of Leeds. It was also not clear what to do with places on the edge of larger cities – for example, are Bury and Solihull towns or suburban centres?

Nevertheless, the 81 places for which we have Experian data include just under 55,000 shops and 160 million ft^2 of floor space (15 million m^2 – although, in the UK, retailing is always measured in square feet). According to the Office for National Statistics there are 257,250 retail outlets in the UK so our case studies represent a 21% sample.[3] As well as showing the big picture, the data is gloriously detailed; we know how many beauty salons there are in Aberystwyth and can see how the fishmonger in Welling did not make it through COVID. We can chart the death of the video rental store alongside the modest revival in record shops and the exponential growth in 'tobacconists' (vaping shops).

The picture that emerges from our high street tales is rich and complex and – spoiler alert – doesn't really show a crisis on the high street. Some places, it is true, are really struggling but elsewhere new sectors are emerging and independents are filling the voids left by the collapsed chains. Each high street has a different story to tell and by knitting them together in this book we hope to tell an alternative story of the British high street, how it is resilient and evolving and what we can do to help it.

David Rudlin, Vicky Payne, Lucy Montague – September 2022

Cities

Smaller Cities / Larger Towns

Towns

Smaller Towns / Villages

Suburban Centres

Out-of-Town Centres

DUNDEE

Portobello · Edinburgh

Paisley

Derry

Belfast

Ashington
Gosforth
Newcastle · The Metro Centre
Carlisle
SUNDERLAND

Scarborough

Skipton · Harrogate
Todmorden · BRADFORD
Slaithwaite
PRESTON · Bury · Barnsley · Doncaster
Bootle
Liverpool · Cheadle · Manchester
Lark Lane · Trafford Centre · Stockport · Meadowhall
Garston · Altrincham · Sheffield
Chester · Eccleshall Rd · Lincoln
Winsford
Trentham Gardens · Nottingham
WREXHAM · Stafford
Wisbech
Belgrave Rd · Norwich
Leicester
WOLVERHAMPTON
Ladywood Rd · Birmingham · Corby
Aberystwyth · Solihull · COVENTRY
Cambourne · Cambridge
Cardiff
MILTON KEYNES
Colchester
Gloucester · Bicester Village · Aylesbury · Chelmsford
Stroud · Uxbridge
SWANSEA · Cwmbran · London · London
St Marks Road · Marylebone · Westfield
Bristol · Kingston upon Thames · Welling
Bath · Peckham · Canterbury
Frome · READING · Dover
Epsom
Winchester · Guildford · Tunbridge Wells
Exeter
BOURNEMOUTH · BRIGHTON
Totnes
Penzance

INTRODUCTION

L et us start in the bar of Kommune in Sheffield, a vast bar/food hall on the ground floor of the old Co-operative Department Store (Co-op) in Sheffield. The publicity blurb tells us that Kommune is an 'innovative concept that brings together some of the most acclaimed, independent kitchens, brewers and retailers in a unique, urban space'.[1] That said, it is the sort of space you will find in many of the towns and cities we write about in this book ... all exposed plumbing and upcycled furniture, sourdough pizzas and craft beer often occupying former mainstream retail space.

SHEFFIELD, THE CITY THAT LOST ITS SHOPS

The Co-op was one of five vast department stores in the Castlegate district of Sheffield City Centre. Local hero Jarvis Cocker was taken there as a kid, reminiscing to *The World of Interiors* magazine about being allowed to look at the fish tank 'as a reward for not causing too much trouble during a shopping expedition.'[2] The unfortunate fish were set within the wall of a subway in Castle Square – a 'bold' piece of late 1960s modernist planning at the heart of Castlegate, with a heavily trafficked roundabout at ground level and pedestrian subways dominated by a dramatic oculus (a circular opening in the centre of the roundabout which was dubbed by locals 'the hole in the road'). The designers were apparently going for a 'Japanese style' underground city with the C&A and Walsh's department stores taking their main entrance from the subway level. As Jarvis went on to say: 'When it was first built, I guess it was seen as a symbol of Sheffield's determination to be a "city of the future", but it soon became the favourite hang-out of the local wino population.'

The Co-op's extraordinary early 1960s building was the finest and largest of the department stores in the area. Designed by the Co-op's in-house architects, it stood at the top of Angel Street with a windowless black granite facade below a 'floating' concrete roof with a zigzag canopy over the pavement. Across the road once stood the Peter Robinson department store where, in the 1960s, an enterprising merchandise manager called Tony Colman rebranded the fashion department as Topshop (because it was on the top floor).[3] With the explosion of fashion and the burgeoning spending power of young people, Topshop grew and grew, eventually subsuming the rather fusty Peter Robinson brand to become the UK's leading fashion retailer.

Nearby was Sheffield's main Burton store, a company also created in Sheffield. Montague Burton, a Lithuanian immigrant, opened his first store in 1903 believing that 'good clothes develop a man's self-respect'. He catered initially for the city's steelworkers who would hire a suit for the weekend or go 'the Full Monty', as they called it. Both Topshop and Burton became part of Philip Green's Arcadia empire which collapsed at the end of 2020, but long before this they had departed this part of Sheffield. Another of the area's department stores, British Homes Stores (BHS), was the scene of the Dominic Chappell pensions scandal and closed in 2016. The

C&A closed after the company withdrew from the UK market in 2000 and Walsh's, which was Sheffield's House of Fraser store, closed in 1998 long before the group was bought out of administration by Mike Ashley.

Our story therefore starts in a city centre that no longer really exists, at least not as a shopping destination to which the young Jarvis could be dragged by his mum. The city has big plans for the Castlegate district, as Simon Ogden, former regeneration manager of the city told us.[4] They include a park on the site of the original castle, the redevelopment of the old market and the promotion of the sort of independent businesses found in the old Co-op store. But the plans don't include mainstream retailing, as local butcher Anthony Birks told the BBC: 'Castlegate hasn't been the centre of town from a retail point of view for some 30 years ... [it] used to be the centre of the universe but now it's bypassed.'[5]

Castlegate stands at one end of what used to be an exceptionally long retail drag in Sheffield. So long was the shopping centre that many chains (Woolworths, Marks & Spencer, BHS, Co-op and Littlewoods) maintained two branches in the city. So, before we write off Sheffield as a shopping centre, we should explore the rest of the city's retail spine that once stretched from the Co-op department store to Moorfoot nearly two miles away.

Some attribute the city's retail problems to an ill-fated attempt during the war to divert a bombing raid away from the city's steelworks. The unfortunate result was that the bombs fell instead on the city centre, the damage severing its retail spine in two places. Post-war planners exploited the gaps by constructing a dual carriageway inner ring road called the 'Civic Circle' with no sense of irony. This was the road that trundled around the 'hole in the road' and it had the effect of chopping the city's retail spine into three distinct pieces: Castlegate, Fargate and The Moor.

Let us walk up to Coles Corner at the end of Fargate. Coles Corner was immortalised by another Sheffield songsmith, Richard Hawley, as the place where young men used to wait nervously for their date outside the old Coles Brothers department store. The store was a Sheffield institution, established by silk merchants and hosiers John and Thomas Cole in 1869. The company was later bought by Selfridges and then in 1940 by John Lewis, to which we will return.

Fargate is where you will find Marks & Spencer, Boots and WHSmith. Until recently, it was the city's 'Zone A' retail area where the highest rents were to be commanded. This was the home of fashion retailers including Topshop, New Look, H&M, Next and River Island. Topshop is no longer with us, following the collapse of Arcadia, and the other fashion stores have largely moved away. A *Sheffield Star* article in August 2020 suggested that 25% of the shops on Fargate were vacant, while the remainder included five banks and six phone shops.[6] Fargate is still just about holding on as a shopping street, but it is touch and go. A partnership between the University and the City has secured £15.8 million from the government's Future High Streets Fund to regenerate the area, the aim being to repurpose the street away from a reliance on retailing by introducing residential and employment uses, digital infrastructure and outdoor events.

The bad news continues as we leave Fargate and walk past the Town Hall to Barker's Pool where we find the John Lewis building, an elegant modernist structure erected in 1963 on a site that was rather off-pitch in terms of the city's retailing at the time. But if you are Coles, or more to the point John Lewis (the store name was not changed until 2002), you can trade wherever you want. As the store manager told us when we visited in 2014, its affluent clientele used to drive in from the

Fargate Sheffield:
Once Sheffield's premier shopping street, Fargate has lost many of its fashion retailers and is barely holding on as a retail location.

Peak District in their Range Rovers and Jaguars, park in the store's multistorey car park, walk over a bridge into the store, to do their shopping and head home without venturing into the rest of the city centre.[7] Nevertheless, it was a major achievement for Sheffield to have a John Lewis at a time when the company hadn't yet opened branches in Manchester, Leeds or Birmingham.

For the last 25 years, the council had been trying to capitalise on its John Lewis by making the store an anchor for a new shopping centre that has variously been called the 'New Retail Quarter', 'Seven Stones' and the 'Heart of the City II'. It was a scheme conceived in the mid-1990s when a report by Hillier Parker and the Oxford Institute of Retail Management brought home to the council the damage that the Meadowhall shopping centre was doing to the city centre.[8] At one point the scheme included a brand-new John Lewis store together with a $100,000\text{ft}^2$ ($9,300\text{m}^2$) Next, 100 other shops, leisure uses and a 10-storey car park. Planning was granted in 2006 but the scheme fell foul of the 2008 financial crisis. Afterwards there was a major redesign precipitated by John Lewis announcing that it would retain its existing

The Moor in the 1970s when it was still open to traffic and ran out of the city centre into south Sheffield.

store. The council's development partner Hammerson pulled out in 2013, but still the council pressed on. Work finally started on a first phase in 2019, the main part of which was taken up with a new office block for HSBC. It included a couple of large retail units and an upmarket café bar but is no longer a retail-led scheme.

Then, in July 2020, towards the end of the first COVID lockdown, the unthinkable happened. John Lewis announced its Sheffield store was being considered for closure along with its Birmingham and Luton branches. The council moved quickly and decisively, agreeing a £3 million package to buy the building and lease it back to John Lewis on a 'turnover rent'. There was a good deal of scrutiny in the local press about whether this spending could be justified given the other pressing needs in the city, but John Lewis was so important to the survival of Sheffield as a retail centre that drastic measures were required. It wasn't enough; within seven months John Lewis had announced a further eight store closures, the Sheffield branch included, leaving the city feeling bereft and betrayed.

Walking south from the now-vacant John Lewis store, there is a sense that we have reached the edge of the retail centre, but have patience – this is the second break in the spine exploited by post-war planners. If we press on through the construction site of the HSBC offices we eventually will come to The Moor – Sheffield's other retail street, anchored, until recently, by a Debenhams department store.

The Moor was originally part of a street that ran for miles out of the city along the London Road through south Sheffield. The top end of the street was so successful that it became part of the city centre with a Burtons, Woolworths, its own Marks & Spencer, the independent Atkinson's department store and Debenhams. The street was rebuilt after wartime bombing and was pedestrianised in 1979. Later the huge Moorfoot office block was built across the southern end of the street, with

an archway for pedestrians that was unfortunately closed due to security concerns, blocking the street.

Like the rest of Sheffield, The Moor struggled in the 1990s as its Habitat, Hamleys and Marks & Spencer closed, and other retailers were lured by the bright lights of Meadowhall. However, since then a partnership between the council as freeholder and Scottish Widows as leaseholder has seen a programme of investment that means it is now the one bright spot on our walk through the city centre. The city's main markets have been relocated from Castlegate to a new building at the southern end of The Moor. Refurbished and new buildings have attracted the fashion retailers from Fargate and a new Primark has opened, along with a leisure scheme in the former Woolworths including a cinema, restaurants and a bowling alley.

This is what remains of Sheffield's once celebrated retail drag. The successive retail crises that we describe in the first part of this book have effectively killed off the city as a major shopping destination. This is something that we can see in many US cities, but in the UK is relatively rare, particularly in a city the size of Sheffield. We should stress that Sheffield is no basket case. Elsewhere the City Council has been very effective at promoting development and regeneration, including the Peace and Winter Gardens, the Heart of the City scheme, Sheaf Square, Grey to Green, the Cultural Industries Quarter and Kelham Island. All of these have been widely acclaimed as good practice and Sheffield is generally considered a competent council. But in terms of its shopping centre, the last 30 years have been a disaster. So, what happened 30 years ago?

On 9 September 1990 the doors opened on what, at the time, was the second largest out-of-town regional shopping centre in the UK. Built on the site of the East

Hecla steelworks, 10 miles away from the city centre, it contained 1.5 million ft^2 (140,000m^2) of retail space with 280 stores and 12,000 parking spaces.

The history of Meadowhall, as told in Sheffield, is that it was imposed on the city by a government-sponsored development corporation in the face of local opposition, but the truth is more complicated. Back in the 1980s, Sheffield was known as 'The People's Republic of South Yorkshire'. It was coined as a damning criticism by Max Williams in the *Yorkshire Evening Post*, but was taken up as a badge of honour by the council who flew a red flag over the town hall on May Day and declared the city a nuclear-free and demilitarised zone. However, they could not stem the catastrophic decline of the city's steel industry, which lost almost two-thirds of its jobs over the course of the decade, leaving vast areas of dereliction.

In desperation and against its better judgement, the council turned to the private sector. One of the only prospects at the time with the capacity to create a significant number of jobs was a new breed of regional shopping centres encouraged by the free market Conservative Government under Margaret Thatcher (as we describe in Chapter 3). At the time, there were proposals for 50 of these vast shopping centres in the UK, including two near Sheffield: Parkgate in Rotherham and the East Hecla site in Sheffield. As Les Sturch, Sheffield's then Director of Planning, told the BBC many years later: 'Rotherham had already decided to go for something big out at Parkgate so Sheffield was going to suffer one way or the other ... the question was where would that be.'[9] The city decided that the promised 10,000 jobs may as well be in Sheffield.

Meadowhall shopping centre:
Built on the site of a former steelworks on the edge of Sheffield, it may have brought jobs to an area of deprivation but it has done huge damage to Sheffield City Centre as a shopping destination.

Planning permission was granted in 1987, a year before the Government imposed a development corporation on the city. Indeed, the council at the time was irritated that the development corporation would take the credit for Meadowhall. In a further irony, the Sheffield planners insisted that the new mall be accessible by train, bus, tram and cycle, as well as having a vast car park, making it the most accessible location in the region with its own transport interchange. There were concerns, of course, about the impact on the city centre, but the council took comfort from the way that Newcastle held its own against the Metrocentre, and pointed to plans to build three new shopping schemes in the city centre – the planners concluded that Sheffield would also be OK. Unfortunately, the town centre schemes foundered and Sheffield was not OK. It was left uniquely ill-prepared to deal with a new mega mall on its doorstep attracting 30 million visitors a year.

In the early 1990s, when we were doing research on town centres, there were anecdotal stories that trade in Sheffield City Centre had dropped by a third on the opening of Meadowhall and that retailers were only remaining in the city centre because they were tied into leases.[10] An impact study undertaken by Elisabeth Howard in 1993 found that Meadowhall was attracting about 12% of shopping trips in the region and that Sheffield City Centre's share of shopping trips had fallen from 23.3% to 18%.[11] What is more, average spend per trip was £50 in Meadowhall, more than twice the average in Sheffield (so the anecdotal reports may not have been far off).

DIAGNOSIS BEFORE TREATMENT

Sheffield is a good place to start when diagnosing what ails the high street. The city shows how traditional town centres are at the mercy of economic forces over which they have little control – making it impossible to hang on to a John Lewis store, however much money is offered, or to realise long-nurtured plans to build a new shopping centre no matter how much they are needed. Councils like Sheffield get the blame, and it is true that there are always things that can, or could, have been done better, since some places have weathered the storm better than others. However, it is important to recognise that town centres are more often the victims of the crisis on the high street rather than its cause.

The aim of this book is to understand the wider trends affecting our high streets and to explore what built environment professionals can do about them. Public policy has been working to revitalise our high streets since at least the mid-1990s, with varying degrees of success. Too often we have been proposing town centre strategies without fully understanding the problems they face. As part of the research for this book, we have delved deeply into the literature on retailing and it is clear there is a world out there that built environment professionals are only dimly aware of. In 2020, the retail sector employed 2.9 million people and its 200,000 VAT registered retailers turned over £403 billion.[12] This overlaps with the hospitality sector, which employs 3.2 million people, the third largest employment sector in the UK.[13] Unless we understand these huge industries, we will continue to prescribe treatment for our town centres and high streets without having done a proper diagnosis of the problems they face.

To give just one example, planners have for years assessed the success of a town centre based on its retail ranking. Systems like Venuescore rank town centres based directly or indirectly on the number of multiple retailers.[14] Retail consultants are commissioned to undertake retail assessments, pointing out that the town centre is slipping down the rankings (often because a rival centre has built a covered shopping centre).[15] The consultants point out that the town is unable to offer the large modern units required by multiple retailers and is therefore 'missing' some of the top 100 retailers that you would expect to find in a town of its size. The recommendation is generally that the town should build its own shopping centre to make itself more 'competitive'. It is the story of several case studies detailed in this book, such as Stafford, Bradford, Wrexham and Bury. Unlike Sheffield, these places managed to build their new shopping centres, often anchored by a Debenhams department store. Now, with older parts of the town abandoned by retailers who moved into the new centre, and with the new centre struggling without its anchor store and other key retailers like Topshop, the advice doesn't seem so sensible. Town centres have found themselves competing with each other for a shrinking pool of retailers while doing damage to their existing centres. So, new reports are written, suggesting that the solution to these problems is to plant more trees or to change the paving in the town square.

Our objective is to explore the wider economic trends that lie behind the crisis on the high street, to better diagnose the problem and feed into more informed decision-making. In doing this, we take the long view of the crises that have beset our high streets going back to the emergence of the supermarkets after the Second World War. Since that time – and probably long before – town centres have seemingly been in a cycle of regular crises. Each generation worries about the death of the high street, and yet, within a few years, they have bounced back stronger than ever. Entire retail sectors, which seemed like they would last for ever, have disappeared, but others have emerged to take their place. This would probably almost certainly have been true of the current crisis that started in 2018. The threat of the internet, like the threats in the past of supermarkets and out-of-town malls, would have done their worst, but town centres would have evolved and bounced back. Then came COVID lockdowns and social distancing and the question is being asked whether this has put us in a different place? Will the current crisis change retailing and town centres forever? Will some places never recover?

Sheffield may be an extreme example of a post-retail city, but it is also a good place to start because, despite its decline as a shopping centre, it is thriving as a city. It is a centre for culture, music and leisure, and has a lively creative and small business sector. It has two strong universities, is a leader in advanced manufacturing and a great night out. Sheffield is important to our story, not because it has failed as a retail centre but because it has thrived *without* its retailing.

FROM WOOLWORTHS TO VICTORIA'S SECRETS: THE CRISIS ON THE HIGH STREET

Before we go further, it is worth taking a moment to understand a bit more about the current high street crisis. Figures from the Centre for Retail Research show that retail job losses were running at 117,000 in 2018, 143,000 in 2019, 182,000 in 2020 and 106,000 in 2021.[16] Data from the early part of 2022 suggested that the trend was slowing, although it appears that this was a post-lockdown bounce. The figures released at the end of 2022 showed 151,474 job losses, almost as bad as the peak of the crisis, probably as a result of the cost of living crisis. Over this period there have been just over 75,000 store closures, although the trend is changing, with 80% of these closures in 2018 being the result of companies closing down whereas in 2022, 68% of closures were as a result of rationalisation. The view was that the multiples that have survived the crisis were now putting their houses in order by closing down unprofitable stores.

Since 2007, there have been 558 retail company failures, the roll-call including: Woolworths, Blacks Leisure and MFI in 2008, Zavvi and Ethel Austin in 2009, JJB Sports, Peacocks and Game in 2012, Comet, Blockbuster and HMV in 2013 and BHS in 2016. There was a brief respite before the collapse of Toys'R'Us, Maplin, Poundworld and House of Fraser in 2018 (along with HMV for a second time). 2019 saw the demise of Jessops, Clinton Cards, Mothercare, Bonmarché, Thomas Cook Travel (with 560 branches), Karen Millen, Jack Wills and Debenhams, which entered administration in April although 115 of its 165 stores continued to trade. In 2020, we lost Beales department store, Oddbins, Laura Ashley, Cath Kidston, Oasis, Warehouse, Harveys Furniture and Bensons Beds, Edinburgh Woollen Mill, Peacocks and Jaeger. The Arcadia Group also collapsed including Topshop, Dorothy Perkins, Burton, Miss Selfridge and Wallis, which together had branches on virtually every high street. 2020 saw the final demise of Debenhams with the closure of all its stores and the collapse of Intu, owner of 13 shopping centres including Lakeside, Manchester's Trafford Centre and both shopping centres in Nottingham. In 2021, the rate of closures seemed to have slowed. We have lost Paperchase, Victoria's Secrets and a number of smaller chains but the great retail clearance sale seemed to be coming to an end.

Of course, many of these familiar high street names have not disappeared. Some have been bought out of administration: House of Fraser is still trading and seeking to reinvent itself under the ownership of Mike Ashley; HMV (as we describe in Chapter 10) is under new ownership and confident it can return to profit after two collapses; Jaeger was bought by Marks & Spencer but its stores were all closed. Online retailer Boohoo bought Debenhams together with the Arcadia brands Burton, Dorothy Perkins and Wallis, while ASOS bought Topshop and Miss Selfridge. These will be online brands from now on, with their hundreds of stores all having been closed.

The reason for this crisis has been much debated. Back in 2012, when retail guru Mary Portas was appointed to lead a review into the future of Britain's high streets, she was dealing with the tail end of 2008 financial crisis, which had a huge impact on retailers. The situation was already improving when she produced her report and the years 2013–17 were a period of relative prosperity for retailers, with increasing consumer spending. Then in 2018, the retail crisis returned as if out of a clear sky, unconnected to problems in the wider economy. It is true that the level of internet shopping had continued to rise, the 2017 business rates revaluation was a factor, policies like the minimum wage were pushing up costs and the weak pound was increasing the costs of imports. Yet none of these really explain the 2018 crisis. What seems to have happened is that years of complacency and under-investment had left the retail sector vulnerable and that a tipping point had been reached (as we discuss in Chapter 4).

THE IMPACT ON THE HIGH STREET

These wider economic problems may not have originated on the high street but it is where the most obvious effects are to be seen. The British Retail Consortium's Local Data Company Vacancy Monitor indicated that the vacancy rate on the high street peaked at 14.5% in the second quarter of 2021, just over 2% higher than the same quarter in 2020.[17] The highest vacancy rates (19.5%) were in shopping centres, most exposed to the collapse of the big retail brands. The high street was doing better, with a vacancy rate of 14.1%, while retail parks, taking advantage of customers avoiding public transport and city centres, had 11.1% of their units

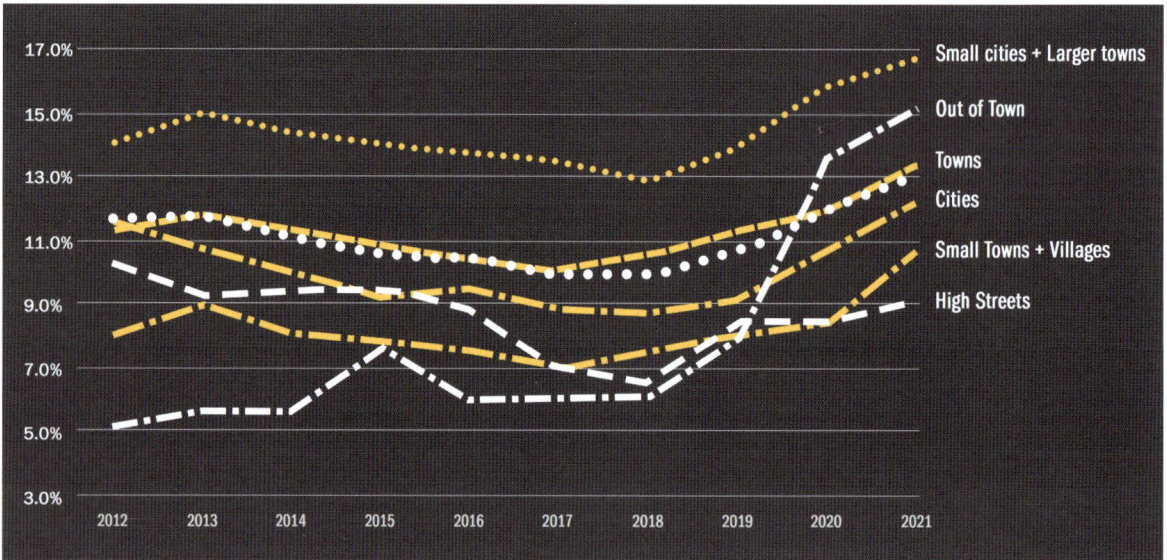

Vacancy rates by type of centre: This graph shows the percentage of units vacant in our case studies, based on data from Experian.

vacant, although this was also rising. The latest data at the time of writing (covering the first quarter of 2022) shows a small drop in these vacancy figures, with the overall rate dropping to 14.1% and shopping centres down to 19%.

Data from the 100 case studies that have fed into this book show a slightly lower vacancy rate.[18,19] It was 11.7% in 2012, fell to 10% in 2017 and then started to rise again pre-COVID, spiking at 13.2% in early 2022. The overall trend was the same across all categories but what is striking is the way that out-of-town malls have gone from having the lowest vacancy rate to the second highest, while high streets and suburban centres have been affected least of all.

When the media discusses these issues, they use 'high street' as a catch-all term to describe all physical retailing (sometimes using the equally misleading term 'bricks and mortar retailing'). By contrast, when built environment professionals use the term 'high street' they are referring to a traditional type of place: a town, city or suburban centre or an arterial route lined with shops. Much of the media talk about the 'crisis on the high street' therefore refers to locations that built environment professionals would not recognise as being high streets, indeed much of it is out-of-town and is as much of a threat to our high streets as the internet.

The vacancy figures don't always help in this respect. They break down the data into 'high streets', 'shopping centres' and 'retail parks', the last of which is almost certainly out-of-town. But shopping centres are not so clear-cut. In the US, shopping malls were generally built in the suburbs and the damage to traditional downtowns was severe and sometimes terminal. In the UK, notwithstanding mega malls like Meadowhall, policy has dictated that many UK shopping malls have been built in town centres, so the figures for shopping centres include space that is both in-town and out-of-town.

Most retail data is collected by sector rather than by location, which means it is not easy to understand the split between in-town and out-of-town space. The Portas Review drew on data from 2011 from various sources to suggest that 42.5% of retail spend in the UK was in town centres, a further 16% was 'neighbourhood sales' (local high streets) while just under a third was out-of-town.[20] Even with the subsequent growth of online retail it is likely that pre-lockdown, 50p in every retail pound was spent in traditional town centres or high streets.

The big change since then has been the growth in online retail, which had risen from 8.3% in 2011 to 19.2% just before the first lockdown,[21] a level exceeded only by China and South Korea.[22] During the pandemic, online sales have, inevitably, been much higher, peaking at 46.2% of non-food sales during the first lockdown while the average for all sales in 2021 was 30.7%.[23] It is not yet clear where this figure will settle once things are back to normal and post-lockdown bounces have worked their way through the system.

However, what these figures do tell us is that the UK high street is far from moribund and that even now it takes a greater share of retail spending than either out-of-town or online retailing. The question is, how does it need to evolve to protect and consolidate this position? One thing is clear, it is not going to involve building very much new retailing. Research from Savills suggests that the UK may have 40% more retail space than it can support.[24] Retail analyst Mike Prew told the *Financial Times*: 'Our working assumption is rents will fall 30 per cent from current levels. And you have to shrink the floor space by 30 per cent as well, meaning a 51 per cent cut of incomes from the shopping centre.'[25]

This suggests a drastic change to our high streets and, of course, the impact will depend on how the reduction in floorspace is distributed. Before the pandemic, the assumption had been that retailing would concentrate in the big city centres. Retailers would once have needed 400–500 shops to cover the whole of Great Britain. Now with greater mobility and online sales they can achieve the same coverage with 80–100 stores, which is bad news for any town centre outside the top 100 – or so it was thought. And yet during the pandemic the tables have been turned, with the big cities, deprived of their office workers and tourists, doing particularly badly compared to suburban centres that are able to tap the homeworking market. No centre is therefore immune to these changes and the next few years will be critical. A centre that gets things wrong, as Sheffield did, could find itself facing a future without, or at least with far less, retail. It will therefore need to reinvent itself (as Sheffield has done) or face collapse.

* * *

This book is divided into three sections. In Part 1, we take the long view of the crises on the high street. In Chapter 1, we look at the emergence of the retail sector and consumer society in the Victorian period. We trace the history of markets and shopping arcades and the origins of the great department stores. In Chapter 2, we look at the first great challenge to what many people still regard as the archetypal high street of butchers, bakers and grocers, with the emergence of the self-service supermarket. In Chapter 3, we look at the crisis of the 1990s when a relaxation of planning controls allowed the building of a series of huge out-of-town regional shopping centres and hundreds of retail parks, threatening the existence of the high street. In Chapter 4 we trace the roots of the current crisis from the boom of the clone town years of the early 2000s to the bust of the financial crisis, a brief recovery and then the onset of the current crisis and how the pandemic has made it much worse.

Part 2 looks at future trends in retail and leisure and is organised like a department store. Chapters 5 to 11 cover the grocery business, fashion and beauty, home and garden, music and film, restaurants and bars, the independent sector along with the emergence of the internet giants of Amazon, Alibaba and eBay and their impact on the high street. In each case we explore how the sector has evolved, the pressures it currently faces and how it is adapting.

Part 3 looks at the future high street and how these trends will potentially affect different types of retail centre. Chapters 12–15 cover the City, the Mall, the Town and the High Street. Drawing upon tales from our 100 case studies, we describe how places are dealing with the retail crisis and draw out lessons that others can learn.

In the conclusion, we pull these strands together to paint a vision for the future high street and how it might be achieved. This is not intended as a handbook or good practice guide. Our hope is that it goes a little way to bringing together the worlds of retail and the built environment to develop a shared agenda for the revival of high streets that are so important both to our economy and the life and spirit of our communities.

Harrogate: Every town has its own story that the national data doesn't capture. Harrogate's centre is large and affluent because of its conference trade and while it was affected by lockdown it has benefitted from homeworking.

Solihull to the south of
Birmingham has one of
the largest catchment
areas in our case
studies but one of the
lowest percentage of
independent shops.

PART 1

THE ROOT OF THE CRISIS

We often act as if the current crisis is the first to affect the high street and yet, town centres are in a process of perpetual change, some might say crisis. This is not the first time that the death of the high street has been predicted and probably won't be the last. In the first part of this book we explore the history of our high streets to better understand the roots of the current crisis.

1 PLACES OF EXCHANGE

For centuries the high street was pretty much all there was to Skipton – a wide street running from the gates of the castle with a market charter dating back to 1203. Halfway along what was once a single wide street now stands a narrow row of buildings. These were originally market stalls whose traders, at some point in the distant past, were granted permanent rights over their pitch allowing them to erect buildings. Similar phenomena can be found in many market towns such as Ludlow and Chesterfield and an argument could be made that these were some of the first shops.

SKIPTON: THE ORIGINS OF A MARKET TOWN

These shops in Skipton are now occupied by estate agents, well-known retail chains, a pub and a couple of cafés. Such is the history of our town centres, most of which have their origins as markets but which have been taken over by mainstream retailers. Skipton has done better than most, being cited by the New Economics Foundation as an example of a place that has resisted becoming a 'clone town' dominated by the same chain stores that are found in every town.[1] Our data shows that 70% of the retailers in the town are independents, even before the closure of the town's House of Fraser department store, Edinburgh Woollen Mill and Laura Ashley.

Unlike many market towns, Skipton's market still plays a central role and gives an insight into what all towns were once like. As Kevin Reid-Griffiths, Skipton's town crier, told the *Daily Telegraph*, 'we have a market here most days where you can buy everything from cheese, meat and vegetables to car parts and telephones'.[2] The market has no fixed stalls and operates on a first-come-first-served basis and so is not particularly pretty. There are none of the striped awnings and picturesque market furniture that you find elsewhere; the attraction of Skipton's market comes from its vitality and variety and the activity that it generates.

To accommodate the market the street is divided into three strips: the road, which carries traffic even when the market is on, the footpaths that run in front of the shops, and between the two, the 'setts'. The latter look like cobbled parking spaces – which is what they are when the stalls have been packed away – but their main function is to accommodate the market. The stalls face away from the road, trading towards the shops so that the space becomes two shopping streets on market days, creating a circuit that would be recognisable to any shopping centre developer. In a final innovation passed down through history, the rent paid by each stall goes to the adjacent shop owner rather than the market authority, creating a

Skipton High Street with its market dating back to 1203 may not be pretty but its appeal comes from its vitality.

symbiotic relationship between retailer and stallholder. This is how all towns used to be, centres of exchange long before the advent of the retail chains.

THE ORIGINS OF TRADE

Archaeological finds from Northern Europe, dating back 30,000 years, include shells from the Mediterranean. This is clear evidence of trade long before the first settlements when humans were still hunter-gatherers. Yuval Noah Harari, in his book *Sapiens*, suggests that trade is one of the features that distinguished humans from Neanderthals.[3] He describes how 10,000 years ago the agricultural revolution created food surpluses, population growth and the foundation of the first villages, towns and eventually cities. These first settlements couldn't have existed without trade; the townspeople trading goods and services for food from the surrounding countryside. These early towns also traded in more exotic goods imported along trade routes from distant lands. To facilitate this trade these early settlements included the first retail outlets, merchants' premises and markets. Urbanisation and retailing go hand in hand, and one wouldn't have been possible without the other.

In Britain the 'market town', like Skipton, is the embodiment of this union of urbanism and trade. A law by Edward the Elder in the 10th century decreed 'no one shall buy or sell except in a market town'.[4] At the time, most towns were market towns, separated by a day's walk (so that most of the population could walk to market and back in a day). The markets operated daily in the larger towns and at least weekly in the smallest, allowing farmers to sell their produce and to spend any surplus on goods and services from the townspeople.

Winchester: A town that was Alfred the Great's capital with its town clock presented by Queen Anne in 1731.

Deptford High Street:
Like many London centres the street supports a lively and slightly chaotic market that dates back centuries.

There were also fairs that happened once a year, often on religious festivals. Most towns had a fair, but some grew to be huge and lasted for weeks, with their own laws, systems of weights and measures and even courts. The biggest were the Stamford Fair at Lent, St Ives at Easter, Boston in July, Winchester in September and Northampton in November. These fairs attracted merchants from across Europe and were the forum where international trade was transacted until the merchants of London took control in the 15th century.

These fairs may have been huge but they left no permanent structures. The first retail structures were built for the daily and weekly markets for the 'poore market folkes to stande dry when rayne cummith'.[5] Market crosses like the one in Malmesbury, where this quote comes from, provided shelter for regular traders. Open-sided market halls were also constructed, sometimes with a guildhall or court on the upper floor. The oldest surviving shop in the UK is purported to be the 'Jew's House' in Lincoln which dates from 1170. Abbey Row cottages near Tewkesbury Abbey date from the late Middle Ages and were originally a row of 20 small shops that would have been let to tradespeople and artisans. By Tudor times many towns like Winchester had developed high streets, lined with shops and inns, some even developing covered arcades like the Butterwalk in Totnes or the Rows in Chester.[6]

THE BIRTH OF MODERN RETAILING

The pattern of retailing that dominates our high streets today is the result of the retail revolution that started in the 18th century, driven by changes in society particularly the emergence of a middle class. New industries like silk manufacturing, ceramics, glass-making and metalwork created luxury goods in an era when people with disposable incomes started to see shopping as a leisure activity rather than a necessity. The middle classes indulged in the new fashionable activity of buying things they didn't really need, as well as items that were far more expensive and elaborate than their function dictated. Luxury goods became status symbols, so that a finely wrought snuffbox or cane would denote membership of polite society. Manufacturers like Wedgwood exploited this by producing bespoke products for the aristocracy in the knowledge that their tastes would filter down to the 'aspirant' classes where they could sell their mass-produced goods. The fashion industry was also established at this time, creating a constant demand for consumers seeking the most up-to-date look while creating a built-in obsolescence of perfectly serviceable clothes that were unwearable once they became last year's fashion.

The consumer society brought with it a revolution in the design of retail premises. The early shops would have been open-fronted, trading directly into the street with wooden shutters that were closed at night. However, the 18th century saw the invention of plate glass, leading to the shopfront and window displays, together with the radical idea of letting customers come into the shop to browse the goods on offer. Over the course of the 19th century these trends created a number of new forms of retailing:

The shopping arcade
Middle-class shoppers demanded pavements where they were protected from traffic, mud and other unpleasantness. Over time this demand evolved into shopping arcades, protected from the weather and often also by security guards from the 'lower' classes. The first modern shopping arcade was le Passage du Caire, built in Paris in 1798, while the Burlington Arcade in London opened in 1818 as a glazed shopping street lined with luxury retailers and guarded by its own police force. The aim was to create a safe, exclusive environment for genteel society, particularly women, who could shop unaccompanied in arcades (and department stores) without risking their reputation. In the mid-1800s there was a boom in shopping arcades and most UK cities have examples, the largest collection being those in Cardiff which make up much of the city centre. The grandest arcades ever built are the Galleria Vittorio Emanuele II in Milan, completed in 1877.

Covered markets
The 19th century also saw the use of cast iron technology to build large indoor markets, which were aimed at a very different type of clientele. The earliest of these was St John's Market in Liverpool (1822), while the first to have a glass roof was Birkenhead (1845). Soon every Victorian city and large town was building increasingly ornate covered markets such as Kirkgate Market in Leeds (pictured), where Michael Marks established a stall that would become Marks & Spencer. Most markets had permanent stalls in the centre of the space, while the walls were lined with small shops and cafés as well as around balconies on the upper floors. The markets allowed new retail businesses to become established and M&S is not the only household name to have its origins in a market stall. Jack Cohen started selling groceries from a market stall in East London and when he later bought a shipment of tea he created the brand 'Tesco Tea'. Morrisons was a stall in Rawson Market in Bradford from 1899 until 1952, when the founder's 21-year-old son Ken Morrison took over the business and decided to expand. Julian Dunkerton started out in the 1980s on a stall in Cheltenham market which evolved into the Superdry retail brand. Meanwhile in Manchester a young Mahmud Kamani was cutting his teeth on a market stall owned by his Kenyan refugee father which sold handbags, before going on to develop a business empire that would become Boohoo. The Victorian covered

Kirkgate Market Leeds: One of the grandest municipal markets in the UK and the place where Marks & Spencer started.

markets were the malls of their day, catering to the masses rather than the middle classes; most were publicly owned, built and managed by local councils.

Chain retailers

Many of the retail chains that came to dominate town centres in the 20th century can trace back their roots to the great Victorian retail boom. In addition to the retailers who started as market stalls, most of the big department stores date from this period, as does the oldest of our supermarkets, Sainsbury's, founded in 1869 in Drury Lane, London. Lipton was founded two years later and grew to 500 stores by the end of the century before being eaten up by competitors, the name only surviving as a brand of tea.

Boots started as a family herbal medicine store in 1849 in Nottingham before growing into a multinational pharmaceutical company and a chain of shops with almost 2,500 branches. WHSmith is older still, starting as a news vendor in Little Grosvenor Street in 1792. As is often the case it was the second generation of Smiths who expanded the business, opening a store in Euston Station in 1848 and then riding the great railway expansion to open stores in railway stations across the country. The company now has 1,100 stores, of which 560 are to be found in stations, airports and motorway service areas.

Other stores were imports, including Woolworths that started in 1879 in the US as a syndicate of six retail chains with shared purchasing. In the early 20th century the chains merged and floated on the stock market, the company becoming so powerful that its new headquarters in New York was, for a time, the world's tallest building, all paid for in cash. The first Woolworths in the UK was opened in Liverpool in 1909, and by the time of its collapse in 2009 there were just over 800 Woolworths stores in the UK.

These chain stores may be well-loved brands but the process by which they emerged in the late 19th century was anything but friendly. Woolworths pioneered the 'five and dime' format, undercutting and putting out of business their local competitors. The rise of these retail giants was similar to the more recent growth of online retailers as a small number of companies captured a large market share at the expense of their smaller rivals. However, for the most ruthless companies to emerge from the 19th century retail revolution, we need to turn to the department stores.

Department stores

The pinnacle of the 19th-century retail revolution was the department store. These great palaces of consumption were, in their economic impact, the Amazon of their day, publishing catalogues and using the newly international postal service to ship their goods to all corners of Empire. The earliest department stores, like arcades, were targeted at the newly wealthy middle classes and particularly at women who were able to shop unaccompanied in the safe environment that the stores provided. However, over time, department stores expanded to serve a mass market, being described by HG Wells in *The History of Mr Polly* as 'those large, rather low-class establishments that sell everything from plants and furniture to books and millinery'.[7] Indeed, the chairman of the very grand Browns of Chester admitted that

St Pancras Station: The expansion of the railways from the 1840s onwards helped WH Smiths become a national retail brand. Today stations like St Pancras are major shopping centres in their own right.

OXFORD STREET

Oxford Street was once a muddy track along which convicts were paraded to the gallows at Tyburn. It was as London expanded and the stylish districts of Mayfair and Marylebone were developed that Oxford Street emerged as a shopping destination. A German visitor, Sophie von La Roche, described in 1784 how she had walked 'for half an hour past brilliantly illuminated windows, with pavements of people standing six deep'. By 1800 there were so many shops selling women's fashions that it became known as the 'Ladies' Mile'.[8]

Towards the end of the 19th century the street evolved with the arrival of department stores: Marshall & Snelgrove (which later became Debenhams), Bourne & Hollingsworth, Waring & Gillow, Swears & Wells, Lilley & Skinner and Peter Robinson (that would become Topshop). John Lewis started in 1864 as a drapery store on Oxford Street and in 1909 the US retail magnate Harry Gordon Selfridge chose the street for his first UK store.

These retail palaces lined the sunny northern side of the street while the southern side was always more down-market. Here tourists mixed with street vendors, prostitutes and even the human billboard, Stanley Green, with the slogan 'Eat less protein to reduce lust!'

Today, Oxford Street is a phenomenon. Before COVID it attracted a quarter of a billion visitors every year, making it, by some distance, Europe's busiest shopping street. Its shops had an annual turnover of £5 billion, a must see on the itinerary of every London tourist. And yet by common consensus it was also a 'hellish urban environment'. The planner Colin Buchanan described it in the 1960s as 'the most uncivilised street in Europe'.[9]

It was also the shopping street most severely impacted by COVID in the UK. And yet, as we will return to in Chapter 12, the fundamental strength of the street means that it will always bounce back.

they targeted 'the C class of customer' – artisans and lower middle class groups who aspired to middle-class values.[10]

The stores were revolutionary when they first opened. The produce was out on display with price labels rather than hidden behind counters. Customers could handle the goods, compare quality and prices and admire the clothes on mannequins. The name comes from the fact that the stores had different 'departments' selling women's, men's and children's fashions along with furnishings, homeware, appliances, books, toys – every conceivable product. They were ruthlessly commercial institutions, selling off-the-peg fashion and undermining the bespoke tailors, drapers and haberdashers that had formerly dominated retailing. In shades of the 2020 Boohoo scandal, they were accused by the Victorian social reformer Henry Mayhew of selling luxury fashion manufactured by 'sweated labour'.[11]

Some of the first department stores were the bazaars that emerged in the early 19th century. The Soho Bazaar was opened in 1815 by John Trotter, who had made his money supplying the army during the Napoleonic Wars. He created an emporium on Soho Square where the 'destitute' wives and daughters of soldiers could hire a stall and sell home-made items such as gloves, toys, and arts and crafts (one stall was frequented by the adolescent JMW Turner, where he bought art materials and sold his drawings).

Bennetts of Derby lays claim to being the world's oldest department store, having been trading since 1734, but for much of that time it was a hardware store. The first true department store was Bon Marché in Paris, which opened 1852 and created a model for all future stores, so much so that one of the first UK department stores, which opened in 1876 in Brixton, was also called Bon Marché. The years that followed saw a number of the larger and more successful drapers' shops develop into department stores, outcompeting their neighbours and cornering their local market. Harrods started as a general store in 1824 but was operating as a department store by the 1870s. Liberty's opened in 1875, Debenhams and John Lewis both started out as drapers' shops in 1878 and 1864, respectively. In Manchester the Watt's Bazaar was taken over by Kendal, Milne & Faulkner, evolving into a department store that proclaimed itself the largest outside London. In Liverpool, Lewis's was founded in 1856 and grew into one of the largest UK chains before closing in 2010. On Kensington High Street in London there were three grand institutions: Barkers of Kensington, Pontings and Derry & Toms, the latter with a 1.5 acre roof garden with streams and a pond stocked with flamingos.

John Stobart has undertaken a review of department stores based on the Kelly's Trade Directories and estimates that there were as many as 600 in England at their peak in the 1930s.[12] Large cities had multiple department stores while even small market towns could boast a modest institution. They were particularly popular in the booming industrial towns of the north where institutions like Binns, founded in Sunderland, expanded into great retail empires, while on the South Coast Bobby's opened a chain of stores catering to the tourist trade.

In addition to Kendal Milne, Manchester had as many as 10 department stores (depending on how they are defined). One of the grandest was Affleck and Brown, which started as a drapers in 1860 and developed into one of the city's main department stores between the wars, advertising fur coats in 1937 for 75 guineas (the equivalent of more than £5,000 today).[13] However, one of the city's most extraordinary stores was Paulden's, which stood on Stretford Road in Hulme, one of the most impoverished neighbourhoods and well outside the city centre. Yet

Paulden's was the first store in the city to introduce electric lighting, lifts, escalators and plate glass display windows, as well as being the first place in the country to sell Danish pastries![14]

Paulden's was acquired by Debenhams in the 1950s, who funded a major refurbishment but, just as the store was about to reopen, it burned down and a week later a double decker bus crashed into it and fell into the basement! So, instead of rebuilding, Paulden's moved into a grand building on Piccadilly Gardens, which later became Debenham's flagship Manchester store. Debenhams also bought Affleck and Browns and, once the new Piccadilly store was complete, this too was closed, later becoming Urban Splash's first major development. Things come full circle since the name lives on in Afflecks Palace, a Manchester institution that occupies the adjacent building. Established in 1982, this is a bazaar filled with independent stalls selling alternative clothing. Afflecks is scruffy, chaotic, cluttered and creative and its influence has spread to the whole of Oldham Street and the surrounding Northern Quarter, which has filled with bars and vintage clothes shops also nurturing a generation of creative businesses, from Red or Dead to Urban Splash.[15]

The story of Paulden's illustrates the process by which independent department stores and even regional chains were gobbled up by competitors. The Binns network became part of House of Fraser, while Bobby's was acquired by the Drapery and General Trust (that would later become Debenhams). The story ends with the collapse of Debenhams at the end of 2020, marking the end of the department store era. Data from CoStar in 2021 estimated that 80% of the UK's department stores have closed since 2016, some 388 stores.[16] At that time there were plans to repurpose only 52 of these stores for uses as varied as housing, offices, trampoline centres and indoor karting.

THE PATTERN OF PLACES

The other great legacy that we have inherited from the past is often overlooked. The pattern of retailing and the location of high streets was established long before the planning system existed to guide such matters. We have heard how market towns tended to be a day's walk apart, but this was never planned, it was a pattern that emerged organically over time (as we described in a previous book *Climax City*).[17]

The same is true in urban areas – there are examples of planned shopping centres but generally they just emerged where there was business to be done. From the location of the main shopping street in a large city centre to a local parade, shopping streets developed where there was passing trade. The company Space Syntax creates plans of cities with the streets colour coded according to their accessibility, from red for the most accessible through to dark blue for the least.[18] This accessibility is based on an algorithm that calculates the extent to which every street is connected to every other street. There is a strong correlation between the streets that show up as bright red on Space Syntax plans and the location of shops. The plan of London, for example, has Oxford Street in the brightest red despite the fact that the algorithm doesn't know Oxford Street is a major retail centre.

A joint project by the Office for National Statistics and the Ordnance Survey has mapped all of Britain's high streets.[19] They used an algorithm to identify all retail areas that are on a named street (thereby excluding retail parks) with 15 or more retail units within 150m. On this basis, they have identified just under 7,000 high streets in Britain. If you overlay these retail centres with the Space Syntax maps there is a clear correlation between the accessibility of a street and the number of shops it is able to support.

Many of these streets are actually called 'High Street'; a survey by Halifax Estate Agents in 2009 identified 5,300 streets in Britain called 'High Street' or variations like 'High Street West'.[20] In the 17th century the improved roads between towns in the UK became known as 'highways', the 'high' meaning 'improved'. When these streets passed through towns they became 'high' streets and were first and foremost traffic routes. It's hard to imagine now that a pedestrianised shopping street like Northumberland Street in Newcastle was once the A1, carrying all traffic between England and Scotland. However, it was this traffic that attracted the shops and over time the term 'high street' came to denote a shopping area.

We have inherited this pattern of high streets even when the conditions that created them have changed. Roads may have been blocked, traffic may have been diverted onto ring roads, populations may have shifted, retail parks may have stolen all the trade, but still the high street holds a special place in our national culture and economy. They provide vital services and have a huge influence on how people feel about their local area. Successive governments have seen the high street as something that should be preserved and protected. Such has been the case for the last 70 years and, in the following chapters, we tell the story of a series of high street crises and the policy response to them. We start with the first of these crises – the decline of local high streets precipitated by the arrival of the supermarkets.

Steep Hill in Lincoln was once the main Roman road to the north. The shops along its length were never planned but grew up there because of the passing trade.

2   DEATH BY SUPERMARKET

At the beginning of his book *Sold Out: Who Killed the High Street*, the veteran retailer Bill Grimsey reminisces about a childhood in the 1950s when he and his mother used to walk down to the High Street in Radlett, Hertfordshire every day to shop.[1] It was a time before most households had refrigerators or cars and he still remembers the name of 'Winkle' the fishmonger, Baz and Ron who worked in the butchers, Freestones the bakers, Hills the greengrocers, Wickins the newsagent where, if he played his cards right, he might get a jamboree bag of sweets, and finally the Post Office with its 'woodblock flooring and solemn glass counter'. He still recalls the sounds and smells of each of the shops, the displays of goods 'jumping about and shouting buy me!'. Such is the image conjured up for many people by the term 'high street', even though it has not really existed for decades, at least not since the arrival of the supermarkets.

My (DR) experience of shopping with my mum in suburban south Birmingham a few years later was initially very similar. I can, however, remember the moment when the retail revolution arrived. Walking into our local grocers *William's Corner*, I can remember my mum's confusion when, rather than queuing up and asking Mr Williams and his assistants for all the items on her shopping list, she found that she was required to find her own way through the store, picking what she wanted from the individually priced goods on the shelves and placing them in a wire basket before making her way to the checkout.

THE SELF-SERVICE REVOLUTION

These were all innovations that had first been introduced by an American grocer called Clarence Saunders when he opened the first Piggly Wiggly store in Memphis, Tennessee, in 1916. With their turnstiles, individually priced items, wire baskets (to deter shoplifting), uniformed staff and checkouts, these stores were quicker, more convenient and needed less staff than the old over-the-counter formats. More importantly for retailers, they increased turnover, not least because of the 'impulse buy' – that thing not on your shopping list that you hadn't realised that you needed until you saw it on the shelf, perhaps on special offer.

The new retail format quickly came to dominate US grocery retailing but it was slow to be adopted in the UK. As late as 1947 the trade journal *The Grocer* was writing 'the people of this country have long been accustomed to counter-service, and it is doubtful whether they would be content to wander round a store hunting for goods'.[2]

St Mary's Road in Garston: A shuttered high street that has been bypassed and struggled to compete with surrounding supermarkets, but as we describe in Chapter 15 is showing signs of recovery.

However, as wartime rationing came to an end in the 1950s the self-service revolution took off. The early skirmishes took place on the high street; shop units were knocked together to create sufficient space and store formats changed, as happened with William's Corner. Before long, we bought our first car and my mum switched her allegiances to the new Mac Fisheries supermarket a few miles away.

Mac Fisheries was part of the Unilever empire and between the wars Lord Lever had invested in a supply chain to bring fish from the Northern Isles of Scotland to English markets. As part of the plan, Unilever opened a chain of fishmongers called Mac Fisheries. After the war there was a decline in wet fish sales, caused in part by the invention of processed foods such as Unilever's own best-selling brand: the Birds Eye Fish Finger. This was the age of the retail brands, from Heinz Baked Beans to Kellogg's Corn Flakes and Surf washing powder, all of which were created to stand out from the competition in a self-service store. Unilever started converting the fishmongers into multi-line retailers, adopting the new self-service format with freezer cabinets for the frozen fish. Soon it became clear that the old stores were too small so in 1964 the company bought Premier Supermarkets from Express Dairies (for £1 million) and went into the supermarket business. This was the moment when the supermarkets started to challenge the high street.

THE BIRTH OF THE SUPERMARKET

There are many candidates for the first supermarket in the UK. According to some histories it was the Premier Supermarket opened by Express Dairies in 1951 in Streatham in South London – the opening ceremony 'performed by 1,500 housewives'.[3] Others say it was the Co-op store in Manor Park London opened in 1949, while Tesco's claim that it was their first self-service store opened in 1949. The truth depends on how we define a supermarket, because it was at about this time that the second stage of the supermarket transformation took place and the self-service format expanded along with the addition of a car park and shopping trolleys. The growth in car use and the widespread ownership of fridges meant that the 'weekly shop' came to replace the daily trips to the local shopping parade. The new large format stores were built outside, or on the edge of, high streets and served a much larger catchment. They were soon sucking in the lion's share of spending on groceries through their sliding doors, sending many high streets into a steep decline – within a few years William's Corner had become an estate agent.

At the beginning of the 1960s there were 572 supermarkets in the UK and by the end of the decade numbers had grown to 3,400.[4] At their peak in 2012 there were 8,000 supermarkets in all formats in the UK, accounting for an astonishing 97% of grocery sales (which in turn makes up half of all retail spending).[5] Meanwhile, the number of independent butchers, bakers, greengrocers and fishmongers had declined from 120,000 units in 1950 to less than 30,000 today (figures on candlestick makers are not available).[6] We once did a strategy for the town of Tipton in the West Midlands and were told by our retail agents that turnover of the delicatessen counter in the local supermarket was greater than the combined total of the rest of the high street.

The new Mac Food Markets (which was how Mac Fisheries rebranded the Premier stores) were large and built in a modernist style with a sleek horizontality, marble floors, freezer cabinets and over-bright lighting. Mac Food Markets traded until 1978, Unilever finally realising, as Express Dairies had before them, that there was a conflict of interest in being both a wholesaler to supermarkets and an owner of one of their competitors.

THE BIG FOUR SUPERMARKETS

Sainsbury's: The oldest of the big four, founded in 1869 in Drury Lane in Holborn. Between the wars Sainsbury's was the largest food retailer in the UK, based largely around London but expanding into the Midlands with the acquisition of the Thoroughgood chain in 1936. They operated like food department stores with sections for dairy, meat and game, cooked meats and groceries, with a comprehensive home delivery service. Following a trip to the US by Alan Sainsbury they opened their first self-service store in Croydon in 1950.

Tesco: As we have heard, Tesco started as a market stall run by Jack Cohen in the East End of London after he was demobbed from the First World War. In the 1920s he went into partnership with the tea trader M.T. Stockwell, combining their names to create Tesco Tea and going on to open their first store in 1929. After the war Jack Cohen also travelled to the US to understand how self-service retailing worked, coming back to open his first self-service store in St Albans in 1949.

Asda: In Yorkshire, the merger of two retailers would create Asda. The Asquith family, who had started off as butchers in Knottingley, went on to create a small chain of supermarkets called Queens (because the first branch was in

the converted Queen's Cinema in Castleford). Meanwhile a group of dairy farmers including Arthur Stockdale had come together to form Associated Dairies and Farm Stores in 1949, which had also developed a retail division. The two groups merged in 1965 combining the 'As' of Asquith with the 'Da' of 'dairy' to form Asda. In 1999 the company was acquired by the huge US retailer Walmart for £6.7 billion, making it part of the largest supermarket group in the world. However, in a sign of the times, Asda was sold again in 2021 for about the same price to Zuber and Mohsin Issa, two brothers whose Gujarati parents had owned a petrol station in Blackburn that the brothers had grown into an international chain of petrol stations and convenience stores.

Morrisons: For almost 50 years Morrisons was a series of family-run stalls selling eggs and butter on Rawson Market in Bradford. In 1952 this was taken over by the 21-year-old Ken Morrison who went on to open Bradford's first self-service grocery store in 1958. Through aggressive expansion and merger, Morrisons had grown to just over 100 stores by 2004 when they bought the Safeway chain for £3.3 billion. With 479 stores Safeway were at the time the fourth largest chain in the UK, a position taken by Morrisons.

At the time there were lots of supermarkets serving the UK 'housewife'. Names like Safeway and Somerfield, Presto, Lipton's, Fine Fare and Kwik Save have long disappeared, the victim of years of consolidation as stores have eaten up the competition, culminating in Morrisons' acquisition of Safeway in 2005 to create the big four (Tesco, Asda, Sainsbury's and Morrisons), which have come to dominate UK retailing.

BIG IS BEST

The story of how the big four grew to dominate in the UK has a number of chapters. On returning from his trip to the US, Alan Sainsbury concluded that stores should be around 1,000m^2 and should 'ideally' have car parking. The Mac Food Store frequented by my mum is now a Poundstretcher and while it seemed huge to a small kid, it is only 1,100m^2 (12,000ft^2) with just 30 parking spaces, equivalent to a small Aldi.

The next big step happened in Bridgford on the edge of Nottingham, the location of the first out-of-town superstore.[7] This was opened in 1964 by the American retailer GEM, a company that had started out as a discount store for US government employees (GEM stood for Government Employees Mart). In the early 1960s the company launched an ill-fated foray into the UK market and the Bridgford superstore at 10,000m^2 (110,000ft^2) was ten times larger than the typical supermarket at the time. It was a large, windowless box with 1,000 parking spaces and 50 departments, including a pharmacy, toys, records, shoe repairs and even carpets. The headline in *The Times* was 'Windowless store makes its debut', this being the most remarkable feature at a time when window displays were seen as crucial to attracting passing trade. As the store manager Herman F.E. Frost told *The Times* reporter: 'We need the wall space for our merchandise, and windows in general are out for the car shopper – he drives in, he stops at our parking lot, and he walks right out.'[8]

The opening weekend attracted 30,000 people and 5,000 cars, gridlocking surrounding streets. However, the store was an unmitigated failure and after two years it was turning over just £6,000 a week, having cost £500,000 to build with a further £700,000 in fit-out and stock. The company blamed its problems on 'the innate conservative outlook [and] the ingrained prejudices of the trading community in this country'. It is probably true that the store was a few years ahead of its time but it is also true that the format – more a horizontal department store than supermarket – was confused. The real revolution took place in 1966 when the loss-making store was sold to the newly established Asda supermarket chain. They transformed it into a superstore that we would recognise today, turnover increasing ten-fold within six months.

The birth of the mega store coincided with the repeal of a law that had maintained retail prices after the war, allowing the large supermarkets to slash prices. It was a period in which more women were going out to work and car ownership was booming so that the high street was left behind as the supermarkets expanded massively. Most of the new stores were still not as large as the Bridgford store. Sainsbury's enlarged their store format to 2,000m^2 in the 1970s while Tesco and Asda went for larger formats, the former opening its first 4,000m^2 superstore in Crawley in 1968.[9] These stores sold a range of household products and clothing as well as food. Petrol stations were added in the 1970s and gradually the stores started cannibalising the high street, including pharmacies, newsagents, off licences, clothes, key cutting and shoe repair.

THE STORY OF ALDI

Al-di is short for Albrecht Discount, a company created by two German brothers, Karl and Theo Albrecht, who took over their family shop in Essen. Their mother had started the shop in 1913 when her husband's emphysema prevented him working in the mines. When the brothers returned from the war they found Essen in ruins but the shop miraculously intact and they started selling cheap goods to the austerity-hit nation. Initially the tight range of goods was a necessity of rationing and they had intended to expand where they were able. However, it became clear that there were many cost savings to be had in restricting the range of the shops. As the book on the company's history says, 'a completely new business model was created ... by accident'.[10]

The brothers expanded into a chain of shops tapping into Germany's post-war mood of frugality. The chain expanded and in the 1950s they were the first to import the self-service format to Germany. In 1961 the two brothers, unable to agree on policy, decided to split the 300-store business into Aldi North and Aldi South, with the dividing line running through their hometown of Essen. The stores carried different product ranges but in terms of appearance the only difference was the colour of the floor.

This formula remained unchanged when Aldi expanded into first the US and then the UK. The stores are basic, the layout confused and the till stressful. The latter has led to the term 'Aldi panic', which refers to that moment when the checkout is so rapid that you find yourself holding up the queue. In the early days speed was achieved by training the checkout operators to memorise the price of all 600 products. Now the products have barcodes on all sides to speed the scanning process. As Xan Rice writes, the 'thrill of the till' as Aldi managers call it, is part of the attraction: 'The rushed, no-frills experience isn't something you merely endure for the sake of saving money; the awareness of your savings makes that experience a pleasure in itself.'[11]

The expansion entered a new phase in the late 1990s with the opening of the first Tesco Extra store at 10,000m^2 in Pitsea, Essex and the company's largest store is the 17,230m^2 store in Walkden, Greater Manchester.[12] These larger stores finally realised the Bridgford vision of the horizontal department store, often built on former industrial sites on the edge of town, capturing a huge proportion of retail spend. Sainsbury's had followed suit with their SavaCentres and Asda with their Supercentres, the largest of which is 11,000m^2.

A further phase happened with the introduction of Tesco Express stores, the first opening in Barnes, South West London in 1994. Since then Tesco has opened 1,740 Express stores while Sainsbury's has 770, Asda 209 and Morrisons 70. These local stores were aimed at extending their market reach even further into the convenience sector, dominated by players like the Co-op and SPAR. However, it also brought them back to the high street where they had started. Some saw this as the final *coup de grâce* as the big retailers took trade from the independent convenience stores that had made a living by being local and open all hours. However, there may also be a benefit in bringing customers back to high streets, and away from out-of-town stores, as we will see in Chapter 6.

THE DISCOUNT SUPERMARKETS

On visiting the UK's first Aldi in 1990, a reporter for *The Times* wrote that 'one looks in vain for avocados or kiwi fruit'.[13] Like most other people in the UK, including the established supermarkets, the reporter had completely missed the point. By 2019 the discount supermarkets led by Aldi and Lidl were challenging the big supermarkets, having disrupted the UK grocery market not through innovation or technology but by keeping things simple and cheap.

That first Aldi opened in Stechford in Birmingham with only 600 lines and one brand of many basic items like butter and tea, all stacked on wooden pallets or in torn-open boxes and all at very low prices. The consensus in the industry was that this would never work in the UK. Unlike those in Germany, customers here placed much more value on service and choice and were less price sensitive. Research by Professor Peter Jackson at Sheffield University has chronicled how in the UK our choice of supermarket, like the newspaper we read, or the car we drive, has always been a signifier of class.[14] As *The Guardian* suggests 'British mums once worried about their children being embarrassed to find Aldi food in their lunchboxes'.[15]

In the early years there seemed to be some justification in this view. Up until the 2008 financial crisis, Aldi and Lidl had each only achieved a 2% market share in the UK. This all changed as the global recession caused many British shoppers to try a discount supermarket for the first time. David Harvey, a brand and marketing academic from Huddersfield University, suggests: 'The recession … broke people's shopping habits and loyalty to the Big 4 as they looked around for the best prices from a variety of outlets.'[16] This has squeezed profit margins in the supermarket sector which, at 7%, had been the highest in the world. In the words of its CEO Aldi has been 'sucking the profitability out of the industry' and margins have fallen to just 2–3% as the big supermarkets cut prices to compete.[17]

The discount supermarket model has evolved over time. The number of products has risen to around 2,000, still a fraction of the 25,000 products carried by the big supermarkets. The reporter from *The Times* would be happy to find that it now includes avocados and kiwis along with sourdough bread, Parma ham, hummus and fresh pesto. The brands are unique to Aldi but they look strangely familiar, designed to look like the brands we know but with different names (Mars bars become Titans, for example). There have been court cases over Kit Kat and the battle lines in 2021 concerned Aldi's Cuthbert the Caterpillar who, Marks & Spencer claim, is a copy of their Colin the Caterpillar. But it has worked, as Aldi has expanded its customer base. Research in 2017 by David Harvey at Huddersfield University found that 77% of households earning more than £50,000 a year have used a discount supermarket compared to 73% of households earning less than £15,000.[18] As the retail analyst Richard Hyman told *The Guardian*: 'Aldi's customer profile is now classless … The supermarket is as strong with affluent people as it is with people on low incomes.'

This has been achieved with a low-tech approach; until 2009 Aldi didn't accept card payments and still has no loyalty programme and so knows very little about its customers. Until the pandemic they also didn't have an online grocery offer and figures from Kantar in March 2021 show Aldi losing market share to the big four for the first time since its arrival in the UK.[19] There were questions about whether Aldi's model, born of post-war German frugality and reflecting the personalities of the dour Albrecht brothers, could prosper in the fast-moving world of online retail. However, as we write, the cost of living crisis has seen Aldi's market share overtake Morrisons' to disrupt the hegemony of the big four retailers.[20]

MARKET SATURATION

The impact of the discounters on the big four supermarkets came to a head in 2014. At the beginning of that year the supermarkets had been busy working on their ongoing programme of new store openings in all formats. By the time it ended most uncommitted projects had been cancelled and Tesco had announced 43 store closures.[21] When the discount retailers had first appeared on the scene in the 1990s, Tesco's managing director David Malpas had been quoted as saying 'We welcome the advent of Aldi and others to come, we can live quite happily in our part of the market and they can live in theirs.'[22] However, as household budgets are squeezed Aldi and Lidl have prospered. Demographics have also been a factor, with the rise of single-person households, healthy eating and lower levels of car ownership, which means people shopping daily on their way home from work. The weekly shop has become the monthly shop and convenience stores have taken up the slack. Meanwhile, the internet had eaten into supermarkets' non-food sales, if not yet into their grocery trade.

The real problem is saturation of the market. At their peak the big four had a 76.3% market share so that any further new stores simply cannibalised trade from their existing stores. Some towns ended up with all four of the big supermarkets surrounding the town centre, competing to take each other's trade. By contrast, the value retailers have been able to open stores where they have no customers, allowing them to grow their market share far more rapidly.

The impact of these trends took time to land, but by 2014 Tesco were forced to issue five profits warnings, exacerbated by an accounting scandal. They eventually saw a 92% fall in profits and announced £250m in cost savings and laid off 2,000 staff. The effect of this was to halt the growth of the big supermarkets and since that time the big four's market share has fallen by almost 10%.

We will return to the grocery market in Chapter 6, looking at future trends in online retail, dark stores, contactless shops and home delivery. With almost half of all retail spending going on food the future of the grocery sector will have a huge impact on our high streets. Our nostalgic idea of the idealised high street may have been killed by the supermarkets, but trends towards convenience shopping, 'real' food movements, artisan retailers and home delivery could see a revival.

3 HEADING OUT OF TOWN

There is a picture taken on 13 October 1986 of three men in suits cutting a ribbon. The one on the left is Nicholas Ridley, Conservative Secretary of State for the Environment, who appears to be making a joke, with the other two in fits of laughter. On the right is Councillor George Gill, leader of Gateshead Council and in the middle stands Sir John Hall, clearly having the best day of his life. The occasion is the opening of the Metrocentre in Gateshead, the UK's first out-of-town mega mall, which was to precipitate the second crisis on the high street.

THE BIG CLARTY FIELD

We will return to Nicholas Ridley in a moment but it is worth starting with John Hall, the son of a miner from the pit town of Ashington in North East England. He started his career as a mining surveyor working down his local pit, however he was a bright lad and the National Coal Board (NCB) agreed to support him in qualifying as a chartered surveyor. On leaving the NCB he set up a company, Cameron Hall, with his wife Mae (Cameron being her maiden name) and started buying and doing up houses in Sunderland. Later they graduated to retailing, building a Co-op store in Gateshead, but soon they were thinking much, much bigger.

Following a trip to the US where he had visited a number of large malls, John Hall realised that they were ideally suited to the cold, wet and windy northeast of England. As he told the *Northumberland Times*: 'I tried to find a site but I was ahead of my time, no local authority was ever going to let an out-of-town shopping development go ahead'.[1]

At about this time, Geoffrey Howe, then an opposition shadow minister, was giving a speech at the Waterman's Arms pub in London's Docklands.[2] Pointing to the derelict land that stretched in all directions around the pub, he made the case that investing public money in declining industrial areas was just propping up failed markets. A better solution was to lift the shackles off enterprise and allow it to revive itself, free from government regulation and taxation. In the speech he quoted an unlikely source, 'Non-Plan – An experiment in freedom', an article that had been published in *New Society* in 1969.[3] Written by a group of counter-culture architect/planners and journalists, Paul Barker, Cedric Price, Peter Hall and Reyner Banham, the piece argued that the 'natural desires and spontaneous whims of the population are being repressed by state planning'. They called for a radical experiment in which parts of Britain's inner cities should be exempt from all planning regulations to free them from the heavy hand of state regulation. These were no free market neoliberals, it was an idea that had grown out of the anarcho-libertarian movement

The Metrocentre in Gateshead: Opened in 1986 this was the UK's first and for two decades its largest out-of-town mall.

of the New Left in the 1960s. The enemy, as far as the authors were concerned, was the controlling, overbearing state and they held up as evidence the disastrous results of post-war planning.

Back in Gateshead John Hall had bought a large site, known as the 'great big clarty field',[4] the waterlogged ash tip of Dunston Power Station on the southern bank of the Tyne about five miles from the centre of Newcastle. With no road access and major contamination issues it wasn't viewed as having any great potential and Hall bought it for just £100,000. However, in the budget of 1980 Geoffrey Howe, then Chancellor of the Exchequer in the newly elected Conservative government, was able to put his deregulated vision for the inner cities into practice by announcing the first tranche of 11 Enterprise Zones. These covered relatively small areas of London Docklands, Glasgow, Belfast, Hartlepool, Liverpool, Trafford in Manchester, Wakefield, Swansea, Corby, Dudley and an area of Newcastle/Gateshead including a certain clarty field. These zones would be free of planning regulations, business rates and capital allowances, they were exempt from Development Land Tax, industrial training boards and requests from the government for statistical information. It had also been suggested that they be exempt from fire and building regulations, taxi licensing and even laws on sex and racial discrimination but the government stopped short of going that far.[5]

Whether the policy was effective is a moot point. Centre for Cities in their report *What would Maggie Do?* suggested that the first two rounds of Enterprise Zones created 58,000 jobs but 40% of these were as a result of companies relocating into the zone to avoid tax.[6] They calculated that each new job cost £26,000 (2010 prices), a good deal more expensive than other inner city programmes.

However, from the perspective of the high street the main impact was that Enterprise Zone policy allowed for the development of the first two regional shopping centres in the UK, Merry Hill and the Metrocentre, and indirectly to a third, Meadowhall. Most of the zones excluded retailing from the relaxation of planning controls, the exceptions in the first round being Dudley and Gateshead. In Dudley two local businessmen, Roy and Don Richardson, built one of the largest retail parks in the UK, which evolved into the Merry Hill shopping centre. In Rotherham, which was a second-round Enterprise Zone, there were plans to build the Parkgate Shopping Centre, which wasn't built but did persuade Sheffield that it had no option but to approve the Meadowhall Centre.

In Gateshead the Enterprise Zone allowed the development of retail units up to $250,000\text{ft}^2$ without planning consent. This was initially intended to encourage the development of a retail park, but John Hall, fresh from his experience of visiting the US, had something else in mind. He reasoned that if access could be improved, there were 4.5 million customers within an hour's drive of the site and it could possibly be developed as the UK's first true regional shopping centre.

As the presence of Councillor Gill in that photograph suggests, this was all done with the enthusiastic support of the council and local regeneration agencies. The pain and unemployment caused by the deindustrialisation of the North East was such that a development creating up to 6,000 jobs was seen as a huge achievement and £1.75 million of public money was allocated to build an access road to the site and a railway station was also provided in 1987. In 1984 the council staged an exhibition of the proposals at the Five Bridges Hotel, part consultation, part promotion.[7] The event attracted more than 1,000 members of the public, but more importantly, led to pre-lets from the retailers Boots, the Burton Group, Carrefour and Marks & Spencer – the first time the latter had agreed to open an out-of-town store.

The Metrocentre opened in stages between 1986 and 1988 and when complete it included 2 million ft^2 (194,000m^2) of retail and leisure space and 10,000 free parking spaces, making it the largest mall in the UK by some margin (it retained this distinction until Westfield London opened in 2008). It includes elements imported from US malls that would become the template for regional shopping centres in the UK. It was open and airy, with malls under a glass roof built in a slightly kitsch classical style to provide the shopping public with a sense of luxury and escape. It was also very practical, with baby changing rooms, mobility schemes and even a chaplain. The centre was organised into zones, each with a colour; the Red Zone was the first to open, anchored by a Carrefour supermarket, followed by the Green, Blue and Yellow Zones. The central mall has since been named the Platinum Zone for more upmarket stores and the Red Zone has been redeveloped with the supermarket replaced by a Debenhams. Until 2008 the centre also included Metroland, Europe's largest indoor theme park. Soon after completion Hall sold the centre to the Church Commissioners for £250 million who, in turn, sold it on to Capital Shopping Centres in 1995 who later rebranded it as Intu Metrocentre until Intu went into administration in 2020.

THE ORIGINS OF THE MALL

The first out-of-town shopping mall is credited as being the Country Club Plaza in Kansas City, opened in 1923, but it was after the war when the mania for out-of-town retailing took hold in the US. The person who did most to shape the mall was the architect Victor Gruen. He had worked in Vienna designing modernist boutiques, but fled to the US in 1938 and after cutting his teeth on Fifth Avenue he moved to Los Angeles. Gruen was described in the many profiles that were written of him as 'short, stout and unstoppable with a wild head of hair and eyebrows like unpruned hedges'.[8] *Fortune* magazine described him as a 'torrential talker, with eyes bright as mica ... famous for keeping two or three secretaries working full time ... dictating non stop in his thick Viennese accent'.[9]

In 1948 he did a deal with Detroit's largest department store J.L. Hudson, persuading them to build four new stores in the city's sprawling suburbs. The stores would be surrounded by parking and smaller leased retail units to feed off the department store's footfall. The format was a wild success and the resulting malls hailed by *Architectural Forum* as an 'architectural classic'. A few years later he tried the same trick with the Dayton Brothers' department store in Minneapolis. However Dayton Brothers had a rival, Allied Stores, who were planning something similar. Gruen's masterstroke was to negotiate what Mennel described in the *Journal of Planning History* as 'a remarkable power sharing agreement between firms that were otherwise well-matched enemies'.[10] Each of the department stores would sit glaring at each other, as far away as possible at either end of a mall, creating the classic dumbbell model that pretty much every subsequent mall has followed.

The result was the world's first true mall, the Southdale Center in Minneapolis, which opened in 1956. Due to Minnesota's harsh climate it was also the first mall to be covered and air-conditioned. The requirement for climate control meant that Southdale also became the first 'introverted' mall, whereas previously stores faced both outwards towards the car park and inwards onto the mall. In Southdale, the external walls were left blank and customers passed through shared entrances from which they accessed stores. The stores, in turn, could get rid of their doors and open directly onto the climate-controlled mall. It was also the first mall to be built on two levels to reduce walking distances and to include a central 'garden court' with fish ponds, sculpted trees and a 6m cage filled with brightly coloured birds. As Malcolm Gladwell wrote in *The New Yorker*, 'Victor Gruen didn't design a building he designed an archetype'.[11]

Within 30 years there would be 1,800 malls in the US. Atlanta, with a population of 2 million, had 12 regional shopping centres and even small places like Charlotte (pop. 400,000) had three.[12] In the early days US department stores like Macy's would open satellite stores in these new malls while retaining their flagship stores downtown. However, from the 1970s onwards they started closing their downtown stores as trade transferred almost entirely to the malls and traditional town and city centres died. This unrestrained retail growth means that the US has 23.5ft^2 of retail per head of population compared to 4.6ft^2 in the UK and 2.3ft^2 in Germany.[13] The only reason why the development of malls slowed in the US was the saturation of the market – the result was the devastation of downtown areas, most of which lost their retail role almost entirely.

REGIONAL SHOPPING CENTRES

Despite its reputation for imitating the US and the experience of supermarkets, the UK did not initially take to the idea of the out-of-town mall or regional shopping centres as they were called. France was the most enthusiastic adopter, building 15 large shopping centres in the 1970s, 11 in peripheral locations.[14] The same happened on a smaller scale in Germany, Belgium and Holland.

In the UK, there had been proposals in 1964 for a million square foot regional shopping centre at Haydock, between Liverpool and Manchester.[15] This was refused after a landmark planning appeal, as part of which Manchester University had been commissioned to assess its potential impact. Their report concluded that increases in wealth, the sale of durable goods, population, car ownership and self-service retailing all meant that conditions were ripe for the development of out-of-town retailing in the UK – 'the difference between the two countries are more a matter of timing and degree'.[16] However, the report used a gravity model to estimate that the Haydock scheme would lead to a loss of trade of 34–46% in St Helens, Wigan and Warrington with 'measurable but not great impacts on Manchester and Liverpool of 12%'. The findings were later used in a government report leading to the conclusion that the 'diversion of trade to out-of-town regional shopping centres would imperil the urban renewal programme of sizable industrial centres and might "kill" trade in smaller towns'.[17]

The UK was therefore the only country to build its regional shopping centres *within* town centres. The 350,000ft^2 Bull Ring Centre in Birmingham was one of the first when it opened in May 1964, while the Arndale Centre in Poole (now called the Dolphin Centre) was the largest at half a million square feet. Soon every other council was busy clearing large parts of their town and city centres to build a shopping centre, including the Merrion Centre in Leeds (1964), the Elephant & Castle in London (1965), the Tricorn Centre in Portsmouth (1966), the Victoria Centre in Nottingham (1972), the Kirkgate Shopping Centre in Bradford (1974), Eldon Square in Newcastle (1976) and, biggest of them all, the Arndale Centre in Manchester (1979). Wikipedia lists 413 shopping centres in the UK, ranging from

THE TRAFFORD CENTRE

Proposals to build a major shopping centre at what was then called Dumplington date back to the 1980s. However, a decade of planning battles meant that the Trafford Centre (as it was renamed) ended up being the last regional shopping centre to be built in the UK.

Planning permission had initially been granted by Trafford Council in 1988 but the decision was called in by the Secretary of State. Following this, there were two planning enquiries, at which eight of the 10 Greater Manchester authorities opposed the scheme. Planning permission was eventually granted in 1993 but this was challenged through the courts all the way up to the House of Lords, who finally gave approval in 1995.

The developer was Peel Holdings, a company shaped in the image of its founder John Whittaker.

The company had been the Manchester Ship Canal Company, part owned by the Greater Manchester local authorities, but Whittaker built up a controlling stake and eventually bought the company outright in 1993. Rebranded as Peel it set out to exploit its huge land holdings through a series of controversial developments, prime amongst which was the Trafford Centre.

The centre that finally opened in 1998 had 1.94 million ft^2 of space (180,231m^2) and 230 retail units including Selfridges, John Lewis and Debenhams, generating a footfall of around 35 million per year. It was sold to Capital Shopping Centres in 2011 for £1.6 billion, then the largest ever property deal in the UK. Capital later rebranded as Intu until its collapse in March 2020.

big cities down to the smallest market towns and suburban centres and less than a dozen of these are built out-of-town.

There was an outcry about the damage being done to the built environment. Dan Cruickshank and Colin Amery, in their book *The Rape of Britain*, were appalled by the devastation wrought by these town centre schemes, writing of the 'brutal obliteration' of the historic city by a 'mind that seriously believes that the centre of Manchester should look like a futuristic vision of a barbaric new city borrowed from Le Corbusier'.[18] The following year Save British Heritage was set up as a pressure group to campaign against these schemes.

Damaging as they may have been, the decision to build regional shopping centres in town almost certainly saved UK town centres from the fate suffered by their US counterparts. The only UK out-of-town regional shopping centre built in the 1970s was Brent Cross, built in suburban northwest London in an area supposedly without any large established town centres (something with which the local traders in Hendon took issue).[19] It opened in March 1976 with three-quarters of a million square feet of space anchored by John Lewis and Fenwick department stores and served by 5,000 parking spaces. The other big shopping centres built at the time were in the new towns. Shopping City, which was built as Runcorn's town centre opened in 1971 with 600,000ft^2 and centre:mk in Milton Keynes opened in 1979 with just over a million square feet, far larger than was justified by its population, so clearly meant to draw on a regional catchment.

The 'town centre first' policy held until the election of the Conservative government under Margaret Thatcher elected in 1979, who viewed planning as an impediment to the free market. Enterprise Zones may have been the start but much more damaging was the belief that government had no business deciding where people should shop. Government guidance, first issued in 1985 and repeated in subsequent guidance notes, included a phrase that was to become infamous: 'commercial competition as such is not a land use planning consideration'. This meant that the commercial impact of out-of-town retailing on existing town centres could only be considered in 'exceptional circumstances' where it 'could *seriously* affect the vitality and viability of a town centre *as a whole*'.[20] The emphasis is our own but gave plenty of scope for developers to argue their case at planning appeal, which is how many schemes were eventually approved. So, just at the time when other European countries started to restrict out-of-town retailing, the UK was rowing in the other direction.

This is where we return to Nicholas Ridley, who was Secretary of State for the Environment between 1987 and 1989. At no other time has the planning system been the responsibility of someone so ideologically opposed to its very existence. He told *The Times* that out-of-town-retailing 'is a bigger force than I. It is a mistake to say that I must stop it, or that it can be stopped ... I don't think it can be stopped with the powers that government has'.[21] This led to a feeding frenzy as developers all over the country sought to promote new out-of-town regional shopping centres.

In the early 1990s there were 50 schemes in various stages of development across the UK, far more than could ever have been built.[22] Those that were realised included Bluewater in Kent, Cribbs Causeway near Bristol, Lakeside in Essex, the White Rose Centre in Leeds, the Trafford Centre in Manchester and, depending on your definition, the Cheshire Oaks outlet centre near Chester. These were in effect alternative city centres and, as we saw with Sheffield in the Introduction, posed an existential threat to existing town and city centres.

RETAIL PARKS

While attention was focussed on the headline-grabbing regional shopping centres an even greater threat was the rash of retail parks and supermarkets that government policy allowed to be built on the edge of virtually every town. We described the expansion of the supermarkets in the last chapter but the retail park (or 'strip mall' as it is called in the US) was an even greater threat to town centres. They involved large individual 'big box' units arranged around a shared car park and had initially been intended for the retail of bulky items, like furniture, carpets, white goods and DIY. Planners had accepted that there was not enough space for these retailers in town centres. However, national planning guidance now said that planning had no role in determining the *type* of retail, so that these restrictions were lifted and retail parks soon filled up with shops selling clothes, shoes, toys, consumer electronics and other goods that previously had been the preserve of the high street.

Wisbech: The retail park that stretches along Cromwell Road south of Wisbech contains more shopping floorspace than the town centre.

Retail parks come in all shapes and sizes, from the upmarket facilities anchored by a John Lewis or a Marks & Spencer, to those feeding off a supermarket car park. There are places like Wisbech in Cambridgeshire where they have eclipsed the town centre in terms of floor area. In less affluent areas they are populated with bargain outlets and discount grocers, while a few like Fort Kinnaird in Edinburgh and Fosse Park in Leicestershire, have grown into 'super parks' with a floor area of more than half a million square feet.

Nicholas Ridley's tenure saw a huge number of these retail parks receive planning consent, often on appeal after an initial refusal by local planning authorities. As Russell Schiller documented in 1994,[23] this caused some commentators to question the very existence of traditional high streets, pointing to what had happened in the US. He cites the example of Marks & Spencer, whose chairman wrote in their 1984 annual report:

> 'The use of family cars for shopping has increasing importance to our customers. Where local authorities have recognised this need and worked with retailers to improve parking facilities and good access roads, the public continue to prefer to shop in the high street. Unfortunately, the response by some local authorities to the requirement of the car-shopping public is inadequate. Unless there is a change of attitude … the importance of the high street in some localities will decline. When considering future store development plans, the company will have to review what steps are necessary to ensure that our investment is directed to locations where our customers will prefer to shop.'

Of the 535,000ft^2 of floorspace developed by M&S over the next 10 years, most was in 'edge of town' locations. By the 1992 annual report the chairman was able to state that the trade in their town centre stores had not been 'cannibalised' by their new out-of-town offer. As Schiller described, the impact on confidence was profound – if M&S didn't believe in the high street, who else would? Soon most large retailers were exploring out-of-town formats including John Lewis, Next, the Burton Group, electrical retailers, shoe shops, pet shops, sports outlets, even stationers. Schiller argues that retailers saw themselves as having no alternative, but, despite the assurances of the M&S chairman, the combined sales of in-town and out-of-town stores rarely justified the increased costs of operating in two locations, thereby weakening a retail sector forced to ride two horses.

For retail developers the economics were more clear-cut. The derelict industrial sites that existed in abundance on the edge of most towns could be bought cheaply and turned into a car park surrounded by retail units that were little more than tin sheds with fancy fascias. The rents may have been lower than town centre units, but the costs were lower still, so that the yields were incredibly attractive. In the absence of planning control there was a gold rush and between 1987 and 1990 half of all new retail space was built in retail parks, which grew over the period from 1 to 25 million square feet.[24]

THE IMPACT ON THE HIGH STREET

The impact of out-of-town retailing was much debated. Critics predicted that it would devastate town centres, while every new planning application was accompanied by a retail impact assessment 'proving' that the impact would be minimal.

Elizabeth Howard and Ross Davies of the Oxford Centre for Retail Management undertook a number of longitudinal studies into the impact of regional shopping centres. Their report on the Metrocentre in Gateshead found that its shoppers were more affluent than those in Newcastle, stayed longer and generally spent more.[25] You would think that Newcastle city centre would be struggling but, as the authors pointed out, this was not the case. The Metrocentre was in fact drawing more people from a much larger catchment than their models had predicted, 40% driving more than 20 minutes to get there compared to 25% travelling that far into the city centre. Newcastle had lost 12% of the trips that it would otherwise have attracted but the drop in retail spend had been offset by the impact of investment in the city centre Eldon Square and strong growth in the national economy. Newcastle city centre had thus been able to shrug off the impact of the Metrocentre, much as Manchester did with the Trafford Centre a few years later. Howard and Davies concluded that the impact of regional shopping centres was 'not necessarily in the largest or the closest centres but in the weaker centres and the weaker parts of existing centres'.

The exception to this was Sheffield (as we saw in the Introduction). This was also subject to a study by Elizabeth Howard, who found that Meadowhall had captured 12% of regional shopping trips, reducing Sheffield's share by 23%.[26] She concluded that in Sheffield people remained loyal to their local centres for regular shopping but switched their occasional big shopping trips from Sheffield to Meadowhall. Sheffield was unfortunate in that Meadowhall's opening coincided with a recession, but the city had also failed to invest in its own town centre. So, while the raw trade figures for the Metrocentre and Meadowhall are not that different, the impact on Sheffield was far greater.[27]

By the early 1990s there was widespread concern about a developing crisis on the high street, with retail vacancies rising. The government commissioned a major review of the impact of out-of-town retailing by BDP and The Oxford Centre for Retail Management.[28] The report was a bit of a disappointment because, while the authors clearly believed that out-of-town retailing was damaging town centres, they failed to find a smoking gun. As a commentator wrote about the report at the time: 'With a few exceptions, [its] conclusions tend to be that actual examples of severe impact upon existing retail facilities are hard to find: the processes by which impacts are realised are tortuous and often obscured by other events, such as booms or slumps in consumer spending'. The following year a government-commissioned impact study of the Merry Hill Shopping Centre by Roger Tym and Partners was much less equivocal, using telephone surveys of shoppers to show that Dudley town centre had lost about 70% of its trade.[29]

VITAL AND VIABLE TOWN CENTRES

The mood had changed and in 1992 government published a draft revision to their planning guidance on retailing, which was adopted the following year.[30] Crucially this was about town centres rather than just retail developments, and accepted for the first time that planning should protect existing town centres. While not going as far as many planners would have liked, it required out-of-town schemes to be assessed in terms of their impact on the 'vitality and viability' of existing centres, the first time that phrase is used. It also specified that new regional shopping centres would only be considered if they were allocated in a statutory local plan, shutting the door on any more unsolicited proposals.

The new policy emphasised the need for positive planning to enhance existing town centres and guidance on how this was to be done was the subject of another major study by URBED. The report, called 'Vital and Viable Town Centres: Meeting the Challenge', was published in 1994.[31] It was based on 36 case studies and a survey of local planning authorities, concluding that many town centres 'felt' that they were declining and that local policy was failing to stem the dispersal of retail and other functions to out-of-town locations. The report suggests criteria that can be used to measure vitality and viability and creates a framework for town centre strategies based on the four 'A's:

- Attractions: Asking what are the uses that attract people to the town centre.
- Access: Exploring how easy it is to get there by a variety of means.
- Amenity: The quality of the environment when people get there.
- Action: The ability of the town centre to act on all of these issues.

These factors work in tandem, so a town centre with strong attractions can afford to make access more difficult by, for example, restricting parking. By contrast, centres with weaker attractions maybe need to make parking free and look to improve their environment. The 'Action' theme was important in promoting the idea of town centre management and one of the report's main authors Simon Quinn went on to be town centre manager of Reading and then head of the Association of Town Centre Management. The Vital and Viable Town Centres report provided a template for scores of town centre strategies that were carried out in the years that followed.

In tandem with the URBED report, the *House of Commons Environmental Audit Committee* was taking evidence on town centres.[32] Following a site visit to Merry Hill and Dudley they were tempted to recommend a ban on new out-of-town retailing. Instead, they recommended an intervention that would become a crucial part of planning policy on retailing – the sequential test. This is a policy test that says that a retail development should be refused planning permission if there is a substitutable site within, or nearer to, the town centre. The government accepted the committee's recommendations and within a year planning guidance had been updated to incorporate the town centre health check methodology from the URBED report and the sequential test.

Despite a great deal of scepticism at the time, this policy has been remarkably effective. There was a major test case at Duxford near Cambridge, where a large out-of-town retail scheme was refused on appeal, following which the number of new out-of-town retail consents fell dramatically. In 1994 86% of new retail space was being developed out of town and yet by 2001 86% of development was being built in existing town centres.[33] As we will see in the next chapter, it was to lead to what some called a renaissance and others called an unsustainable boom in town centre retailing that led over time to the next crisis on the high street.

Norwich city centre: Policy changes in the 1990s led to the revival of city centres like Norwich, although much of this was through multiple retailers rather than the city's market.

4 FROM BOOM TO BUST

Debenhams finally collapsed in December 2020 with the closure of its remaining 124 stores and the loss of 12,000 jobs. It had struggled for a number of years, falling into administration in April 2019 and, after a High Court battle with its landlords and disgruntled shareholders, making a Company Voluntary Agreement allowing it to renegotiate its rents. A series of store closures and redundancies would follow but the chain remained in a weakened state going into the first COVID lockdown. In April 2020, it entered a 'light touch' administration, with 6,500 redundancies, but the final nail in the coffin was the collapse of the Arcadia Group on 30 November 2020. Without the Arcadia concessions that occupied large parts of every Debenhams store, there was no way it could survive. The venerable store that had been trading since 1778 was no more. Except, of course, as an online brand following its acquisition for £55 million by Boohoo. The story of Debenhams illustrates the wider trends that have affected the high street in the last 20 years, as we describe in this chapter.

THE FALL OF DEBENHAMS

The heyday of Debenhams was the 2000s, in the retail boom that followed the government policy changes described in the last chapter. The new policy emphasis on the health of town centres and the sequential test for planning applications, with its presumption against out-of-town development, persuaded investors to put their money into existing town and city centres. So much institutional money flowed into town centres that it seemed 'they existed to deliver money to pension funds', in the words of a leading property expert.[1] They were no longer really about shopping – and certainly not about community – but about generating a return on capital.

We will see in a moment how the decade saw a rash of proposals for in-town shopping centres as towns and cities, desperate not to fall down the retail rankings, promoted schemes. This is where Debenhams came in, because while the big cities might have been able to anchor their shopping centre with a John Lewis or a Selfridges, the schemes elsewhere were all anchored by Debenhams.

Debenhams was run by Belinda Earl at the time, who had started work as a Saturday girl at the age of 16. Twenty-four years later she had risen to become chief executive, introducing the 'Designers at Debenhams' brand, which worked with leading designers to produce 'runway fashion' at high street prices. Debenhams was the hottest name on the high street and in 2006 announced plans to double the number of its stores to 240. The financial logic seemed irresistible – shopping centre developers would offer Debenhams attractive terms to secure their signature

Chelmsford: Debenhams was the anchor of many high streets and shopping centres but its fate was sealed during a brief period of ownership by a private equity consortium in the early 2000s.

on a pre-let. Having got them in place they were able to sign up other retailers keen to feed off the footfall that the Debenhams would attract. Once a certain percentage of the space had been pre-let then the pension funds would be willing to invest and the scheme could proceed. Debenhams continued to open new stores until 2017 despite its annual losses rising to almost half a million pounds a year.

As Sir Ian Cheshire, Debenham's former chairman told the BBC, its stores became a 'straitjacket' that made it almost impossible to save the company when trading conditions deteriorated.[2] They may have secured advantageous rent deals, but they overexpanded and many of the new stores didn't trade particularly well while business rates, staffing and maintenance costs crippled the business. As the headlines started to emerge about the company's problems, it became difficult to attract top staff and the company was unable to invest in its stores, which were dominated by concessions that could be had elsewhere on the high street. Such is the death of the department store, not just Debenhams.

But there is a wider story of corporate greed and bad decisions that explains the death of Debenhams. In 1985 Debenhams was bought by the Burton Group, the retail empire of Sir Ralph Halpern that, at its peak, ran 2,800 stores including Topshop and Dorothy Perkins and employed 60,000 people. In 1998 Debenhams was floated as a separate company on the London Stock Exchange while the remainder of the group was rebranded as Arcadia. As Tony Colman, former director of Burton and later a Labour MP told us, Burton was run as a social business and many of the directors were socialists.[3] They set ethical standards for suppliers and treated their staff well, from comprehensive graduate training schemes down to 60% staff discount for their 'Saturday girls'. They owned all their stores, the original Burton's shops often including a snooker hall or dance hall on the upper floors. It did however mean that a huge amount of value was left in the business, making it vulnerable to takeover. Arcadia was bought by Philip Green a few years later with borrowing from the Royal Bank of Scotland. Having acquired the company, he sold the stores to repay the borrowing while leasing them back on 20-year leases with upwards-only rent reviews.

Something even worse happened to Debenhams, which was sold to a private equity consortium in 2003 for £600 million.[4] The consortium owned the company for only a few years, taking out £1.2 billion in dividends before 'flipping' it by refloating on the Stock Exchange. A company that had been virtually debt-free was now saddled with more than £1 billion of debt as stores were remortgaged. A further 23 stores were sold to British Land for £495 million and rented back to the company on 35-year leases with guaranteed rent rises of 2.5% a year. This is the real reason for the death of Debenhams – all of its other problems stem from this brief period of brutal private equity ownership. As the retail analyst Richard Hyman told *The Guardian*: 'At the very time when the sort of massive changes we're seeing today were embryonic, Debenhams' wherewithal to react, i.e. money, was removed. It was removed into the bank accounts of private equity investors. That is the truth of it.'[5]

THE AGE OF THE SHOPPING CENTRE

So, while the 2000s could be seen as a success for government policy, the foundations of the high street crisis were being laid. The genie of out-of-town retail had been put back in its bottle and town centres across the country were being regenerated with huge levels of investment. Much of this investment was directed into new shopping centres, indeed this could be seen as the golden age of the

Birmingham: The
redevelopment of the
Bullring Shopping
Centre with its iconic
Selfridges store was
the high point of the
retail boom in the
2000s.

Birmingham: The
redevelopment of the
Bullring Shopping
Centre with its iconic
Selfridges store was
the high point of the
retail boom in the
2000s.

in-town mall. In cities and towns up and down the country, councils were being advised by retail agents that they risked missing out on the retail boom because their town centre shops were too small and cramped to attract the major retailers. Lack of representation by these 'multiple retailers' would see town centres sliding down the retail rankings, which was something that local councils simply couldn't allow. So the same retail agents were employed to help councils assemble sites and promote schemes for new covered shopping centres.

As is so often the case, Birmingham led the way, as it had been seeking to redevelop the Bullring Shopping Centre for some time. The Bullring had been one of the first in-town malls and was showing its age. A number of schemes had been developed, finally resulting in planning permission being granted in 2000 for a scheme designed by the architects Benoy. The plans proposed a curving covered mall with Selfridges at one end and a huge Debenhams at the other. But in a radical move the mall was bisected by an open street curving down the hill to the historic St Martin's Church. The centre opened on 4 September 2003 and soon became the busiest shopping centre in the UK with 36.5 million visitors a year.

A series of ambitious proposals followed, including the Highcross Centre in Leicester, Cabot Circus in Bristol, St David's in Cardiff and the two huge Westfield Centres in London. Most influential of them all was Liverpool ONE (covered in Chapter 6), which led the way in the transformation of shopping centres from inward-looking malls to light airy spaces integrated into the surrounding city centres. The Grand Arcade in the middle of the St David's Shopping Centre in Cardiff was promoted by its designers as a direct descendant of the city's arcades. But it was the absence of a roof that provoked the most debate. As shoppers in Liverpool ONE were quoted as saying 'it is strange that they made the shopping centre outside, with all the bad weather'.[6] More importantly, Liverpool ONE was far more integrated into the city centre, opening up the original street pattern with no doors, so people soon forgot where it began and ended.

The evolution of the shopping centre was set to continue, with the redevelopment of the Broadmarsh Centre in Nottingham and the Sevenstone iteration of the New Retail Quarter in Sheffield. The latter would have been an open-air retail quarter with each building designed by different architects, however as we saw in the Introduction, it was a victim of the credit crunch and its developers Hammerson eventually pulled out in order to concentrate on the completion of the Victoria Gate scheme in Leeds.

The same process was at work in smaller towns, who were developing ambitious plans to build new shopping centres. In our case studies they include the evocatively named Eagles Meadow in Wrexham, the Princesshay Centre in Exeter and the Rock in Bury. All of these were built without roofs, indeed Princesshay was shortlisted by the Academy of Urbanism for a Great Place Award in 2011.[7] Remarkably, these centres were all opened in 2008 or 2009, Bury being the last to complete after its developer collapsed in the first year of the financial crisis and it had to be bailed out by Hammerson. Of course, the other thing that all three have in common is that they were anchored by Debenhams stores that have since closed.

Not all town centres were so 'lucky' and many of the retail schemes under development were not sufficiently committed by 2008 and the plans therefore collapsed in the face of the financial crisis. Not that councils gave up easily on their dream, many spending years negotiating with developers and seeing the plans dumbed down as cost savings were made. Some schemes, like the Retail Quarter in Sheffield, could never be revived, at least as a retail scheme, but others did emerge in a brief clutch of shopping centre openings in 2013–15. It is perhaps these later schemes that have done the most damage to town centres, as the stories of Stafford (case study box) and Bradford illustrate.

BRADFORD PLAYS A DANGEROUS GAME

Bradford is a place that has long suffered from being overshadowed by Leeds, but historically its retail centre punched above its weight. A historical review of retail rankings showed that until the 1980s Bradford's retail status was one level greater than its urban status and not far behind Leeds.[8] However, its position started to slip in the 1990s, causing the council to decide that they needed to promote a new retail scheme. Little did they know that it would come close to undermining the entire town centre.

In 1998 the council formed a partnership with two local developers, Magellan Properties and Caddick Developments, to build the new centre. This was actually a redevelopment of Broadway, a tired retail scheme that had been built over the culverted river in the 1950s. The new Broadway would transform the city centre, the council were told; it would include 100 shops, with new stores for C&A and BHS (who were already in Broadmarsh); would be anchored by a new Debenhams and see the relocation of the Marks & Spencer from the top end of town.

Within a couple of years, the partnership had been sold on and was eventually bought by Westfield. By that time planning consent had been granted and work had started on demolition, with the new centre scheduled to open at the end of 2007. It was then that things started to go wrong. The demolition of the old centre created a huge 4.5ha (11 acre) hole in the city centre but, as the local press started to put pressure on the council, Westfield went strangely quiet. The promised dates came and went and when construction failed to start, suspicion grew that Westfield were stringing Bradford along while they finished their new centre in Derby. By October, Councillor Mallinson, the Council's executive member for regeneration, was telling the local paper: 'On a number of occasions, we have aired our frustrations and

City Park in Bradford with its mirror pool that fills during the day. The success of Bradford city centre is as much to do with this as the redeveloped shopping centre.

have continued to beat our chests ... threatening to take the site off Westfield if construction hadn't started by Christmas.'[9] The reality was that in the background Westfield had been struggling to sign up retailers and were still below the number of pre-lets they needed to commit to construction.

Then in 2008, the financial crisis hit, with no sign of Westfield, and it dawned on the city that it might have made a monumental mistake. Who demolishes a quarter of their city centre for a scheme that apparently wasn't viable even before a global recession and now looked like it might never happen? The hole left in the city centre was turned into a temporary park, with a series of artworks and a performance area, but as the financial crisis spread and the government started worrying about a crisis on the high street, the city's position seemed hopeless.

The situation continued for six years, until a brief period when retail fortunes recovered between 2013 and 2015, allowing Westfield to resurrect the scheme. The shopping centre was completed and opened its doors ready for Christmas trading in 2015. Since then, the centre has traded well and helped restore the city's position in the retail rankings, at least before the pandemic and the loss of Debenhams. The impact on the town centre as a whole is more questionable. In 2019 and 2021 Bradford had the worst vacancy rate of all our case studies, peaking at 24.1%, as the upper end of town, shorn of its M&S, has struggled. Shoppers may have returned to Bradford but many of them park in the huge Westfield car park, and shop in the new centre without frequenting the rest of the city centre.

The upper end of the town centre is dominated by the Alhambra Shopping Centre, a brutalist concrete box which the council has recently acquired with the intention of redeveloping the area for housing. The council is promoting the surrounding area as the city's Independent Quarter but in a city where around half of the population are Muslim, the scope to develop a culture of independent bars is limited.[10] As with the Stafford case study (see box), the overall effect of the new shopping centre has been to damage the town centre and to make it far less resilient to the current retail crisis.

CLONE TOWNS

The boom years for retail in the early 2000s created other problems. In 2005, the New Economics Foundation published an influential report called 'Clone Town Britain'.[11] This was prompted by concerns that: 'Real local shops have been replaced by swathes of identikit chain stores that seem to spread like economic weeds making high streets up and down the country virtually indistinguishable from one another.' A major target for the report were the big supermarkets, which were then in a vigorous expansion phase both in terms of numbers and size of stores and the range of goods they stocked, with the introduction of in-store fishmongers, bakers and butchers, pharmacies, clothes, newsagents, record stores and even post offices. One by one the retailers lining the high street were being extinguished as their markets were stolen by the supermarkets. The report quotes a US study that documented how, in the 10 years after Walmart moved into Iowa, the state lost 555 grocery stores, 298 hardware stores, 293 building suppliers, 161 variety stores, 153 shoe stores and 116 drug stores, a total loss of 1,326 businesses.[12]

The Clone Town Britain report was based on a self-completed survey covering towns and villages with populations between 5,000 and 150,000. Around 150 places participated but the results are based on 130 complete survey forms. These documented the retailers in each town centre to generate a clone town score allowing towns to be categorised as 'home towns' full of individuality and independent businesses, 'border towns' which were marginal and 'clone towns'. Just over 40% of the towns were considered 'clone towns', rising to 48% in London. The most extreme clone town in the survey was Exeter, with a score of just 6.9 out of a possible 60.

The report raises three concerns about this homogenisation of the high street. The first is the worry that everywhere was starting to look the same. As the report writes: 'Many town centres that have undergone substantial regeneration have lost their sense of place and the distinctive facades of their high streets under the march of the glass, steel, and concrete blandness of chain stores built for the demands of inflexible business models that provide the ideal degree of sterility to house a string of big, clone town retailers.'

The second concern was the impact on independent producers. It worried about niche journals that would never be stocked by supermarkets, independent publishers robbed of their outlet through the closure over the previous five years of one in ten bookshops, and indie-record labels deprived of local record stores, not to mention artisan cheese makers, local farmers, wine producers, etc. The report quotes a legal case in 1998 when the American Booksellers Association filed a lawsuit against Barnes & Nobel, calling it a 'fight about preserving what America is able to read'. The clone town retailers carried a limited range of vanilla products that would appeal to a mass market, thereby strangling diversity.

The third and prophetic concern was that this loss of diversity on the high street was making it vulnerable to collapse. Natural ecosystems are based on genetic diversity; when they become dominated by a small number of species they can be wiped out by climate changes, pests and disease. In the same way, the report writes 'clone towns imperil local livelihoods, communities and our culture, by decreasing the resilience of high streets to economic downturns and diminishing consumer choice'. Which is exactly what happened when the economic downturn of 2008 coincided with the rise in online.

WOOLWORTHS AND THE START OF THE RETAIL CRISIS

As we saw in Chapter 1, Woolworths was created as a 'five and dime' (what would be a pound store today) at the end of the 19th century, quickly growing to be the most innovative retailer of its age. It arrived in the UK in 1909 and grew rapidly through the 1920s until pretty much every town had a Woolworths. At its peak it had 850 stores selling everything from its famous pick 'n' mix sweets, to its own brand of Ladybird children's clothes, records and CDs, household goods, stationery and more. It was a mini department store and when it disappeared many people claimed that it had been their favourite shop, even if they hadn't actually been there in years. In December 2008, the company went into liquidation, along with its 807 remaining stores and 27,000 jobs. The collapse also included its CD and DVD wholesale arm Entertainment UK which in turn led to the collapse of Zavvi – the rebranded rump of Virgin Records, as we will see in Chapter 9.

Even after a decade that has seen the failure of many high street household names, the collapse of Woolworths remains the most shocking. Bigger than Arcadia or Debenhams in terms of job losses and affecting virtually every town in the country, it was all the more alarming for seemingly coming out of a blue sky. The high street had seemed to be doing so well and, while the financial crisis had exploded a few months earlier, it seemed too early for it to be hitting retail.

Part of the problem for Woolworths, like Debenhams, came down to bad property deals. Until 2001 it had been owned by Kingfisher, who had sold 182 of its leases for £614 million, leaving Woolworths with 700 different landlords, often on lease terms of 50 years with upward-only rent clauses.[13] However, most retail analysis put the failure down to complacency, poor management and a failure to innovate. Woolworths didn't spot the threat of pound stores or value retailers like B&M, Home Bargains and Wilko, which were essentially doing the same thing but better and cheaper. On another front, digital music platforms and streaming services were undermining its CD and DVD sales, both retail and wholesale. As one retail analyst told *Retail Gazette*: 'Fundamentally, nobody knew what Woolworths was for, and that included the management.'[14]

In 2008 Woolworths found itself struggling to maintain sales, with £400 million in debts and lenders like GMAC Financial Services that had just taken a huge hit on subprime mortgages and decided to get out of retail. The collapse was swift and inevitable, toppling the 'first domino of physical retail Armageddon', in the words of retail analyst Matthew Hopkinson.

THE PORTAS REVIEW

Within a few years, the Woolworths collapse had turned into a fully-fledged crisis on the high street and big names like Blacks Leisure, MFI, Zavvi, Ethel Austin, JJB Sports, Peacocks, Game, Comet, Blockbuster and HMV followed Woolworths' example. The impression of crisis was not helped by a spate of rioting in 2011, including the so-called 'Tesco riots' against the opening of a Metro store in the Stokes Croft area of Bristol. Much worse riots were triggered later in the summer by the police shooting of Mark Duggan, causing hundreds of millions of pounds of damage, first in London town centres and then in copycat riots across the country.

The government's response was to set up a review of town centres and the Prime Minister David Cameron turned to the retail guru Mary Portas to lead it. Mary Portas had started her career as a 'Saturday girl' at John Lewis and spent 10 years designing window displays for Harrods, Topshop and Harvey Nichols. By the time she was 30, she was on the board of Harvey Nichols, leaving there in 1997 to set up her own retail branding consultancy. However, she was known to the public and David Cameron as 'Mary Queen of Shops' because of her BBC series. The programme would visit a failing independent retailer incognito or when the owners were away. Mary would then tell them all the things they were doing wrong, get them to buck up their ideas and heroically turn the business around. David Cameron reasoned that she was just the person to do the same for the high street as a whole.

In her report she concludes that high streets are indeed at a crisis point and that 'unless urgent action is taken much of Britain will lose, irretrievably, something that is fundamental to our society'.[15] She documents how there had been 10,000 shop closures in the previous two years, one in six units stood vacant and footfall outside London had dropped by 10%. The reasons for this were only partly to do with the recession. The internet had played its part; at the time 10% of sales were online and this had accounted for half of the growth in retail spending since 2003. 'M-commerce' sales on smart phones were an even bigger threat, having grown by 500% in the two years before the report. But even this didn't really explain the problems on the high street.

The problem was that while the internet and the recession only accounted for a 10–15% drop in sales, many high street retailers were so marginal that this was enough to push them below break-even. In the style of one of her programmes, Portas told us that 'we shouldn't mourn the loss of poorly run retail businesses that weren't able to adapt to our 21st century needs'. Many 'mediocre' businesses had thrived in the boom years and were now being found out. By contrast, she spoke admiringly of malls like the two Westfield Centres in London as '21st century urban entertainment centres' that have 'raised and reframed consumers' expectations of high streets and town centres'. She is also full of admiration for supermarkets that have 'delivered highly convenient, needs-based retailing, which serves today's consumers well'. While she recommended that new out-of-town development should be more tightly controlled, her real point was that high streets should get with the game and become more like Westfield or Tesco.

This they would mostly have to do without many of the big retailers, which had gone to the wall. The successful ones that remained would once have needed 400–500 stores to cover the country but could now get by with far fewer because of the reach that the internet gave them. Most small and medium town centres would therefore need to be reinvented as centres for independent shops, community uses and services. We come to a similar conclusion in this book; the question is: how do we bring it about?

The report's recommendations fall under five themes. The first is aimed at running town centres more like businesses by establishing 'town teams', empowering and funding Business Improvement Districts (BIDs) and helping people set up as market traders. The second theme is about creating the right conditions, with three recommendations relating to business rates, three more on planning deregulation plus free parking. The third is about levelling the playing field, with two recommendations restricting new out-of-town retailing and two suggesting that big retailers should support their local high street. The fourth theme targets retail landlords, suggesting that a duty of care to their tenants be put on them and measures taken to stop them leaving units empty. It suggests a register of high street landlords and powers for local authorities to intervene when units are left empty. The fifth theme relates to the community, with two recommendations about the neighbourhood plans, recently introduced by the Cameron government, reference to developer contributions and community right to 'try' to support imaginative use of empty properties.

The final recommendation involved setting up a series of pilot projects that inevitably became known as the Portas Pilots. In 2012, 370 places applied and in May 12 were selected, each to receive a slice of the tiny budget of £1.2 million plus 'a tailored package of support from both the minister and retail guru Mary Portas'.[16] A second round of 12 places was announced later in 2012, plus a further three pilots supported by the Greater London Authority. The pilot schemes included street art and 'bicycle rickshaws', 'guerrilla gardening' and 'yarn bombing', modern-day town criers, a 'school for shopkeepers' and a 'Dragons' Den' style competition for local entrepreneurs. The tiny budget caused Bill Grimsey to describe the pilots as 'little more than a PR stunt to lay the grounds for a lucrative TV makeover show about the Portas Pilot Towns'.[17]

In 2017 the BBC's 'You and Yours' programme commissioned the Local Data Company to review the first 12 pilots, generating a headline that they had lost nearly 1,000 shops since becoming pilots, representing a drop of 17% or one closure every 22 days.[18] However, it did find that in 10 of the pilots the vacancy rate had fallen as the units were converted to other uses, which to be fair, is what the review had predicted. Mary Portas admitted to the programme that she had hoped her review would have led to more government action: 'That didn't happen. It was a weighted PR campaign which looked like "Hey, we're doing something" and I hoped it might kick start something – but it didn't.'

GRIMSEY REVIEW

The quote about the pilots being a PR stunt was part of a public spat between Mary Portas and Bill Grimsey, who set up his own review a year later 'written by professionals for professionals'.[19] Grimsey's anger was as much about the scale of the government response to the crisis rather than Portas' conclusions, which were actually similar to his own. In the book he subsequently wrote entitled *Sold Out: Who Killed the High Street*, his main argument with the Portas Review was that it underestimated the scale of the problem, 'the high street is as good as dead already', and that it failed to understand the retailer's perspective.[20]

Grimsey's book is full of harrowing stories of retail hubris, complacency and recklessness. He is a lifelong retailer, having started as a butcher's boy, risen through the ranks of the grocery chain Bishops before holding management positions at Budgens, Tesco, Wickes and Iceland. He admires retailers like Tesco, who in his view have been more responsive to customer needs than the high street. He puts the failure of the high street down to something rotten at the heart of the industry. Prophetically, despite the upturn in the market when his review was published, he predicted that there was much worse to come. Retailing, he says, is dominated by larger than life characters combining 'business acumen, negotiating skills and more than a little bit of chutzpah'. They invariably sail close to the wind and many of them have ruined their businesses. He describes a tempestuous meeting with a foul-mouthed Philip Green, although at the time he admitted that, while he didn't approve of Green's 'rambunctious' management style, 'he clearly knows what works on the high street'. He may have been wrong on this point but he was right to identify a sector obsessed with finance and property rather than their core business of catering to customer needs. In another story, he described

ASHINGTON

Together with neighbouring Newbiggin-by-the-Sea, Ashington was one of the first Portas Pilots. Known as the world's largest pit village, the area has seen the closure of all of its mines. However, our data shows that its high street is performing at least as well as many much more prosperous towns.

As part of the pilot, a Town Team was set up and local boy Sir John Hall (developer of Gateshead Metrocentre) became its chair. Much work has been done on promotion and events including a new market. However, the key project was a £1.5 million scheme to reopen the high street to one-way traffic and parking. The street was divided down the middle with a row of planting beds. On one side was created a wide pavement, seating areas and trees. On the other, a single carriageway for one-way traffic and 30 chevron parking places. It is not strictly a shared space scheme but shares many of the characteristics of one, with traffic reduced to walking pace and frequent crossings. Al Vaziri, owner of Al's Card Shop, told the *Newcastle Chronicle* 'since the car parking opened my takings have doubled'.

selling the debt-laden Big Food Group (owners of Iceland) to an Icelandic investor for an unbelievable sum. When asked where the money was coming from, the answer was the Icelandic banks backed by HBOS, both of which would collapse under the weight of a huge portfolio of bad debts a few years later in the credit crisis.

When Grimsey said the high street was dead, he meant the high street of the big retailers. His solution is to champion independent retailers and to turn high streets into more rounded community hubs, again not unlike Mary Portas. He proposes consolidating town centres, converting peripheral streets to housing and relocating successful independent shops into the core. He sees the reform of business rates as essential and proposes a stick and carrot approach to getting landlords to bring empty space back into use. This should all be funded by national retail and leisure chains being required to invest 2.5% of their sales revenue in a local fund to support town centres.

None of this is very different to Portas but unlike the Portas Pilots which were little more than a bunch of projects dragged off existing shelves, there is a working example of what Grimsey's package might mean in practice. In Belgium the alderman of the small town Roeselare came across the Grimsey Review.[21] Kris Declercq, who has since been made mayor, drew up a programme of 50 action points and got the support of the town's 300 traders. A key measure was to use property tax relief to refund businesses who moved from a peripheral location into the centre, opened a second store or lived above the shop. Taxes were reduced for new businesses and increased on a year-on-year basis for any property left empty. This was combined with a business finder service, putting landlords in touch with prospective tenants. Parking has been taken out of the central square but made free on the edge of the centre, the shops are required to maintain their shopfronts and window displays, events are organised and antisocial behaviour and littering fined. It is an ongoing and evolving process, with a second round of measures set out in 2020 in response to feedback and experience about what had worked. As Vanessa Dehullu, now responsible for the programme, says: 'Doing nothing is not an option, because you will end up with a dead city centre.'

A BRIEF RECOVERY

A parliamentary briefing paper in 2018 documented how the retail sector contributed £194 billion to UK economic output, employed 20% of the workforce (4.9 million people) and consisted of 374,000 businesses.[22] All of these things, the paper pointed out, had grown in the previous four years, while the rate of retail failures had fallen. In the five years up to 2013, the Centre for Retail Research had documented just under 20,000 store closures and 184,324 job losses, whereas in the next five years there were 7,421 store closures and 83,655 job losses.[23] Vacancy rates were also down marginally and retail sales had risen by 12.7% in the five years to 2018.

This false spring saw the revival of the retail property market. Up and down the country retail schemes that had been put on ice as a result of the global economic crisis were dusted off and restarted, to the relief of many councils. In addition to the Westfield Shopping Centre in Bradford that we have already heard about, these included Victoria Gate in Leeds and Grand Central in Birmingham, both developed by Hammerson and anchored by a John Lewis, as well as centres in smaller places like Stafford and Wrexham. The last new Debenhams opened as late as 2017.

STAFFORD

It was a blessing in disguise when Debenhams pulled out of the Riverside Shopping Centre development in 2014. Construction had just started on the £70 million edge-of-centre mall that was to have been anchored by a Debenhams and a Marks & Spencer, the latter relocating from the town's main square. Fortunately, there was no turning back and the developer was able to sign up Primark as the second anchor. So when it opened in 2016, the centre was fully let, with a cinema, chain restaurants and a good mix of fashion retailers.

Stafford is a typical market town and county town. The town centre is encircled by markets – the Asda, Tesco Extra and Sainsbury's would have been joined by Morrisons had they not pulled out in 2016. Despite the supermarkets the town centre remained busy, but the council were being advised that they compared badly in the retail ranking to competitors like Burton-on-Trent, Telford and Shrewsbury.[24] Stafford, where 71% of retailers are independents, scored badly and the council felt pressured to do something, hence the promotion of the Riverside Shopping Centre.[25] This was designed as a classic small mall but is disconnected from the traditional town centre. It was conceived before the recession and eventually was built in a brief window of viability after 2013. However, far from improving the town centre it has made matters worse. The 170 multiple retailers that had been in the town in 2012 had fallen to 140 by 2019. Many retailers in the mall relocated from the old town centre while others quit the town altogether. The vacancy rate has risen from 11% in 2012 to 19.6% in 2019, twice the average of the other towns in our sample. As a shopper told a local news reporter in May 2021: 'Stafford is a ghost town ... I've lived here for 59 years and it used to be a thriving town centre ... now it's all vaping shops, phone shops and barbers.'[26]

Stafford is a recipient of the Future High Street Fund and is looking to revive the old town centre with new housing, environmental works, a revamped market square and the relocation of the market. The hope is that this will be enough to revive the town centre as a community focus rather than a shopping destination, even if the problems being addressed in the old town centre are largely self-inflicted.

However, as Bill Grimsey reported in 2018 when he reconvened his review,[27] the storm clouds were gathering. Retail problems were being masked by rising consumer spending, even if much of this was being done on credit cards, and retail costs at 2.9% per annum were rising faster than sales growth at 1.9%. The high levels of debt and bad property deals had not gone away and 'zombie retailers' were roaming the high street with levels of debt greater than the value of their assets. The banks couldn't afford to foreclose but at the same time they certainly weren't going to lend more so that companies couldn't invest. Company Watch figures quoted by Grimsey that measure the financial resilience of companies showed that 44% of retail businesses were classed as being financially vulnerable, rising to 64% for small retailers. As a result, the second Grimsey Review predicted (before the COVID pandemic) that 6,000 retailers (including independents) would fail by 2020.

THE CURRENT CRISIS

This brings us back to the current crisis on the high street that we described in the Introduction. It started in late 2017/early 2018, since which time around 50,000 stores have closed, compared to the 10,000 units that had closed in the run-up to the Portas Review. The current crisis has seen the loss of more than 75,000 jobs, starting with House of Fraser in 2018 and peaking with the collapse of Debenhams and Arcadia at the end of 2020.

It is important to note that this crisis predates the first COVID lockdowns in March 2020 and the implementation of Brexit, although both made the situation immeasurably worse. To many, the crisis seemed to have come out of nowhere. The economy may not have been booming but it wasn't doing especially badly. Retailer costs were rising through factors like business rates and the minimum wage but there was not a dramatic change in costs in 2018. Likewise, the internet was gradually edging up its share of retail spend, but there was no dramatic change. The Brexit vote had been a shock to the sector but in 2018 there was still hope that trade barriers could be minimised and of course the COVID virus didn't yet exist.

What seems to have happened is that all the problems of the retail sector that Bill Grimsey had documented in his review finally came home to roost. It wasn't any one thing, it was everything, gradually piling the pressure on a sector that had lost its resilience, saddled with too many physical stores, locked into upwards-only rent deals with too many overheads, too little investment, and perhaps most importantly, too few fresh ideas. In 2018, it all became too much and the camel's back was broken. With markets, of course, the most important commodity is confidence; once that goes everything is at risk.

One factor that may not have triggered the crisis, but is certainly worth highlighting, was the 2017 business rates revaluation. This had been delayed from 2015 and for many of the larger retailers it resulted in significantly higher rates bills, in many cases higher than their rent. Business rates are based on a multiplier of a property's rental value, the rate rising from 34.8p in 1990 to the present rate of 51.2p. The revaluation took place just before the market dipped so that retailers were paying rates based on rental values that had since fallen. To cushion the blow a transitional arrangement was introduced, but all this meant was that retailers in weaker centres that had seen rents fall had to wait longer for their rates reductions. There is widespread consensus that the system is broken, including the Treasury Select Committee.[28] Business rates make it even more difficult for physical retailers to compete with online retail when Amazon, with a turnover of £8.8 billion, paid £63.4 million in business rates in 2018, while Next, with less than half that turnover, paid well over £100 million on its 500 stores.[29]

The effect of these factors on the high street was most clearly demonstrated in December 2019 when one of the UK's biggest investment funds M&G, with £2.5 billion invested in shopping centres and retail parks, was forced to suspend withdrawals from its property portfolio. Investors had taken out almost £1 billion and the fund managers were unable to sell their assets quickly enough to cover the withdrawals, citing 'Brexit-related political uncertainty and ongoing structural shifts in the UK retail sector'.[30]

This brings home the point that shopping centres and retail parks, very much the villains of previous crises, were just as badly hit in 2018. Unlike traditional centres they were far more dependent on the mainstream retailers who were now in difficulty. In 2019 the Local Data Company reported that the vacancy rate had risen by 2.3% in retail parks compared to just 0.5% on the high street.[31] In addition to retail closures, viability was being squeezed by insolvency procedures that had allowed retailers like New Look, Monsoon and Debenhams to renegotiate their rents, while other retailers like House of Fraser were achieving the same thing by negotiation.

The biggest casualty of these trends was Intu, which was forced to admit in March 2020 that it had abandoned attempts to raise £1 billion in equity due to lack of interest from investors. This was a few weeks before the first lockdown, so again it wasn't COVID related. Intu, owners of the Trafford Centre in Manchester, the Metrocentre in Gateshead and Lakeside in Essex, together with 11 other UK shopping centres, had seen its share price fall from £2.8 billion in November 2018 to just £164 million in March 2020, a drop of 94%. With debts of more than £4.5 billion they missed a deadline set by their banks, making their collapse on 26 June all but inevitable.[32] Footfall at the Trafford Centre in the first three months of 2020 had actually been slightly up on the previous year and occupancy rates were steady. Rental income was down by 9.1% but the figures were far from disastrous. The problem was that investor confidence in big retail had collapsed and for debt-laden companies like Intu and many of the big retailers this put them in an impossible position.

THE GOVERNMENT RESPONSE

The government response to the emerging crisis in 2018 was swifter than it had been at the time of the Portas Review. Sir John Timpson, founder of the shoe repair and key cutting chain that carries his name, was asked to undertake a review, but even before his report was published in December 2018 the government had announced the £675 million Future High Streets Fund in the autumn budget.[33] Timpson recommended that this be combined with a High Streets Task Force to provide expertise and advice to local authorities and to support them in bidding for the funds. In July 2019, the new Prime Minister Boris Johnson announced a £3.6 billion 'Towns Fund' targeted at what had become known as the 'red wall' towns of Northern England that had traditionally voted Labour but had turned to the Conservatives in that summer's election. The Towns Fund included a further £325 million for the Future High Streets Fund, bringing it up to £1 billion, more than 800 times greater than the resources committed to the Portas Pilots. An £8.6 million contract was given to a consortium led by the Institute for Place Management at Manchester Metropolitan University to run the High Streets Task Force, which recruited 150 high street experts to support local authorities to prepare a business case as part of their application for the funds.[34] Eventually, 72 places were allocated a share of the funds, with grants ranging up to £25 million, with another £95 million being put towards Heritage High Streets Fund supporting another 69 places.

This amounts to the biggest ever investment of public funds in our high streets and is certainly touted by government as transformational. The biggest recipients were Sunderland and Swindon, each of which received £25 million. Sunderland promised to develop the 'UK's best library', to remodel a major road in order to connect the huge Vaux development site to the city centre and to refurbish the Elephant Tea Rooms and fit out vacant retail units around the square linking the development to the high street. Swindon proposed to create a bus boulevard linking the station and the town centre by remodelling an existing dual carriageway and removing underpasses. Like many of the successful bids these were existing projects that could be pulled down from the shelf, although the role of the High Streets Task Force was to ensure that they were part of a coherent strategy to revive the town centre. In the Introduction we heard about the Sheffield Future High Streets project seeking to repurpose the Fargate retail area and elsewhere the fund has invested in new theatres and even housing. Whether these schemes will succeed in transforming town centres is too early to tell, partly because most are yet to be completed, but also because of an even greater shock to the high street that was just around the corner.

COVID

At the end of 2019 there were reports of a virus affecting the Chinese city of Wuhan. By February it had been given a name; COVID-19 and by the end of that month the first major European outbreak was gripping Italy. On 23 March, UK government imposed the first lockdown banning non-essential travel and closing schools, workplaces and non-essential retail. In mid-April 2020 restrictions were gradually lifted but in the autumn a second wave led to a further lockdown in November and ongoing restrictions through to spring 2021 when the vaccine roll-out enabled restrictions to be eased. However, new more transmissible variants of the virus arrived, first Delta and then Omicron, leading to a third wave in autumn 2021 with restrictions that fell short of a full lockdown, although people were advised to work from home and foreign travel was very restricted.

These restrictions hit non-essential retail and the hospitality and cultural industries. The supermarkets and other 'essential retailers' did well, while other town centre businesses received government support including a furlough scheme for employees, loan and grant schemes, a 100% business rates holiday, a VAT cut for hospitality businesses and a moratorium on evictions from commercial premises. All of this was necessary as the first lockdown saw levels of footfall in town centres drop by 89.8% with the press full of pictures of deserted shopping streets.[35] When restrictions were lifted, there was a brief boom, boosted by the government's 'Eat Out to Help Out' initiative, but many centres struggled to get back to pre-pandemic levels. In autumn 2020 London's Oxford Street's footfall remained down by 68% year on year.[36]

A number of local authorities ran their own business support scheme as well as experimenting with traffic reduction measures, widening pavements to allow for outdoor trading and drinking. In London there was controversy as councils like Lambeth brought forward the implementation of 'low traffic neighbourhoods', blocking roads with temporary planters. Liverpool implemented its 'City without Walls' initiative in summer 2020 to temporarily widen pavements, allowing bars, cafés and restaurants to use the space outside their premises while maintaining social distancing. Bright orange bollards were used to narrow the street in one of our case studies, Lark Lane, making it one-way, although residents complained outdoor drinking was not appropriate for a residential area.[37]

COVID has affected the high street in a number of important ways. It hit traditional shopping centres and retail malls hardest while retail parks, with plentiful parking and easier social distancing, saw something of a revival, reversing the trend of 2018. High street vacancy rates were 14.5% in 2021, rising to 19.5% in malls but being just 11.1% in retail parks.[38]

Prior to the pandemic there was a winner-takes-all trend in which the big cities were thriving at the expense of smaller towns and suburban centres. That all changed as work from home orders deprived the cities of their office workers and travel restrictions robbed them of their tourists. The beneficiaries were smaller suburban centres where home workers were able to pop out for a coffee or visit the local shops. The Centre for Cities has run a High Street Recovery Tracker throughout the pandemic, calculating a 'recovery index' based on a range of factors including footfall and spend, with a baseline pre-pandemic score of 100.[39] At the end of 2020 the index was showing all the major cities at the bottom of the recovery index with scores of 22–45. By contrast the top 10 were all suburban centres or smaller towns. As we write (February 2022), after all restrictions have been lifted, the cities largely remain in the bottom half of the index, with scores of just 50 for London and around 80 for the other cities. Surprisingly, the top 10 are now dominated by industrial towns, with Barnsley, Sunderland, Middlesbrough and Wakefield all having recovery index scores above 100, suggesting they are doing better in terms of footfall and spend than they were pre-pandemic.

The other big change during lockdown has been the growth in online retail. Before the pandemic this was on a gradual, if remorseless, rise from 10.2% in 2011 to 16% in 2019, a level exceeded only by China and South Korea.[40] During lockdown, online sales reached 32.8% in the first lockdown and 37.8% in the

Lark Lane Liverpool: The 'City without Walls' initiative, like many similar initiatives across the country, saw temporary works to widen pavements and create safe cycling routes even if the bright orange bollards did nothing for the appearance of the street.

second.[41] There was another peak as a result of the Omicron restrictions at the end of 2021, but generally between these restrictions it has been running at a level of 26–27% as groups such as the elderly have been introduced to the idea of buying online. It is too early to say but it appears that the retail industry will need to get used to a market in which at least a quarter of sales are online.

THE END OF THE HIGH STREET?

In a post-pandemic world there remain many uncertainties and it will be a number of years before a clear picture emerges of what the future high street will be. The history of previous crises on the high street show how resilient they are. The death knell was sounded in the 1970s and again in the 1990s but in both cases high streets bounced back, fighting off the formidable threat first from the supermarkets and then from out-of-town retailing. Will the current crisis be any different? Much of the analysis indicates that it will be.

Not only has the current retail crisis been deeper than those in the past, as we write in 2022 it is being compounded by a cost of living crisis. Having just started to recover from COVID, retailers are being squeezed by high inflation and energy costs, which both increase their overheads and reduce the disposable income of their customers.

As we quoted in the Introduction the UK may have 40% more retail space than it can support.[42] A reduction will not be evenly distributed and some places may find themselves with much larger reductions in retail space. Stronger centres will see the spaces vacated by the lost multiples filled with a diversity of independent businesses but others may collapse altogether. Town centres rely on customers and, as footfall declines, there is a tipping point, as we have seen in the US where hundreds of malls have been abandoned.[43] Just as serious is the state of the retail property industry. As one of our interviewees told us, building new retail space and, more importantly, refurbishing existing space, is no longer a commercial proposition. The rents that can be charged are too low and the leases too short to make it possible to make a commercial return or even to borrow money on retail property. The town centre model that we described at the start of this chapter is broken and if town centres are to survive we need to create a new one. To do this we need to understand the changing face of the retailing and hospitality industry, which is what we do in Part 2 of this book.

Preston: For many years the council pinned its hopes on the Tithbarn scheme, the last of a generation of huge city centre redevelopments, the likes of which will not be seen again. The centre has, however, been revived through improved markets, leisure and food uses.

Beach Road in
Chorlton, South
Manchester, the UK's
first cashless high
street.

PART 2

FUTURE RETAIL

Urbanists care deeply about the high street but don't always have a good understanding of the retail and leisure sectors. This undermines our capacity to regenerate town centres and too often we are planning for a high street that existed 30 years ago. In this section we look at current developments in the retail and leisure sectors and how they are likely to impact our town centres.

5 INDEPENDENT AND CREATIVE

Like plenty of success stories, Camden Market was only really supposed to be temporary. In the early 1970s, the area was blighted by plans to complete London's 'motorway box', which would have turned much of Camden into a traffic interchange. The temporary market that took over part of the space as a meanwhile use in advance of the construction works has grown into a multimillion pound business. We start this chapter with the history of Camden Market because it is of great relevance to the UK high street.

CAMDEN MARKET

Because of the uncertainty over the site British Waterways were only too happy to grant a seven-year lease on the blighted land to Northside Development Ltd. The company was gambling that the motorway plans would be dropped but in the meantime they needed an economic use for the site. The Dingwalls warehouse was transformed into a late-night 'dance hall' and it quickly became a cool hangout for the likes of the Rolling Stones, Pink Floyd and later The Clash.

Meanwhile, the 27-year-old Eric Reynolds was walking around London searching for a space to open a market. As he says: 'There was an explosion of arts and crafts in the Sixties and Seventies, but there were few places for people to sell their wares.' He came across an old printer's yard owned by Northside, negotiated a lease and opened the first market on Saturday 4 March 1974. As Eric tells the story: 'There were 40 stalls let-out at £3, mostly craftsmen and artists – silversmiths, people selling home-made buttons, knitted children's clothes, plus a woman who sold decorated traffic lights and milk churns. But the weather was appalling and we only got a few hundred people. Later that year, the canal was opened up. Then Sunday trading became legal, so the market opened on Sundays as well.'[1]

Soon, the 'meanwhile' market evolved to sell all the gear that went along with the crowd of 70s mods, punks and bohemians that made Camden their base. With the newest sounds and unconventional fashions Camden Lock became the established home of London subculture, a fertile seedbed for new designers to try their hand. The market stalls required minimal commitment and a receptive audience provided regular footfall – an illustration of the power of independents and creatives to transform a place.

Decades later, the markets are huge and labyrinthine. When Walt Whitman said 'I am large, I contain multitudes' he was talking about himself,[2] but the same could be said of Camden Lock. There are four main markets: Camden Lock, Buck Street Market, Hawley Wharf and Stables Market, with more than 1,100 traders and

Camden Markets: From humble beginnings the markets now house more than 1,100 traders and attract 30 million visitors a year.

30 million visitors a year, of which only 15% are from London. The average age of visitors is 15–35 and the number of repeat visits is 35%, which is very low.[3] It has become a major tourist destination where visitors flock to see London's 'authentic' alternative culture. It is hardly surprising that it has sometimes struggled to retain its independent and creative edge.

One long-term stallholder told us how he remembered better days when there were more freestanding stalls and fewer tourists (notorious for browsing rather than buying). He recalled previous stallholders, including friends who had been pushed out, and feared for his own future at the market. In particular, he noted the growth of food and drink stalls that now dominate large sections of the market, and predicted, with resignation, that they are seen as 'the future'.[4]

However, another stallholder selling vintage clothing told us that she had moved to the market after the pandemic stopped her from attending 1950s and 1960s events where she had previously traded. Her experience of Camden was positive – it had provided an alternative business model at a difficult time and the management had been supportive, taking a pragmatic approach to what were often unpredictable levels of footfall during successive lockdowns and changing guidance.

Urban Space Management, the company set up by Eric Reynolds, sold its stake in the market in 1999 but is still running successful markets elsewhere. Much of the market was bought by the Israeli billionaire Teddy Sagi through his company Market Tech, part of his wider Lab Tech company, which specialises in gambling software. They purchased the Stables and Camden Lock markets in March 2014 for £400 million and then in October paid £95 million for Hawley Wharf and Buck Street Markets.[5] The company's software background allowed it to develop electronic point of sale (EPOS) software and footfall tracking to know exactly who is using the market and how much they are spending. As we write, the *Financial Times* has reported that Teddy Sagi has put the whole complex on the market, seeking bids in the region of £1.5 billion, a valuation far greater than the largest UK shopping mall.[6]

The data collected through Market Tech's terminals confirms the suspicions of our first trader, namely that tourists don't spend very much, and that food stores are the most profitable. As a result, Buck Street is now almost entirely food and large shiny dining pods have been set up on the street with consistent signage. Elsewhere stalls are tending to focus on tourist goods rather than traditional arts and crafts and some are not even independent, but outposts of established brands. Juxtaposed against these polished and coordinated units, the old second-hand vinyl shops, used book stores and vintage clothing stalls look rather tatty and one fears for their future.

Still, the streets of Camden throng with life and the area feels very unlike a traditional shopping area both in terms of its traders and its customers. Camden is important because it shows a potential alternative future for the high street appealing to a very different demographic to the mainstream shopping malls. The problem is maintaining an independent ethos in the face of such financial success, which is worrying when authenticity is so central to the appeal.

THE NORTH LAINE IN BRIGHTON

Preserving authenticity is also a concern in Brighton. The city has a traditional retail core, with the mainstream shops on Western Road running towards Hove, and an increasingly secondary retail area on London Road running inland. But it is the independent retail and leisure area to be found between these two shopping streets

The North Laine in Brighton: Formerly a secondary shopping area this has grown into a lively district of independent shops.

that makes Brighton special. This can be divided into the Seafront, the Lanes and the North Laine. The Seafront with its boardwalk along the pebble beach, lined with independent bars and restaurants, shops and galleries has done much to reinvent the British seaside resort. Behind this, the Lanes is the original Saxon town, a warren of narrow streets full of traditional pubs and speciality shops (gift shops, galleries, jewellers and designer clothing).

However, it is behind this that you will find the focus of Brighton's independent retail culture. The North Laine is a grid of Victorian streets built on the long communal fields (Laines) that used to surround the town. It was originally a secondary shopping area selling hardware, work clothing and other practical things. Like Camden it was blighted in the 1970s by an aggressive road scheme that would have seen much of it demolished. A campaign to save the area evolved into a locally led regeneration initiative that created the unique area that it is today – a mix of independent shops, vintage clothing, bric-a-brac, record stores, galleries and bars, thronged with people and decorated with ever-changing murals. It was here in 1976 that Anita Roddick opened the first Body Shop.

The North Laine has been a centre for hipster retail since before most hipsters were born – a reflection of Brighton's uniquely diverse population. When Richard Florida applied his Boho Index to the UK, Brighton was ranked sixth, the smallest city in the top 10 places, fuelled by a combination of its large LGBTQ+ community and its reputation as an alternative destination.[7] As Florida told *The Guardian* on the release of the report, 'Creative, innovative and entrepreneurial activities tend to flourish in the same kinds of places that attract gays and others outside the norm. When people with varied backgrounds and attitudes collide, economic growth is likely.'[8] A reasonable question is whether the specialist retail areas of Brighton are the result of this diverse community or the reason why such a diverse range of people decided to move to the city. The reality is probably a bit of both.

The question for the North Laine Traders Association is how to keep it this way. For the last three decades it has been a constant struggle against the encroachment of multiple retailers, cafés and restaurants, who will pay higher rents and have threatened to squeeze out the independents that made the area successful and desirable in the first place. Despite having no powers to do this, the campaign to keep the area independent has been remarkably successful. Starbucks and Tesco hustle just beyond the boundary but sustained community pressure, especially on landlords, has preserved the area's unique character in spite of its success – no mean feat.

Authenticity and financial success remain uneasy bedfellows. When the Academy of Urbanism visited the area, one of the traders admitted to owning three units.[9] Each had a separate identity, and each changed its identity every few years to keep up the pretence of being independents. Because this is what customers expect the shops to be – preferably owned by the person who served them with eclectic stock that is a reflection of the owner's personality. A carefully curated illusion.

What we see illustrated in Camden and Brighton is that the independent sector exists as a separate retail ecosystem, located in distinct areas away from mainstream retailers and with a different customer base. Success is a fragile balance – remember that Covent Garden Market in London and Greenwich Village in New York were once thriving independent retail areas. The challenge is one of conservation, as the identity and character created by new designers, artisan bakers and record sellers raises the appeal of these areas, attracting a wider audience, more investment and higher rents, driving out the very businesses that created the appeal. Within a capitalist system, this is perhaps inevitable – the distinctive identity becomes 'marketised', leading to the erosion of authenticity. One person's regeneration is another person's gentrification.

THE INDI INDEX
The question for the future of our high streets is whether this alternative ecosystem of independent retail is confined to the hipster enclaves of London,

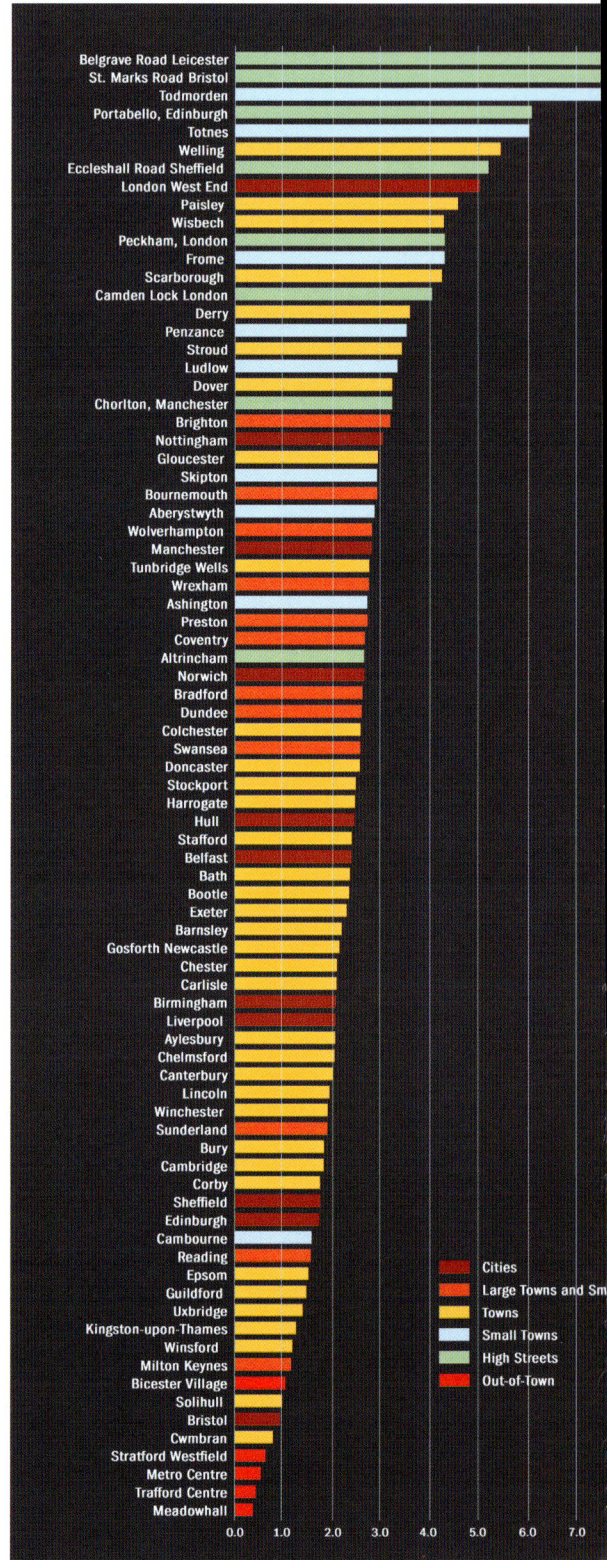

Legend:
- Cities
- Large Towns and Sm...
- Towns
- Small Towns
- High Streets
- Out-of-Town

The Indi Index: Using data supplied by Experian for our case studies, this graph shows the ratio of independent shops to multiples. In Belgrave Road there are 88 independents for every ten multiples, whereas in the Metrocentre there are only three.

Brighton and the other big cities, or whether it might have a role in filling the gaps left by the contraction of mainstream retailing. The data we have on our case studies allows us to differentiate between multiple and independent retailers (Experian define multiples as stores that are part of a network of nine or more outlets). From this we have developed an 'Indi Index', a ratio of independent stores to multiples. In the 81 case studies for which we have data, the average Indi Index is 2.7, in other words there are 27 independents for every 10 multiples. Our town centres are already overwhelmingly independent. The trend is also clear; in 2012 the index was 1.7, meaning that there were 10 fewer independents for every 10 multiples than there are today. While the majority of retail floor space is occupied by multiple retailers (because they are generally in larger units), this data is an important corrective to retail assessments that measure the success of town centres based entirely on the multiple retailers.

The graph ranks our case studies in terms of their Indi Index, showing that there are only seven places with more multiples than independents including, as we might expect, the four large out-of-town shopping centres. But they also include Cwmbran, Bristol and Solihull, with Milton Keynes, Kingston upon Thames and Winsford not far behind. The Bristol figure only relates to the Broadmead retail area whereas the independents are to be found elsewhere in the town centre. Milton Keynes, Cwmbran and Winsford are types of new towns and their town centres are largely made up of single shopping centres. Perhaps more surprisingly, many of the other towns with a low Indi Index are historic places. In our case studies of places like Guildford and Winchester it was explained to us that a shortage of 'modern' has pushed multiple retailers into older buildings, pushing up rents and squeezing independents out of the centre.

At the other end of the graph the most independent place in our case studies is Belgrave Road in Leicester, where there are 88 independents for every 10 multiples. Five of the top 10 places are high streets and the others are smaller towns, with Camden only 14th (40 multiples for every 10 independents, although this does not include the market). Maybe surprisingly, independents outnumber multiples 5 to 1 in London's West End, while quirky Brighton only comes only 21st on the list just above Nottingham, the most independent of the provincial cities.

Before we get carried away with the idea that independent coffee shops and bakers are taking over the high street, we should recall that independents cover a huge range of activities. One of the fastest growing sectors in our case studies is health and beauty, and most beauty salons, nail bars and barbers are independent, as are many fast food takeaways and convenience stores.

THE IMPACT ON TOWNS

Independent businesses have also played an important part in the regeneration of some northern post-industrial towns and villages. The case of Hebden Bridge is well known – a mill town nestling in a deep Pennine Valley that was once famous for manufacturing trousers but was recently described by *High Life* magazine as the 'fourth funkiest place on the planet'. Its cheap housing attracted what became known as the 'Hebden Bridge Hippies', who in 1965 convened a public meeting to agree a four-point strategy for the town: to clean it up, to put on events for visitors, to convert those visitors to residents and to use their money to rescue the town's industrial buildings. One of the people at the meeting was David Fletcher, a lecturer at the School of Architecture in Manchester. Now in his 80s he still has lunch every day in the Hebden Bridge Mill that he bought and renovated in the 1970s. As he told us, the strategy worked like a dream. The visitors really have become residents as the town has become a magnet for a 'motley mixture of artists, writers, photographers, musicians, alternative practitioners, teachers, green and New Age activists and, more recently, wealthier yuppie types'.[10] The town centre is full of independent shops selling arts and crafts along with alternative therapies and coffee, such that it was described by the New Economics Foundation as the 'least cloned town in Britain'.[11]

Hebden Bridge may be an extreme example, but it is not alone. A few miles away is Todmorden – home to Incredible Edible, which we will return to in a later chapter, but perhaps more telling is the case of Slaithwaite because of its similarity to hundreds of small towns and villages scattered across Northern England. Just to the west of Huddersfield, Slaithwaite (pronounced Sla-wit) is a collection of tumbling Victorian stone terraces and monolithic former textile mills threaded along the River Colne and the Huddersfield Narrow Canal. The canal once proved a useful route for the trade in illegal liquor – a practice still celebrated annually with the Moonraking Festival. The industry has long gone, but Slaithwaite has thrived in recent years and done so with a rare authenticity, thanks to grassroots initiatives.

Two co-operatives are at the heart of the story of a revitalisation that has seen the high street fill up with independent businesses. The first was The Green Valley Grocer, created in 2009 by the quick action of residents facing the loss of the town's only greengrocers. They created a co-operative and within a month they were able to issue shares and raise the finance to take over the shop. The members of the co-op have the same voting rights regardless of their stake and the structure created a ready-made customer base for the reopened shop. The model keeps money in the community, as one of the co-founders Graham Mitchell told us: 'It's a virtuous circle. The money raised and spent protects and creates jobs and supports the rest of the local economy.'[12]

Slaithwaite: The crowd-funded Handmade Bakery now occupies a canal-side warehouse in the former industrial town.

At about the same time Johanna and Dan McTiernan started what has become another key feature of village life – The Handmade Bakery. Lacking capital, they initially borrowed a restaurant kitchen after hours and used space at the back of The Green Valley Grocer. As they became established, they also turned to the community to raise capital, creating the UK's first 'bread subscription service'. Members commit to buy at least one loaf a week and those that have invested receive their interest in bread. Now a local hive of activity, the bakery is housed in a canal-side unit with a lively café, open kitchen and workshops for the public.

In the decade since these two businesses opened, Slaithwaite has seen many more independent shops and food and drink outlets open, leading to the revival of the high street. This success has gone hand in hand with an influx of young professionals, attracted by the easy commute by train into Leeds and Manchester. It would be easy to put the town's revival down to gentrification, but there are many places with equally good connections that have not been revived in this way. It is a question of chickens and eggs: are the young professionals drawn to the town because of the co-operatives and other independent shops, or are those shops there because of the influx of professional people? As in Brighton it's a bit of both.

MOVING MAINSTREAM

The resurgence of independents on our high streets is not purely a tale of co-ops, grassroots community action, artisan bakers, boutique retailers and alternative culture. In our case studies the proportion of units occupied by independent retailers was 56% in 2012, had risen to 61% pre-pandemic and is now at 63.1%. The majority of shops on our high streets are independent, and they are a vital part of most town centres. The highest representation of independents is on high streets and in small towns where they occupy just over 71.3% of units. Next is the large cities, where 66% of the units are independent, with slightly lower percentages (58–60%) in the small cities and large towns. Lowest of all are the malls, where just 25% of the units are independents, which explains why they have proven so vulnerable to the crisis in mainstream retail.

The main areas of growth in recent years have been in vaping shops, nail bars, hairdressers/barbers, tattoo parlours and of course the ever-present fast food takeaways and chicken shops. The biggest sector, however, remains convenience stores, of which there are just under 50,000 in the UK, 71% of which are independents.[13]

Research by the Local Data Company for the BBC programme 'You and Yours' showed a substantial increase in independent retailers in town centres in the last few years as they moved into the void left by the contraction of mainstream retailing.[14] This was seen as a good thing, although there was a worry that this growth is not always balanced – the programme reported that one in six shops in Stockton are hairdressers or beauty salons. As one of the businesses interviewed by the programme explained, this is largely because landlords were desperate and businesses that would previously have traded in suburban parades can now afford to be in the town centre. Independents are therefore emerging from their niches in markets like Camden or suburban parades to populate town centres. Whether hipster cafés or vape shops, these are tenants that can quickly fill vacant high street units, providing hope for stalled town centres.

However, we can't just assume that independent retailers can fill the gaps in our high streets. As the British Independent Retailers Association points out, independent retail is a precarious pursuit and the small annual change in the number of businesses disguises huge churn beneath the surface.[15] In 2018, for example, 34,500 new independent retailers were established but 35,500 ceased to trade. Prior to the pandemic, figures from the Centre for Retail Research show that store closures and job losses in the independent sector were far higher than with multiples.[16] In 2018, the independent sector lost 11,280 stores and 55,030 jobs compared to 3,303 multiple store closures with the loss of 38,433 jobs. Even in 2021 when the independent sector was growing, there were 8,801 independent store closures and just under 26,000 job losses compared to 2,517 multiple store closures and just under 68,000 job losses. The failure rate in the independent sector is huge, it is just that there are always new businesses waiting to take the place of those that have fallen.

The Grimsey Review recently revisited their 2013 'Against The Odds' report, warning that we shouldn't be complacent about the health of the independent sector.[17] While the sector proved resilient during the pandemic, this came at a huge cost to business owners and the amounts of debt carried by the sector. The report estimates that the 68,000 independent retailers and 56,000 independent hospitality businesses are carrying a collective debt of £2.2 billion, five times pre-pandemic levels. The report concludes 'having survived the worst public health crisis in a generation, their loss would be catastrophic ... it would not only be the small independent business owners that would suffer ... it will hit the people they employ, the companies that supply them and landlords of the properties they occupy'. The report concludes that if we are going to reinvent town centres, we need a strategy to avoid a lost generation of independent retailers.

This high failure rate means that independent retailers are not always attractive to retail landlords who are largely risk averse. Many landlords have traditionally seen independents as a liability and, at best, a stopgap tenant to fill a unit until it could be let once more to a multiple. Independents were seen as paying little rent, being reluctant to sign long leases and unable to fund fit-out, so that the costs to the landlord often outweighed the income. The world has changed; there are very few multiple retailers looking to lease space and when they do, they also refuse to sign long leases, demand rent holidays to cover fit-out costs and seek to link the rent they pay to the turnover of the store. Still, institutional investors and retail landlords remain reluctant to deal with independent retailers.

James Kingston, head of property for Stockport Council, and previously an agent for retail landlords, explained to us that, it's all well and good letting a vacant unit to an independent business, you may need to do so to stop your shopping centre looking empty. But he warned against falling into the trap of believing that this is a viable property strategy, as the rents paid will hardly cover the landlord's management costs and certainly will not provide a commercial return on the investment which went into building the unit. His worry was that without a commercial return you not only cannot build new retail space, more importantly, you can't fund essential refurbishment. Independents therefore, cannot sustain the institutional property investment model that has come to dominate our town centres.[18]

This is reinforced by our case study of Coventry, where there have been long-term plans to redevelop the southern part of the town centre. As the market for mainstream retail became more difficult, the City Centre South scheme evolved into a residential-led development with some ground floor retail. The centrepiece was to have been the Pavilion. In the words of its publicity this was to have featured 'a dynamic variety of pop-up retail and leisure providers ... allowing the mix of offers to change and evolve to promote new local independent initiatives and artisans'.[19] It was an attempt to incorporate independent retail into mainstream retail property development. However, enquiries with the developer revealed that they have been unable to make the numbers work and that The Pavilion has since been dropped.

This doesn't rule out independents as a solution for struggling town centres. The problem lies not with the independent retail sector but with the institutional investment model that lies behind town centre development. It is a model that is broken, even though many people in the industry are yet to recognise this. Independent retail quarters like Camden are incredibly profitable but their viability and investment value is based on cash flow rather than blue chip tenant-backed capital. There is more than one way to judge viability, as can be seen through the reuse of some of the department stores that have closed in the last few years.

BOBBY'S OF BOURNEMOUTH

Bournemouth:
The Debenhams department store in Bournemouth before it became Bobbies once more.

Founded in 1880s, Bobby's was a department store chain with eight outlets along the South Coast of England. When the founder Frederick Bobby retired in the 1920s he sold the business to the Drapery Trust, a retail conglomerate that also owned Debenhams. The Bobby's name survived until the 1970s when the store was rebranded as Debenhams. But local people still thought of it as Bobby's, part of

their retail heritage for over 100 years, and were devastated when it closed in 2020. But within a year, the name 'Bobby's' had been reinstated as the store reopened to queues that stretched around the block, accompanied by uncharacteristically positive reactions in the comments section of the local paper. What had risen from the ashes was a new type of department store. It couldn't paint a clearer picture of the way the high street is evolving.

The second floor of the building now hosts GIANT – a new free art gallery that opened with an exhibition of the work of world-famous artists Jake and Dinos Chapman. Cultural institutions being used to regenerate towns on the South Coast are nothing new – think Margate and St Ives – but GIANT is no publicly funded lottery project, but rather a private initiative by local artist Stuart Semple, sitting in the retail heart of Bournemouth, rubbing shoulders with Primark, Wetherspoons and Burger King. In addition to the gallery, the new department store includes an ice cream and coffee parlour, a beauty hall with organic skincare from local producers, a microbrewery, artisan makers and craftspeople and a market space run by South Coast Makers. The headlines have focussed on Drool, a food hall for dogs, but the scheme itself is much more than a gimmick. It is an attempt to entirely reimagine the department store, going back to its Victorian roots as a bazaar before it was taken over by a limited number of big brands.

The scheme has been developed by a company called Verve, just as the rest of the property industry is running a mile from retailing. As the company's director Ashley Nicholson told *The Guardian*, 'As everyone was exiting, values were falling and it meant properties that had previously been only in the ownership of pension funds and large property companies were becoming accessible to more normal scale investors and property companies like ourselves.' As he points out, they bought a 'perfectly good, functioning retail store' for about a third of what it would have cost to build a new one, creating a huge commercial opportunity if they could get the offer right.[20] Their aim is to make the building a destination (which is where GIANT comes in) and to pack it with independent retailers of all kinds.

This is a good example of an alternative economic model that has the potential to revive not just vacant department stores but whole town centres. As always, Jane Jacobs put it best when she wrote:

> 'Cities need old buildings so badly it is probably impossible for vigorous streets and districts to grow without them ... for really new ideas of any kind – no matter how ultimately profitable or otherwise successful some of them might prove to be – there is no leeway for such chancy trial, error and experimentation in the high-overhead economy of new construction. Old ideas can sometimes use new buildings. New ideas must use old buildings'.[21]

It is a model that is emerging in many towns, sometimes through entrepreneurs, sometimes through pop-up initiatives like Box Park in London, sometimes through the public sector. If town centres are to be revived by and for independents, the creation of new models of retail property development are essential.

THE FUTURE OF INDEPENDENTS

The future of retailing may very well be independent. The sector has proved nimble at filling the gaps left by the multiples, both in terms of empty units on the high street and in terms of market sectors. Indeed, as we will see in Chapter 8, online platforms like Etsy have done much to promote independent and creative businesses by giving them access to millions of customers. Also, in an age when anything is available online, people want town centres to be something different, to be authentic and to offer an experience rather than just stuff. The clone towns of the 2000s, with identical retailers lining every high street, are part of the reason why we got into this mess in the first place. Independents provide a possible solution.

If we can get this right, then there is a huge opportunity for independents to fill the vacuum left by the withdrawal of multiples from the high street. It is a trend that predates the pandemic but has been accelerated by it as multiples retreat to online platforms, leaving behind the infrastructure of town and city centres. This might seem like a 'the-end-is-nigh' type moment to the high street, but instead it could be a huge opportunity to reinvent the sort of diverse town centre that was squashed by the clone town.

6 GROCERS AND PURVEYORS OF FINE FOOD

When you shop at online grocery purveyor Ocado for the very first time, you not only receive a £20 discount on your shop, you also receive a rather handsome branded wooden spoon (offer valid at the time of writing, terms and conditions apply, see store for details etc). It's this kind of freebie that Ocado uses to signify its superiority: 'You won't be getting nice free spoons from Asda now, will you?'. At Ocado you also have the option of shopping from that greatest of British institutions, Marks & Spencer; Ocado achieved something of a coup in 2020, setting up its 'M&S at Ocado' partnership at the expense of its previous partner, Waitrose. What you don't get at Ocado though is value; they regularly hover around the expensive end of the *Which?* supermarket price comparison rankings. What you also don't get is a shop to walk into, because unlike most of the online supermarket players, Ocado has no bricks and mortar stores at all. You will never walk into an Ocado and be hit in the face with the tantalising waft of the bakery section, you won't get to have a clandestine squeeze of their avocados, and you certainly won't be making any 'linked trips' to your local high street. In that sense, when Ocado was founded in April 2000, it was both ahead of its time and foreshadowed a break between physical stores and grocery shopping.

HOME DELIVERY

In April 2021, a new grocery delivery app arrived in Manchester.[1] At any time between 8am and midnight Weezy allowed you to order from a selection of products including baked goods, fresh produce and alcohol, bringing it to your door in under 15 minutes. Together with Ocado this illustrates a potential revolution in the grocery market. While Ocado target the 'big supermarket shop', Weezy (and the many speedy grocery delivery apps like it) is targeting the corner shop and the 'metro' style supermarkets, those nearby places that you pop into on the way home from work or pop out to when you realise you've run out of toilet paper, teabags or washing up liquid. Alec Dent, co-founder of Weezy, said in an interview with *Charged Retail* that in most cases the app gets items to customers faster than they can go out and get their own shopping.[2]

When large supermarkets can promise, at best, delivery within a matter of hours, how can apps like Weezy dispatch in minutes? The secret is their 'hyper local

The independent high street may be threatened by online retailers and delivery services but offers an entirely different experience that is likely to remain popular.

Ocado: Its vans have become a familiar site and the company pioneered home delivery. In recent years it has been challenged by services promising delivery in as little as 15 minutes, but Ocado's hive warehouses are a much greater threat to the high street.

fulfilment centre model'. Translation: your groceries come not from a shop, but from a warehouse a mile or so down the road, ominously nicknamed 'dark stores'. When you order from a conventional supermarket, you're participating in the 'store picking model'; someone goes around the supermarket for you. They weave in between other customers, diligently selecting your products (definitely not judging you along the way) and hope that what you want is in stock. Weezy's warehouses, devoid of customers, allow for greater efficiency, a higher degree of control and much lower overheads.

However, questions remain about the viability of these fast delivery services. Wired tells the story of Jokr, which dominated New York's billboards in late 2020 with its promise of a free 15-minute delivery service.[3] The company raised £430 million in capital, promising to build 100 micro-warehouses in New York alone. It expanded into cities across the world and yet in the first half of 2021 it generated just $1.7 million in revenue while making a $13.6 million loss. Just 14 months after launching it announced it was pulling out of New York and Europe, although it continues to trade in South America. Other services like Buyk, Fridge No More and Zero Grocery disappeared altogether, and the investors who sunk nearly $8 billion into the six rapid delivery services that were competing in New York have largely lost their money. These investors hoped that they would pick the company left standing in a particular market, or better still the company bought for a silly valuation by a bigger company seeking market domination – back in Manchester, Weezy was acquired by competitor Getir in November 2021.[4] But there are questions about whether even market domination will bring with it profits. McKinsey, in their *State of Grocery Retail 2022* report, estimate that mainstream supermarkets make a 4% margin on in-store sales and lose 13% on each online order.[5] And this is on a £70 order delivered next day as opposed to an impulse buy of a single tub of ice cream delivered in 15 minutes at 10pm. The reality is that 15-minute delivery services currently lose money on every order and many doubt whether they can ever become efficient enough to alter this hard truth.

The other question is whether this is just a pandemic trend, or one that will have a long-term impact on the future of high streets and local centres. Much of Deliveroo's growth during the pandemic was made up of grocery deliveries (the 'store picking' kind) when social distancing meant there were long queues outside the big supermarkets. This didn't stop Deliveroo, who we will come back to shortly, having the 'worst IPO (initial public offering) in London's history' in March 2021.[6] As the country opened up after COVID, Weezy's founder Alec Dent was keen to stress that the app would only increase in popularity post-pandemic. It would, he said, prevent people from becoming 'hostage to their fridge', allowing them to make impromptu plans with mates again without the silent judgement of their near expiry foodstuffs back home.

Knight Frank's Intelligence Lab agreed, their property market insights observing in April 2022 that demand for 'quick-commerce' or 'q-commerce' was driving competition for urban logistics, pushing up rental and land values for warehousing.[7] Although expansion of the 'dark supermarkets' has slowed as the main players near their current targets and the market consolidates, Knight Frank predict that consumer adoption of q-commerce is likely to see further growth, and demand for suitable units will continue – provided they can find a route to profitability.

This is a problem that Ocado has solved, although its 'dark stores' are on an altogether different scale. Its 'hive' warehouse in Erith, to the east of London, covers 36 acres (15 hectares) and houses 3,500 robots operating as a swarm capable of picking a grocery order of 50 items in about a minute. Where the 'big shop' disruptor and the corner shop disruptors align is that their dark stores are much more likely to be located on an industrial estate than on a high street. Of course, many of the big supermarkets are also out-of-town, but their preferred sites tend to be on the edge of existing town centres, maintaining the promise of the elusive 'linked shopping trip' optimistically spoken about in town centre strategies. Even if that promise sometimes remains unfulfilled, it must be better for the high street than a customer that hasn't left their home at all.

HIGH STREET GROCERS

What does all this mean for the resilience of high streets and their physical configuration? It's easy to imagine a dystopian future where prospective trolley pushers and basket carriers remain ensconced inside their homes, supplied by delivery bikes (or eventually drones) while our beloved corner shops and possibly less beloved but equally useful small supermarkets disappear. But humans are strange creatures and don't always respond to technological innovation the way that Silicon Valley might like us to. Most of us have said 'thanks but no thanks' to MiniDisc players, 3D home television and computerised eyewear. Speedy grocery apps could turn out to be a fad; tempting introductory offers will dwindle in the face of market consolidation and spent investment, the novelty of delivery speeds may wear off and the cost of living crisis will likely make bulk buying and the value ranges of large supermarkets more appealing.

Even if they don't turn out to be a fad, it is hard to imagine their geographic coverage becoming so large that they create a significant impact on the grocery ecosystem. These delivery apps can only serve urban areas. Market leader Getir, which started in Turkey in 2015 and where it now operates in 50 cities, had a presence in 20 UK cities and towns as of February 2022.[8] This, however, is a long way from national coverage. A delivery model based on short distances between warehouse and consumers only lends itself to areas of high population density. And shoppers are surprisingly loyal to the so-called inefficiency of in-person grocery shopping. Although the online sector is still growing, Ocado shifted their expansion plans down a gear in July 2022 as customers reduced their use of delivery for online grocery orders.[9]

The data on our case study high streets supplied by Experian shows that, far from contracting, physical grocery and other food-related retail uses are doing remarkably well, even in the wake of the pandemic. If you combine the categories 'convenience store', 'supermarket' and 'grocer' (the three most general food shop categories), the data shows an increase of 37% in the number of stores between 2012 and 2022. The majority of that rise (24.8%) was represented by the 'grocer' category, with 'supermarket' seeing a small decrease (0.1%). This might be explained by the trend for supermarkets to move away from large floorplates towards smaller 'metro' style stores that Experian are classifying as grocers. This picture seems to be supported by data from the Local Data Company. Looking only at multiples, they assessed more than 200,000 stores in 2021 and, while the overall trend was for the number of multiple stores to decline, there was a modest increase in their 'convenience store' category (the only food-related grouping).[10]

So, for the moment there appears to be an enduring appetite for food retail on the high street that hasn't been fully satisfied by out-of-town supermarkets, online shopping or speedy delivery apps. And the picture only gets more interesting as we move away from convenience and towards the sensual.

GARDEN OF EARTHLY DELIGHTS

The efficiency of the online world may have lured some shoppers but seeking out and acquiring nourishment is also a deeply visceral experience, driven by more than need or convenience. We are ultimately choosing items to put into our mouths, which will to a greater or lesser extent become part of us. It is consuming in the most literal sense and, for some people, the cold competency of mainstream food retail is not enough. They want to hold products in their hands, to weigh and measure them, to smell and even taste before purchasing, and to connect with another human who knows about what they are selling and can recount the lore of how the item came to be.

There is no better place to satisfy such desires than a food market. Volume food retailing is seeking to please all of the people all of the time, with wide ranges, sourced from all over the world, packaged to grab and pay. At their best, food markets promise the opposite; they are hyper-specific, hyper-local and hyper-sensory. Here you can come over all Nigella, admire the dark shining curves of an aubergine, inhale the indecent oozing scent of a ripe Brie and let the warm floral taste of local honey melt across your tongue. It's not surprising that they are popular; between 2012 and 2022 the number of food market businesses in the UK increased by 104% according to industry research company IBISWorld.[11] The same trend can be seen in our high street case studies, where the number of markets increased by 31.7% between 2012 and 2022.

Successful markets can have significant impacts on the fortunes of high streets and town centres. In 2010 Altrincham, a town to the south-west of Manchester, achieved the dubious honour of having the highest vacancy rate in the country; almost a third of its shops stood empty. By November 2018, it had

Levenshulme Market
in South Manchester: A social enterprise run by the community with 50 stalls that trades every Saturday from March to December together with monthly Friday evening markets.

been crowned high street of the year in the Great British High Street Awards and, by 2021, its vacancy rate was only 8.3%, despite having lost its Debenhams and House of Fraser. What changed? As with any place-based renaissance the answer is complicated and many parties were involved, but the role of the market is a key piece of the puzzle.

Altrincham market reopened in September 2013 under the curation of Nick Johnson, formerly of the developers Urban Splash, and his wife Jen Thompson. The market is made up of two parts, a covered outdoor area with stalls, and a hall with food and drink outlets around its edge that we will return to in the next chapter. There were a few good traders, a fishmonger and butcher but most (in Nick's words) were selling second-hand toilet rolls and were happy if they took £30 a day. Some like Marge didn't really sell anything but opened her stall three days a week for the chat and company. Nick therefore made himself deeply unpopular, clearing out these tenants to 'curate' a mix of stallholders. As he said, he turned his back on the design and branding that had been such a feature of Urban Splash in order to 'curate people doing interesting things'.

The success of the market has influenced the evolution of Altrincham town centre. There are more independent businesses now. Some started life in the market before moving into a permanent space, others are new independent businesses attracted by the town's new image. The Altrincham model has been cited so many times since in town centre strategies and replicated so frequently that it is hard to remember that it was innovative at the time.

The success of independent (often foodie) businesses shows that it's not just markets that offer gastronomes their epicurean kicks. In our research we can see that shops offering specific foodstuffs fared relatively well between 2012 and 2022 despite the much proclaimed 'death of the high street'. Far from declining, bakeries were up by 8.4%, delicatessens by 12.5% and greengrocers by 2.1%. The star performer was, however, dairy produce retailers (we assume cheese shops), up by 46.2%. Vegetarianism seems to have had an impact on the fleshier offerings (the number of butchers decreased by 20% and the number of fishmongers decreased by 13.6%) but generally food purveyors seem to be overcoming the challenges of the modern high street.

One problematic element of discrete food retailers in the modern age, and the veneration of ingredients in general, is affordability. Most traditional bakers were sufficiently affordable for families to rely on them as part of their weekly shop. While you can still find affordable options, it is increasingly common to see their artisan counterparts selling a loaf of bread for upwards of £5, the inevitable minimalism of the shop fit-out not extending to the pricing. Quality produce now feels far less accessible than it once did and the counterpoint to the affluent high street with its artisan food shops is the food desert that exists in many poorer districts, where the health of the population suffers through lack of affordable quality food.

CONVENIENCE

The other trend affecting future food retail is 'convenience' reversing a trend that dates back to the arrival of the refrigerator in the kitchen and the car in the drive. As we saw in Chapter 2, the mass ownership these items caused shopping patterns to change in the 1960s from the daily shop for fresh and perishable goods to the weekly supermarket run. As a result, the numbers of independent butchers, bakers, greengrocers and fishmongers declined from 120,000 units in 1950 to less than 30,000 today.[12] The decline of the corner shop was even sharper, with more than half being lost in the late 1950s.

The latter figure is quoted by the BBC presenter Babita Sharma in her book *The Corner Shop: Shopkeepers, the Sharmas and the Making of Modern Britain*.[13] The corner shops that had stood at the end of virtually every terraced street and had been the main source of food shopping for most people were disappearing fast, until they were rescued by a generation of entrepreneurial South Asian families fed up with the discrimination and lack of advancement that they experienced in factories. They were joined by Asians expelled from Kenya and Uganda, many of whom had a background as small business owners. With the decline in manufacturing in the 1970s and 1980s more families used their redundancy money to set up in business such that by 1991 a quarter of the South Asian community was self-employed.[14]

By working long hours, seven days a week (until 1994 supermarkets were unable to open on Sundays) they carved out a niche alongside the supermarkets. They catered for local needs, top-up shopping, sweets, newspapers and cigarettes and gave birth to franchising operations like Londis and SPAR that provide branding, supplies and support services to independently owned shops. SPAR is a Dutch firm, originally called DESPAR, which is an acronym of a Dutch phrase that translates as 'through united co-operation everyone regularly profits'. It arrived in the UK in 1959 and now has 13,500 stores in 48 countries. Londis (short for London District Stores) was also formed in 1959 and was originally owned collectively by its individual shopkeepers.

The corner shop sector is difficult to separate out in our data. In the past, the sector was dominated by CTN stores (confectionery, tobacco and news). However, as long ago as 2009 Dennis Evans, Director of SPAR distribution, was quoted as saying: 'Many of our convenience retailers need to move their businesses away from what are basically CTN or emergency purchase models to a fresh food store where consumers can buy tonight's tea and do a good top-up shop.'[15] The number of CTN stores in our case studies has indeed fallen, from 347 stores in 2012 to 298 stores in 2021, while convenience stores have risen from 438 to 672.

Rather than doing a weekly shop, people are buying the makings of their evening meal on their way home from work. A 2017 Waitrose report found that one in 10 people don't decide on what to eat until just before they eat it.[16] Wrigley and Brookes have defined convenience culture as shopping 'little and often' and cite the reasons being a 'time poor' society, austerity (with people avoiding the expense of the big shop), as well as an increased awareness of the value of local economies and fresh produce.[17] Because of this, the UK convenience market pre-pandemic was predicted to grow by 17.6% between 2018 and 2023.[18] This trend was accelerated by COVID, sales in corner shops and independent grocers increasing by 63% during lockdown.[19]

The supermarkets have been very aware of this trend and most of them have developed a convenience format; smaller stores, without parking and located on a high street. Tesco opened its first convenience store in Barnes, South West London in 1994. Since then Tesco has opened 1,740 Express stores while Sainsbury's has 770, Asda 209 and Morrisons 70. These local stores are aimed at securing a slice of the convenience market previously dominated by players like the Co-op and SPAR. This has brought the supermarkets back to their high street roots. Some see this as the final blow for the small convenience stores that had made a living by being local and open all hours. However, all retailers benefit from customers coming back to high streets, and away from out of town stores.

None of this is as convenient as a 15-minute food delivery, of course, but the sector is banking on people wanting the human touch and the sense of community that a local store provides. The advent of Amazon lockers in many local stores means they may become part of the online retail revolution rather than its victim. This is also true of the arrival of the first Amazon contactless supermarkets, as well as Alibaba's Freshippo stores (see case study box).

FEAST TO FAMINE

During the height of the pandemic many of us experienced the sight of empty supermarket shelves for the first time. This could become a more common occurrence as supply chain costs (including energy and raw materials) increase and border issues persist post-Brexit. In June 2022, Heinz stopped supplying Tesco with some of its products including beans, ketchup and tomato soup when the retailer refused to increase their prices to reflect increasing costs. Globally, food scarcity is

CONTACTLESS SUPERMARKETS

Amazon has indicated that food is one of its key target markets. It acquired the Whole Foods chain in the US in 2018 and has invested in London-based Deliveroo. However, it is also investing in physical stores. The first Amazon Go checkout-free food stores opened in Seattle in 2017 and at the time of writing there were 27 stores in the US including 10 in New York. The first store in London opened in 2020 under the brand Amazon Fresh and there are now 12 in London with more planned, possibly in partnership with Morrisons.[20]

The Chinese e-retailer Alibaba has also opened a chain of contactless supermarkets in China called Freshippo. The first store opened in Shanghai in 2016 and there are now 246 in China, with Alibaba experimenting with the same format for convenience stalls, breakfast bars and even entire malls.

The Amazon stores use cameras and AI to monitor products that have been taken off the shelf and all customers need to do is to download an app onto their phone. After that they can just walk into the store, pick up what they need and walk out, the payment being debited directly from their account. In the Alibaba stores checkout is by facial recognition (using Alibaba's own system) and payment automatic via Alipay.

The Freshippo stores also act as local fulfilment centres that can deliver online orders within 30 minutes. Pickers drop items into a bag, which is then whipped up onto an overhead conveyor system to the back of the store where the delivery bikes wait.

set to become a growing issue as a result of conflict and the climate crisis, which also impacts price. The UN's World Food Price Index went up 23% year on year as of June 2022. That scarcity brings another, sadly far more common experience – looking at stacked shelves, knowing that you cannot afford their contents. This experience will be exacerbated by rising domestic energy costs.

These trends make predictions about the future of food retailing a risky enterprise. Some see the future as being delivered to your home (although probably not in 15 minutes), others in a return to artisan quality fresh produce, others have predicted that the out-of-town supermarkets will lose out to the convenience of the local high street or alternatively to the value retailers like Aldi and Lidl. All these trends can be found in the data and in the literature and affect different places in different ways. Affluent areas will see an increase in artisan retailers, while urban high streets, particularly those with more ethnically diverse populations, will continue to see a strong independent sector. What is clear is that the story that we would have told 10 years ago, of the ongoing erosion of the high street by the supermarkets, is no longer true. The supermarkets are now back on the high street and in town centres and the future of these traditional centres for food retail is looking more positive than it has done for many years.

7 FOOD AND BEVERAGE

I n the last chapter, we described the transformation of Altrincham, from the town centre with the highest vacancy rate in the country to high street of the year. It is worth returning to the story because food and drink played a vital part in this transformation. Retail agents have a whole category of uses that they call F&B, or food and beverage. It covers bars and restaurants, coffee shops and takeaways, with subsections covering roadside uses, transport interchanges and food courts. The sector encompasses a huge range of retailers, from Michelin-starred restaurants through mid-market dining chains, independent local businesses, fast food takeaways and street food vendors. It includes household names like McDonald's, Nando's, Starbucks, Greggs and Pret A Manger. It also includes pub companies such as Stonegate (with 4,500 outlets including Slug and Lettuce and Walkabout), chains like JD Wetherspoons and traditional brewers like Mitchells & Butlers and Whitbread. None of these explain the transformation of Altrincham.

IS FOOD REALLY THE NEW ROCK AND ROLL?

The story of Altrincham's transformation goes back to a conversation in 2012 between the council leader Matt Colledge and local resident Nick Johnson, who also happened to be a director at the developer Urban Splash. Difficult times after the financial crisis meant that Nick was looking for other opportunities and, in his telling, when he declined an invitation to sit on the town centre regeneration board, the leader asked why he didn't take over the market. Johnson saw this as an opportunity to get back to his roots, in the early regeneration of Manchester. As he put it in a podcast interview a few years later, his generation had been shaped by the attitude of punk.[1] In the years that followed, at least in Manchester, property had become the new rock and roll – bold, irreverent and annoying. However, as always happens, property had become boring and corporate and in the 2010s food was set to become the new-new rock and roll, a place where independent operators could innovate and experiment. So after talking to his wife and business partner Jen, Nick said: why not?

A week later the chief executive came back from his holidays and informed the leader that this wasn't the way things were done, there were tendering rules to follow and the European Union procurement system. So, a brief was written, and tenders issued to appoint a company to take over the market. Fortunately, Nick Johnson's time as a development surveyor had taught him how to write a decent bid and 18 months later his new company Market Operations were given a lease on the market for the princely sum of £10,000 a year.

Stockport: The old market hall has been repurposed as a modern food hall experience, based on its near neighbour Altrincham.

The market at the time was moribund, a ghost of the bustling market that once existed (the market charter goes back to the 12th century). In addition to the covered market, described in the last chapter, there was the Market House, a covered hall with permanent stalls around its edge. It was Jen's suggestion that the centre of the market hall be filled with long communal tables. People could buy food from any of the stalls and then sit together to eat, like a food hall in a shopping mall – although Nick hates that comparison.

The market hall opened in 2013 with just a pizza stall, a coffee shop and a bar. As Nick struggled at the top of a ladder getting the PA system to work, it filled with people, with no branding or advertising. As he says it has been full ever since. The space is run on an entirely informal basis – there are no lease agreements, no lawyers and no borrowing. In the early days, if someone wanted to try their hand at opening a stall, they would submit their idea to Nick and Jen and, if they liked it, they could have a go, and if it didn't work out, so be it. The management company provides the space, communal facilities and front of house staff so that stallholders only need to worry about their business. In the nine or so years since it opened only three businesses have failed and, because there are no legal agreements, these have been resolved amicably with the unit often re-let by the next trading day. Market Operations have since opened similar operations in Manchester's Northern Quarter (Mackie Mayor) and in Macclesfield. Copycat food markets have also appeared in many towns, so much so that it has become known as the Altrincham phenomenon. It has helped transform Altrincham town centre from a place where people shop to a place where they socialise, grab a pint and something to eat. It has made the centre relevant once more to its affluent catchment population.

Altrincham Market:
The repurposed market hall with food stalls around the edge and communal tables in the centre has become a model for similar developments across the country.

The transformation of markets into food and drink outlets is a trend that can be seen elsewhere. There has been an explosion of interest in street food, a trend imported to the UK from Asia via the US. Street food vendors trade from mobile units and have been boosted by the number of pop-up events across the country as well as festivals and other events. It is estimated that the street food market in the UK is now worth £1.3 billion.[2] As in Altrincham, this trend is transforming traditional markets, the highest profile example being Borough Market in London. The turnover and footfall that it generates, particularly in the evenings, has helped to transform even quite traditional markets and, where a balance can be maintained with other traders, the results can be positive. However, as we saw in Chapter 5, the stallholders in Camden Lock worry that food and drink operators, because of the greater profits they generate, are starting to dominate the market. As with all things, a balance is important.

THE FOOD AND DRINK TAKEOVER

The same trend can be seen in many town and city centres, as illustrated by our case study data. Services are coming to dominate town centres, rising from just under 56% of units in 2012 to 63.2% in 2021. The graph shows that the food and beverage sector makes up the biggest proportion of these service uses, with just under 9,400 units in 2012 rising to 11,250 units in 2021 (45% of all service uses in our case studies).

These services include 3,117 pubs, bars and bar restaurants (up 25%), 3,011 restaurants (up 20%) and 2,376 cafés and coffee shops (up 10%). There are also 2,057 fast-food outlets of various kinds in the data (up 28%) and while fish and chip shops have fallen, Chinese and Indian takeaways, and pizza delivery shops have more than doubled. Even the 'pubs' category has increased, albeit only by 2%. This seems to run counter to the national trend, which has seen 7,000 pub closures since 2012 reducing the number in England and Wales to just 40,000.[3] It appears that many of these pub closures have happened in villages and suburban areas where the units have been converted to housing. By contrast, town centre pubs are holding their own despite competition from bars, which have grown by 41%. This hints at a wider trend by which outlets that were previously to be found in suburban areas are moving into town centres. The availability of units and falling rents has created an opportunity for suburban businesses to move into town centres with much bigger catchment areas. We will see the same trend in the health and beauty sector in Chapter 11.

The data also allows us to rank the popularity of different types of restaurants in the UK. Our case studies are home to 36 types of restaurants from 28 nationalities. The most popular remains Italian restaurants, with just under 400 outlets (down 17%), not including the 207 pizza restaurants (up 20%). Second comes Indian restaurants with 274 outlets (down 16%). The biggest increases are Asian restaurants and American restaurants with 258 and 184 outlets, respectively, both of which have more than doubled. Many of these restaurants will be independent businesses although there has also been a growth in mid-market restaurant chains like Carluccio's (400 units), Byron Burgers (69 outlets), Café Rouge (120 units), Pizza Express (470 units) and Wagamama (150 units).[4] The food and drink takeover of town centres is therefore not all about the sort of independent businesses seen in Altrincham – the same tensions exist between independents and multiples as in mainstream retail.

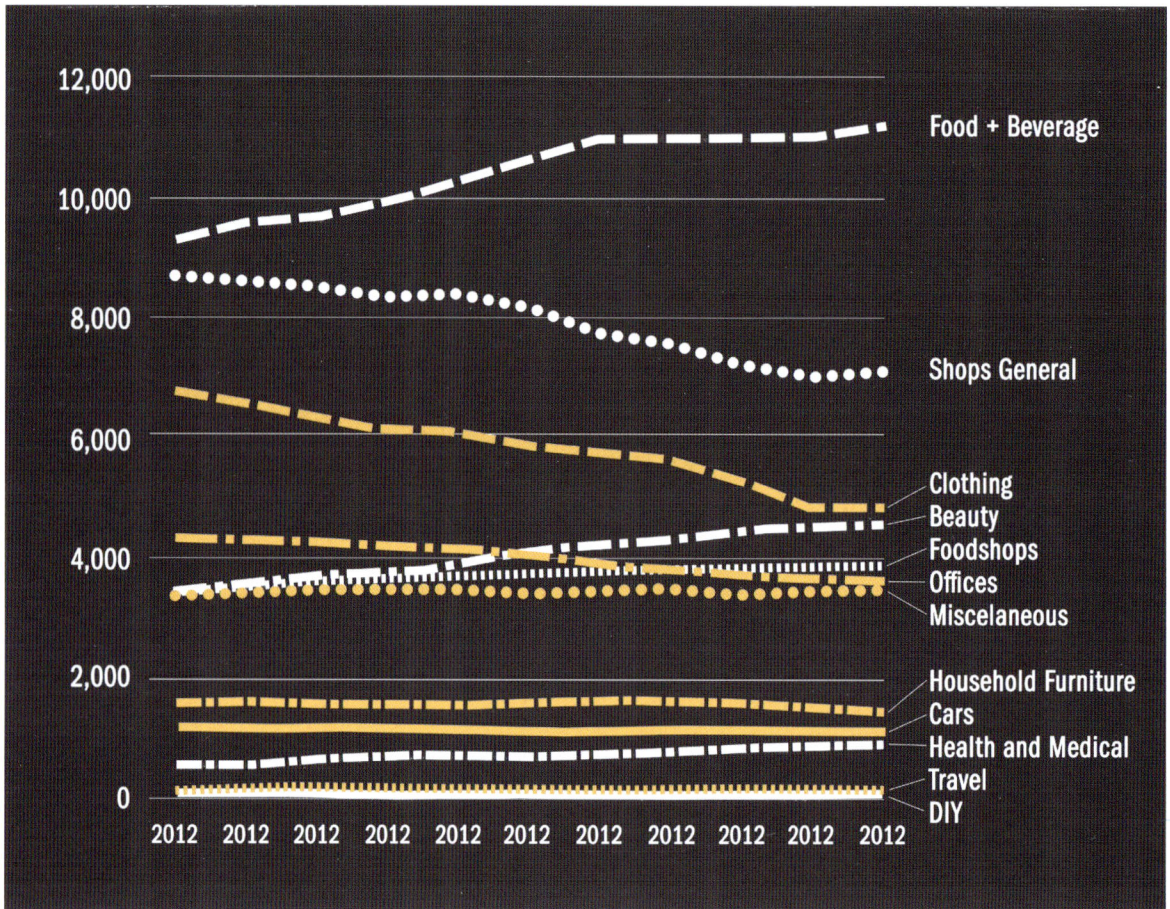

TEA AND COFFEE

The most important beverages on the high street are not alcoholic; for years tea rooms and coffee shops have played an important role. Coffee as a drink emerged from Turkey and was imported into London in 1652 when a merchant trading with Turkey saw two of his servants leave to open The Turk's Head, the country's first coffee house. They became fashionable places for the upper classes and also places of business, Lloyd's of London and the New York Stock Exchange both originating as coffee houses. However, in the 19th century, as The East India Company switched from coffee to the more lucrative tea trade, coffee fell out of fashion.

What emerged instead were tea rooms, the most famous of which were the Lyons tearooms founded in 1894 that became a staple of the high street. The tea rooms served tea, and coffee, initially with waitress service and then cafeteria style. They also had cake counters selling Lyons branded products including tea, cakes and ice cream. The brand also sold through supermarkets, indeed Mr Kipling cakes started as a Lyons brand. The biggest stores were called Lyons Corner Houses and stretched over four or five floors with a series of restaurants, a food hall, delicatessen, cake counter, hairdressers and even a food delivery service.

Numbers of outlets by type: The numbers of shops in our case studies by type based on Experian data.

Some Corner Houses were open 24 hours a day and the largest employed 400 staff.

While coffee had fallen out of fashion in Britain, it remained popular in Europe, but made a comeback in Britain. This happened with the invention by Gaggia in 1946 of the commercial piston espresso machine. The first of these machines arrived in London's Soho in 1952, ushering in a huge expansion of coffee shops and espresso bars through the 1950s and 1960s. At a time when pubs were dominated by middle-aged men and largely off-limits to young people, coffee bars became the centre of youth culture. They were the hangout of intellectuals, beatniks and mods, with a jukebox, dancing and even live music.

Those in the world of coffee talk about three waves of coffee culture. In the first wave, coffee was just a hot drink sold as an alternative to tea. The coffee bars had espresso machines but most people drank 'frothy coffee' (what we call cappuccino today), with no real thought to its quality. Restaurants and cafés sold filter coffee, often with free refills, and the quality was generally terrible. Then in the late 1960s, the second wave of coffee culture started in a small way in Berkeley, California. It was there that Alfred Peet started selling coffee beans, distinguishing them by country of origin and type of roast. The third wave of coffee culture, dating from the early 2000s, saw coffee emerge as a connoisseur's product, with special beans sourced from individual producers. This was accompanied by the rise of the barista and the artisan coffee shop, serving an increasingly discerning clientele. In terms of the future high street it is the second wave companies that have had the greatest impact.

In 1971 three students at the University of California were inspired by Alfred Peet to set up a shop selling coffee beans in their hometown of Seattle. They wanted a strong name starting with 'St' and after rejecting Starbo, alighted on the name of the first mate in *Moby Dick*. Starbucks initially only sold beans supplied by Peet, until he offered to help them train their own roastmaster. Eventually, Starbucks bought Peet's in 1984 and by 1986 they had six stores in Seattle and had eventually started selling coffee, rather than just coffee beans. It wasn't until the company was sold a year later that the expansion started, reaching 46 stores by the end of the 1980s, and an astonishing 33,833 outlets today.[5] Half of these are in the US with the remainder in 80 countries across the globe.

The arrival of the second wave of coffee culture in the UK was also linked to Seattle. It was initiated by two of the city's expats Alley and Scott Svenson who, frustrated by their inability to get a decent coffee in London, set up the Seattle Coffee Company. This had grown to 50 outlets before they sold the chain to Starbucks, allowing the company to enter the UK market. The coffee revolution had started and soon every UK high street would have a coffee shop. The largest UK brand is Costa with 3,400 outlets, of which 2,121 are in the UK. Started by Sergio Costa in London in 1971 the chain was owned by the brewer Whitbread between 1995 and 2019, when it was sold to Coca-Cola for £3.9 billion.[6] The other large UK player is Caffè Nero, also founded in London in the mid-1990s, with 1,000 outlets in 11 countries.

According to the British Coffee Association, 95 million cups of coffee are drunk in the UK every day, from 25,000 outlets.[7] Of these, 27% are independents and 32% are made up of the branded chains, the balance being non-specialist outlets like pubs. The sector was hit hard by the COVID pandemic with a 40% drop in sales.[8] It is predicted that the sector will take at least three years to recover to pre-pandemic levels, particularly as ongoing homeworking dents lunchtime sales to office workers. As always, market analysts are bullish about the prospects for the sector, citing all the innovations that are taking place. But the question is whether we are reaching saturation point – how many more coffee shops can our high streets take? The answer is probably quite a few if towns and cities are to match the density of coffee outlets in London and New York (there are 2,330 branded coffee shops in London, one in four of the total number in the UK, and New York has even more with 3,389 outlets).[9] Whether further expansion will be welcomed is another question. Quite a few of our high streets have seen community resistance to the expansion of branded coffee shops. With the retreat of the big retailers, it seems coffee shops have taken on the mantle of the unacceptable corporate face of the high street.

THE BLANDIFICATION OF FOOD AND DRINK

In a recent blog, 'More Songs About Buildings and Food' the architectural writer Drew Austin suggests that in the 1970s all of New York's culture was in some way connected to music, be it venues, clubs, boom boxes on the street, record stores and the media.[10] Today music is much more available than it was in the 1970s, but its impact has dissipated. It has become a 'decorative backdrop, a form of sonic wallpaper … It has been naturalized and assimilated and somewhat defanged in the process'. Austin argues that 'our sensory experience of the city is defined by whatever physically imprints itself on the landscape, and right now that is restaurants and bars'. Food is indeed the new rock and roll.

But he ends the article by worrying that the rock and roll moment is fleeting and gentrification soon transforms an exciting scene into bland wallpaper. It is a theme taken up by Jonathan Nunn writing in *Dezeen*, who starts his piece by asking whether you have recently had a meal in a new restaurant in a city centre: 'Let me guess,' he says, 'The food was from another country but the menu emphasised that all the dishes are made with local, well-sourced, seasonal ingredients. The decor of the restaurant was chosen to mimic the street food culture of that country, but with a modern, comfortable twist so you know you're not really sitting by the roadside. The menu told you where the food was "inspired by" … the typeface of the restaurant was sans-serif, and the name of the restaurant was one very tasteful word.'[11] He calls this the 'sohoification' of food culture, the commodification of a type of restaurant that was once independent and original but is now everywhere, at least in the large cities. This type of restaurant has become a signifier used by developers to attract a certain type of buyer to their new apartments.

This is part of a wider story of the food and beverage sector. Sure, there are lots of corporate players like McDonald's but, when people go out for a meal or a drink they generally like to think that they are doing so in a place which is distinctive and independent. It is noticeable that all the coffee shops described above are not very old. While the high street, at least before the retail crisis, was dominated by retailers with Victorian roots, the food and drink sector is dominated by companies with a history that rarely stretches back further than the 1990s. The big three coffee companies in the UK all started as quirky independents and they try and retain some shreds of that ambience, even if the experience of buying a coffee is more McDonald's than an independent barista.

The same is true of the restaurant sector, which is dominated by casual dining chains that started out as independents but have expanded rapidly while trying to maintain an independent ethos. Take for example Franco Manca, which started in 2008 on Market Row in Brixton but now has 60 outlets and is in most large British cities. Or Bill's, which started out in 2001 as a grocer in Lewes, East Sussex, and is now a restaurant chain with 78 branches. Even Pret A Manger started out as a single shop in 1983 in Hampstead, London. The first shop failed after 18 months with the brand only taking off after it was bought from the liquidator – 16 years later it was bought by McDonald's (who later sold it on).

This is also true of brewers, led by BrewDog, which was founded as recently as 2007 by two 24-year-olds in Ellon near Aberdeen in Scotland. It now has 78 outlets and sells beer through every supermarket in the country. It once described itself as 'post-punk, apocalyptic, motherfucker of a craft brewery', driving a tank down Camden High Street and projecting naked images of the founders on the Houses of Parliament, but has become the fastest growing drinks producer in the UK.[12] On a smaller scale, craft breweries have mushroomed in all of our cities. None are as big as BrewDog, but many have become substantial businesses. The same is true of 'independent' bars, which have seen huge growth in recent years. In our case studies, the number of bars in the biggest cities has increased by 58% in the last 10 years. Again, most of them appear to be independent but behind the scenes companies own multiple outlets.

The food and drink sector is therefore at a different stage of the economic cycle to mainstream retailing. As the retail sector contracts, the food and drink sector expands and grateful landlords are only too willing to let vacant space to bars and restaurants that remain profitable despite the setback of the pandemic. However, with this expansion comes a danger that the independent spirit that so many customers value is lost as companies consolidate and independent operators become chains able to dominate the market.

FAST FOOD, THE SOUL OF THE HIGH STREET?

There is another side to the food and beverage sector and one that is regarded much less positively. There are just over 57,000 fast food takeaways in the UK, including chains like Subway (2,320 outlets), Greggs (2,181), McDonald's (1,367), Kentucky Fried Chicken (KFC) (900) and Burger King (369).[13] The industry is worth £21 billion, employs almost 430,000 people and continues to grow by just under a percentage point a year despite the pandemic. In our case studies, takeaways make up 18% of food and beverage outlets and have grown by 28% since 2012.

In this book, we have identified the growth of independent retailers and the return of activities to high streets as positive trends but the fast food sector puts a different slant on these conclusions. Even with these huge chains, the majority of takeaways are independent businesses. Indeed many of the outlets operated by the big chains are franchise operations. When we talk about independents, we tend to have in mind craft bakers and artisan coffee shops but there are vastly more independent chicken shops in the country. Furthermore, most of these are located on high streets. While the big chains may have out-of-town formats, even they are predominantly in-town or more specifically high street businesses. Vacancy rates on high streets would be far worse were it not for the fast food sector – indeed many planning authorities are concerned about the prevalence of fast food takeaways and have sought to limit their number through planning policy. Bristol has a policy to prevent new takeaways within 400m of a school and Brighton has increased this to

800m, while Medway has restricted takeaways to 10% of units in town centres and 15% in local centres.

In 2020, the National Audit Office suggested that 20.2% of 10–11-year-old children in the UK were obese; this figure is slightly worse for older children at 21.4%.[14] The figures are closely related to deprivation, with children in the least deprived areas having half the obesity rate as those in the most deprived. It is also clear from the maps in the National Audit Office report that obesity rates correlate closely with urban areas. In 2019 Gehl Associates were appointed by Guy's and St Thomas' Charity to look at the issue. Their report quotes childhood obesity rates of 32% in Peckham and an astonishing 52% in Camberwell. The report suggests that there are 8,000 fast food outlets in London, one for every 1,000 Londoners.[15] Childhood obesity is one of the most pressing health problems we face today according to the World Health Organization, and the high street is at least in part to blame.

The Gehl report was based on observations and interviews with young people and provides an insight into what is happening. The appeal of takeaways is based on the availability and appeal of the food, which is cheap, tasty and energy-dense, even if it lacks nutritional value, has high levels of fat, sugar and salt and is linked to obesity and a range of health conditions, including cardiovascular disease, type 2 diabetes, stroke and cancer. However, more important than the food, according to Gehl, is the role of takeaways as third spaces for teenagers. In their observations, young people are largely absent on the high streets or in parks and public places. As 15-year-old Zihoa told the researchers: 'There aren't any places for kids like us, the only places we can go into are like McDonald's, McNeils and other cheap restaurants …' As the report says: 'They are desirable places to spend time: they are low-cost, have informal seating, provide free Wi-Fi, and large groups can spend a long time there. In a teenager's everyday life this feels like a place where they can

Deliveroo: In just 10 years the company has grown to employ 3000 staff and operates in 10 countries. Some see it as a threat as it opens dark kitchens to compete with the high street.

hang out undisturbed, they can tell their parents where they are, they can get there easily and stay as long as they like. In a neighbourhood of limited places to hang out, and a fear of staying on the street for too long, a fast food place becomes the most obvious choice'. Put that way, takeaways are performing a service that high streets have always provided, it is just unfortunate that eating unhealthy food is the price for accessing these social spaces.

FASTER FOOD

Fast food takeaways may be the villain of the piece in the minds of many people who fear that they are coming to dominate the high street, but they too are under threat from the advent of home delivery apps like Deliveroo, Just Eat and Uber Eats. Like the grocery delivery apps discussed in the last chapter, they allow customers to order food online from restaurants and takeaways, charging the restaurant a commission and charging the customer a service and delivery charge. Deliveroo was founded in 2013 and now has 3,000 staff and operates in 10 countries. These apps received a huge boost during COVID and seemed to have maintained this momentum post-lockdown. In the first half of 2021, Deliveroo reported a doubling in the number of orders to 148 million, while the value of its transactions also doubled.

Initially many restaurants and takeaways embraced these apps as a way of expanding their customer base. On signing up, the outlet is sent an electric terminal that soon starts pinging with new orders, followed by the arrival of a delivery person on a bike. What's not to like? However, as an investigation by *The Guardian* illustrated there is a darker side to these apps.[16] News stories have tended to concentrate on the conditions and minimum wage for the delivery riders but there is also a corrosive effect on restaurants. The initial surge in orders once the terminal arrives soon subsides. Restaurants find themselves having to put up prices to cover the 35% commission, alienating their existing customer base. Then they find those customers leaking away to other outlets, undercutting them on price and appearing above them in the search results on the delivery app websites. What has become clear is that the apps are mining information on the customers of each of the companies they work with and then controlling the gateway between those companies and their customers.

Some of the competitor restaurants offering better prices on the app do not even exist. 'Cluckleberry Finn Fried Chicken', for example, is a brand created by Deliveroo and has no physical outlets, its food being created in a dark kitchen probably located on an industrial estate. Deliveroo has hundreds of these brands, tailoring them to the particular demographics of a local area and produced in kitchens that *The New Yorker* described as 'the culinary equivalent of a multicolour retractable pen', able to produce whatever cuisine is most profitable locally.[17] In China, the market is now dominated by Alibaba and Tencent, and has become so efficient that robot restaurants churn out popular dishes with no human involvement.

Takeaways and restaurants find themselves in an impossible position, having no option but to remain on these apps because their customers expect it, but finding themselves competing directly with dark kitchens owned by the app, which also controls the visibility of their restaurant to their customers. *The Guardian* investigation concluded that it was hard not to suspect that the ultimate aim of the 'venture capitalist subsidised food tech industry' was not to help local restaurants, as the publicity blurb insists, but to do away with them altogether.

The Pantiles in Royal Tunbridge Wells: Perhaps the oldest food and drink area in the UK having grown up around a spa discovered in 1606. Today it is home to 70 independent traders including specialist shops, galleries, cafes, restaurants and bars.

And it is important to remember this is happening in an industry that still loses money on every delivery. Uber Eats lost $232 million during the pandemic causing analysts to ask, if it can't make money when physical restaurants were forced to close, when would it?[18] Just Eat and Deliveroo also continue to lose money and the latter saw its shares crash by 30% within minutes of its listing on the London Stock Exchange in March 2021. Last year it made a loss of nearly £300 million and yet was still valued at £5 billion. In Chapter 6, we concluded that the 15-minute grocery delivery apps could probably never be profitable and that the main players would struggle. The food home delivery business is in a similar position because the costs of providing the service are higher than the amount they can charge. But the outcome may be different. First of all they are dealing with small independent businesses rather than the supermarkets and secondly, they have a huge customer base. *The Guardian* may be right that the only way to become profitable will be at the expense of local restaurants, and that would have a devastating impact on the high street.

The food and beverage sector is at a different stage of the economic cycle to mainstream retailing. It is in a mature phase of the market where consolidation and commodification is the rule, rather than market innovation. The independents that emerged in the 1980s and 1990s have grown to become huge multiples and their dominance of the market has not been undermined in the way that has happened to mainstream retailers. The sector does, however, remain dominated by independents and is constantly reinvigorated by small operators, the most recent trend being street food. However, the vitality of these independents is threatened by home delivery apps. As we describe in the next chapter, while sites such as eBay and Gumtree have opened up new markets for small retailers, the delivery apps, while initially promising the same, have become a major threat. The question is whether this is specific to the food and drink sector or a taste of what is to come with mainstream retailing.

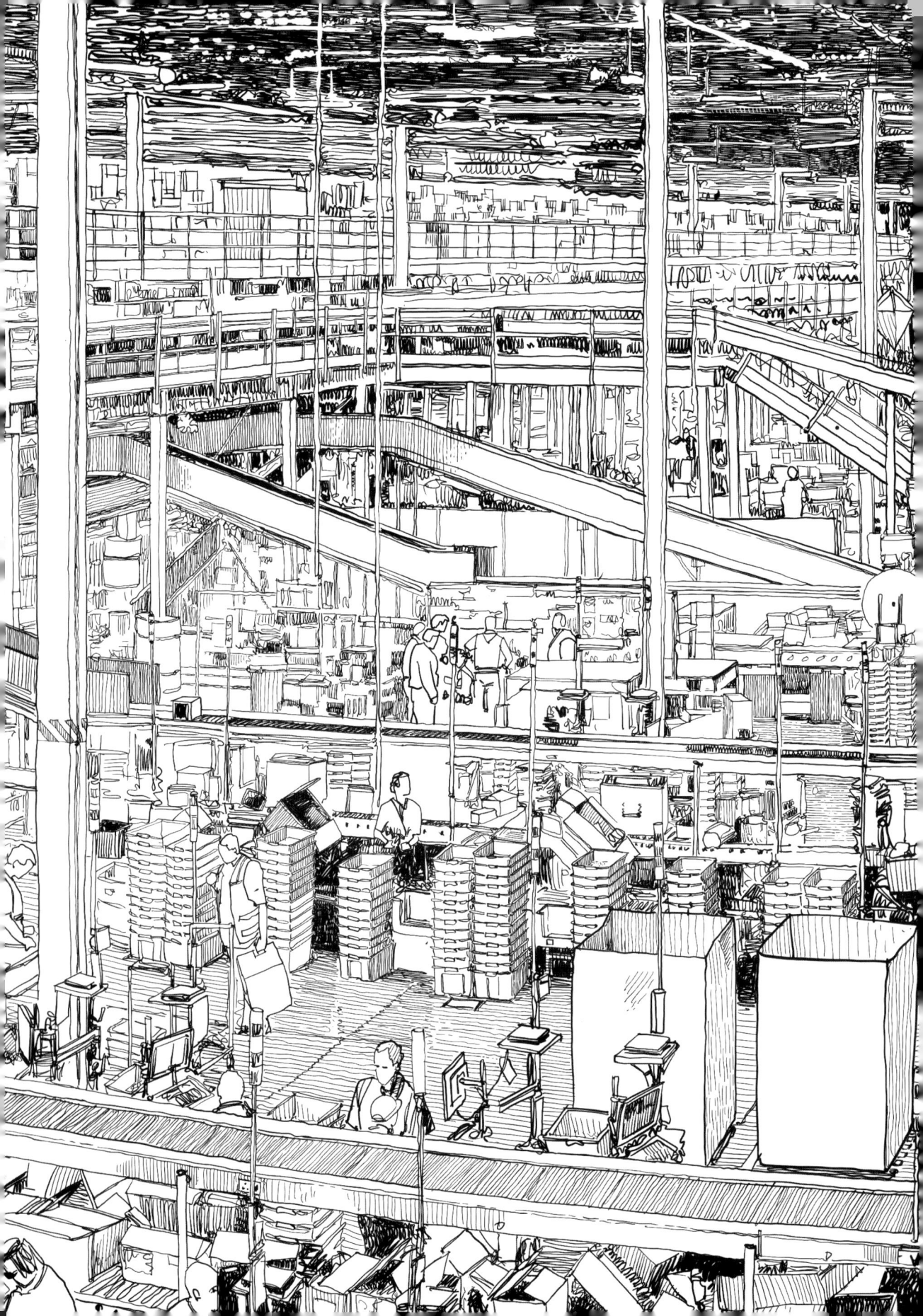

8 ONLINE AND E-COMMERCE

The biggest online shopping day of the year is not Black Friday or even Cyber Monday but 'Singles Day'. This was a tradition started by Chinese students unable to find a partner in the 1990s. They would celebrate their single status by buying themselves a present, the chosen date being 11 November because of its collection of lonely '1's. In 2009 it became an online event in a small way when the Chinese retailer Alibaba had its first Singles Day sale, featuring just 27 merchants. By 2019 Singles Day, sales had topped £30 billion, four times the volume of sales on Black Friday.

Such is the exponential growth of online retailing, with companies like Alibaba, Amazon and eBay dominating the retail market. It seems inevitable that the online juggernaut must crush the high street. However before we lose all hope, it is worth noting that, as we were completing this book in 2022, the online fashion retailers Made and Missguided collapsed. In our early drafts we had explored how the Manchester-based online fashion retailers Boohoo and Missguided, so popular with 'Love Island' contestants, had been seen as the future of fashion retail. Yet as lockdown was lifted and traditional retailers surged back, Missguided got things badly wrong and the brand is now owned by the physical retailer Fraser Group. The boundary between online and physical retail is more permeable than we thought. What we may be seeing is the emergence of a seamless multi-channel offer that creates opportunities as well as threats for the street.

OPEN SESAME: THE RISE OF ALIBABA

It is worth starting this chapter with Alibaba rather than Amazon. While Alibaba is only about half the size of Amazon, it is the only company that comes close to the internet behemoth in terms of the scope of its services and more importantly its ambition. It dominates China, with about 80% of the online market, and has its eyes set on Europe. Founded in 1999 in Hangzhou, it listed on the New York Stock Exchange in 2014 as the largest IPO ever.

A mythology has built up around Alibaba's founder Jack Ma, a man who only passed his college entrance exams on the third attempt because of his weakness in maths and didn't own a computer until he was 33. As an English teacher on a trip to Seattle in 1995, a friend introduced him to the internet. At that point, as he told 'Talk Asia', he had never even touched a keyboard, but he realised very quickly the potential of the technology and the huge blind spot it had for China.[1] When he got back to Hangzhou he organised an internet party to demonstrate the phenomenon to his friends: 'We waited three and half hours for half a page to load

Amazon: The scale of Amazon's fulfilment warehouses makes it difficult to see how the high street can possibly compete.

... We drank, watched TV and played cards, waiting. But I was so proud. I proved the Internet existed.'[2] His first venture was *China Pages*, a company that created home pages in the US for Chinese companies, and later he was recruited by the Chinese government's Electronic Commerce Centre. But in 1999, he returned to his hometown to start Alibaba with a group of 18 friends. The name had come to him in a café in San Francisco, when he asked a waitress what the name Alibaba meant to her. She replied 'open sesame – magically opening a secret door to a treasure trove'. Everyone else he asked that day, whatever nationality, knew about Alibaba. Within a year, the company had secured $25 million of venture capital.

Alibaba is a business to business (B2B) platform, in other words a wholesaler, and its original aim was to expand the market for Chinese businesses. In 2003, once Alibaba had started to turn a profit, it branched out by creating Taobao Marketplace, a customer to customer (C2C) platform – in Chinese 'tao bao' roughly translates as 'to find treasure'. It is essentially the Chinese equivalent of eBay – indeed eBay tried to buy Taobao to establish a presence in China. When their overtures were rejected eBay set up its own Chinese operation but was unable to compete and was forced out six years later. Taobao now has 90% of the Chinese C2C market.

In 2008 Jack Ma branched out again, this time creating Taobao Mall as a business to customer (B2C) platform – like Amazon. This was shortened to TMall and was given its own website in 2010, becoming a separate company a year later. In 2014 TMall Global was launched, opening the site to non-Chinese brands. On the most recent Singles Day, the top selling brands on TMall were Apple, Nike, New Balance, Adidas and Ugg, making this the largest market for Western products in China.

The mirror image of TMall is AliExpress, which is also a B2C platform but operates solely outside China, allowing Chinese companies to sell to the rest of the world. AliExpress is already the largest e-commerce site in Russia and is a major player in Eastern European countries, Indonesia, Brazil and Turkey, with a presence in most Western European countries. As President of Alibaba's wholesale marketplace division Trudy Dai told the *Financial Times*: 'From the very first day that Alibaba was founded we had a global dream.'[3] The company's target is to bring half of its sales from outside China by 2025. The main problem in achieving this has been delivery times, which the company is addressing by establishing an air shuttle service between Hong Kong and Madrid and opening a distribution centre in Liege, Belgium.

As the company expanded it also diversified, buying the *South China Morning Post* in Hong Kong and major stakes in the social media platform Weibo and the video streaming service Youku. It brought together a number of logistic companies to create Cainiao to deliver its packages in China, and bought a controlling stake in the department store chain Intime Retail.[4] It has also opened a chain of supermarkets called Freshippo. These high-tech supermarkets act as local fulfilment centres for online orders, as described in the case study in Chapter 6. Customers in store can scan goods to get details of provenance, cooking advice and recipe ideas and where to find just the right wine in store to go with the meal. Checkout is by facial recognition (using Alibaba's own system) and payment automatic via Alipay. The first store opened in Shanghai in 2016 and there are now 246 in China, with Alibaba experimenting with the same format for convenience stalls, breakfast bars and even entire malls. Alipay is another part of the empire, an online payment platform that is larger than PayPal. This sits within the Alibaba subsidiary Ant Group and because customers prepay money into their accounts, it has become the world's largest investment fund, with a third of China's population as investors.

Alibaba illustrates the power of online retail and also the 'first mover' advantage that comes from being the first company to exploit a particular market. Just as Amazon has done in the US and Europe, Alibaba has come to entirely dominate online retail in China, becoming the equivalent of Amazon, eBay, PayPal and FedEx rolled into one. Unlike Amazon it does not carry inventory, acting purely as a bridge between buyers and sellers. As such, it dominates the marketplace while creating huge opportunities for smaller Chinese businesses to access world markets. However, while Alibaba has helped Chinese retailers find new markets, it also represents a huge threat to those who are unable to compete in this new world. Having been battered by online competition these retailers now face powerful and efficient Alibaba stores on the high street.

Whether Alibaba is able to export its model to Europe depends on the attitude of the Chinese authorities. The dominant market position of online retailers is causing concern in many places, with discussions about antitrust laws to break up some of the internet giants in the US. The Chinese government shares these concerns mixed with political nervousness about the power of companies like Alibaba. In October 2020, Jack Ma spoke at a business summit where, in front of Chinese officials, he criticised the state's attitude to business saying, 'We shouldn't use the way to manage a train station to regulate an airport … We cannot regulate the future with yesterday's means.'[5]

The government was irritated and responded by blocking the flotation of the Ant Group on the New York Stock Exchange and launching an antimonopoly investigation. Jack Ma disappeared for three months – some say he was lying low but there were dark rumours that he was being held. When he reappeared, he was penitent and his comments focussed on charitable work to elevate the rural poor.[6] In April 2021, the antimonopoly investigation concluded and the resulting fine was a lot less than had been feared. Alibaba was ordered to sell its media assets and to restructure the Ant Group, but its share price surged on the belief that the worst was over. Alibaba had been brought to heel but was now free to do business, and having saturated the Chinese market its strategy is expansion elsewhere.

THE ONLINE REVOLUTION

When Mary Portas was undertaking her review of town centres in the UK in 2012, she cited the growth of e-commerce as one of the main threats to bricks and mortar retailing. At the time, online retail accounted for just under 10% of retail sales and had accounted for around half of the growth in sales since 2003.[7] The UK had the highest proportion of online retail in Europe, a level exceeded only by China and South Korea.[8] While the percentage of online sales may have been relatively small by today's standards, Portas worried that many retailers were in such a precarious state that even a 10% drop in sales would push them over the edge – as indeed has turned out to be the case. In the years that followed, the proportion of internet sales crept up by a percentage point a year until 2015 when the rate accelerated to 2% a year, reaching 19.2% in 2019. Then came the pandemic and the rate shot up to 32.8% during the first lockdown and nearly 38% during the second lockdown in January 2021. Government estimates suggest that 46.2% of non-food sales during the first lockdown were online.

The question is where the level of online retailing will settle post-pandemic. The average figure for 2021 in the UK was 28.9% although the most recent figure at the time of writing in March 2022 was 26.1%.[9] The UK still leads Europe but other countries are catching up, with the Netherlands reaching e-commerce levels of 23.9% and Germany 21.9%. Analysts suggest that something fundamental has changed with many people having had their first experience of online retail during the pandemic – 86.2% of shoppers in the UK made at least one purchase online in 2021 – and these people are expected to continue doing at least some of their shopping online going forward.[10]

The process is now becoming self-fuelling – with the failure of so many traditional retailers and the closure of so many stores, the opportunity to shop on the high street is contracting and brands such as Debenhams and Topshop can now only be bought online. The world has changed forever and the levels of online spend will remain at levels much higher than they would have been if the pandemic had not taken place, probably somewhere in the region of 25–30% of total sales. What is more difficult to predict is the ongoing trend – will the 2% a year growth return or will we see stability for a few years as the market adjusts? Is there a point of saturation beyond which online sales can't go, or will their relentless expansion continue until the last physical shop dies?

The latter seems unlikely. A survey by the branding company I-AM prior to the pandemic found that 74% of millennials still preferred physical retailing.[11] This seems to hold true post-pandemic. A report by PwC in 2022 suggested that 65% of under 25s said they loved going to real shops and would prefer in-store to online retailing if they had the time.[12] Lisa Hooker of PwC writes in *Retail Week* how the youngest shoppers, as digital natives, have already factored in the advantages of the internet. These have become expectations but they want more and physical retailing is where they are looking: 'It is a social activity … that whole experience of browsing different shops, visiting favourite retailers and enjoying some food and drink while being able to catch up, [that] cannot be replicated online yet.'

Our view is that there will always remain a significant proportion of sales that take place in physical stores – the internet is not going to destroy the high street. That is not to downplay the challenge that online retail represents, which is greater than any of the previous crises on the high street described in Part 1 of this book. It will mean we need less mainstream retail space, causing rents to collapse and with it, the commercial value of retail property. While the internet will not kill the high street, it has sounded the death knell of many legacy retailers and perhaps more importantly the entire retail property investment model. The high street in the age of the internet is therefore going to be a very different place.

AMAZON: 'DOMINATE EVERY MARKET'

The threat to the traditional retail model can best be illustrated by Amazon, the largest online retailer in the UK by some distance, with 435 million monthly visits to its website and more than twice the online sales of the second place retailer Tesco.[13]

Amazon started life in July 1995 selling books from a garage in Seattle. In just 25 years, it has grown to become all-encompassing, selling pretty much everything. Its head office is called Day 1, representing its obsession with acting like a start-up. Day 1 companies are frenetic and always assume that someone else will do what they do better; they are innovative and expansionist and focussed entirely on the customers rather than the competition. Day 2 in Jeff Bezos's words means 'stasis, followed by irrelevance, followed by excruciating painful decline, followed by death'.[14] Which pretty much sums up the state of many traditional retailers in the face of the Amazon bulldozer.

Amazon's tactic since its foundation has been to identify a retail sector, understand what the customer is looking for, focus on meeting those needs better than the incumbent retailers and then setting out to dominate the market, starting with books and CDs, moving onto consumer electronics and then fashion, e-books via Kindle, streaming services via Amazon Prime, and Amazon Web Services (the world's largest cloud computing company). Current targets include the craft market (Handmade at Amazon), luxury fashion, healthcare and, of course, the supermarkets.

Amazon's mantra is to understand and focus on the customer. To integrate itself fully in people's lives via Alexa and to give people a huge choice of goods that can be delivered to their door within a day or sometimes hours. Amazon's turnover in the first quarter of 2021 was $108.5 billion (compared to $75.5 billion in the same quarter the year previous). It won't be long before it eclipses the annual $560 billion sales of Walmart, the world's largest retailer. Even before the pandemic, Amazon accounted for 2.1% of all US household spending. An ex-Amazon executive told Brian Dumaine, author of the book Bezonomics, 'Everything we did at Amazon was about becoming a tightly woven part of the fabric of people's lives … We're getting to the point when there is going to be a massive integration. Amazon is becoming an operating system for life.'[15] Dumaine illustrates the level of Amazon's dominance in the US where three-quarters of customers said that they did 'most' of their online shopping on Amazon, the next biggest share being Walmart at 8%. He describes how in 2018 a Georgetown University poll asked Americans which institutions they most trusted – Democrats put Amazon at the top of the list and Republicans put it in third place, after only the military and the police.

The UK is not far behind these figures with Mintel estimating that 90% of UK consumers have used Amazon and 70% do so at least once a month.[16] In 2019, it accounted for 30.1% of all online retail sales, three times as much as second placed eBay. In 2022, Amazon's UK revenue was 82% up on pre-pandemic levels. There were 281,257 Amazon Marketplace sellers in the UK in 2019 and 21 of the company's 77 European fulfilment centres are in the UK, employing 27,500 staff.[17] This figure has risen by 7,000 during the pandemic, plus 20,000 temporary workers who were taken on over Christmas 2020.

As Amazon's growth and ambition seem to have no limits, there are real questions about whether many high streets can withstand its onslaught. That is before the playing field is tilted by the fact that Amazon pays virtually no corporation tax (just £6.3 million in the UK in 2019). There are also concerns about the huge amount of data it holds on its customers, and allegations about its anticompetitive practices, fake reviews and the exploitation of third-party sellers. Notwithstanding the entry of new players to the UK market like Alibaba, Amazon looks set to dominate UK retailing for the foreseeable future and if the high street cannot adjust to this it has no future.

Of course, Amazon is also an opportunity; Amazon Marketplace represents a potential outlet for retailers to reach huge numbers of customers. They will need to play the game to ensure that customers are able to find their products on the site and will need to accept heavily discounted prices, but nevertheless the internet is a double-edged sword, as perhaps best illustrated by eBay.

EBAY: THE PERFECT MARKET?

The foundation myth of eBay involves a broken laser pen. Its founder Pierre Omidyar, born in France of Iranian descent but living in California, created an auction on his personal website and was amazed when someone offered $14.83 for the first item he had posted. On contacting the buyer to check that he realised that the laser pen didn't work, Omidyar was told that the buyer was a collector of broken laser pens. The lesson being that, if the market is big enough, there will be a buyer for virtually anything.

This was 1995, the same year that Amazon was founded and the site originally called AuctionWeb was being run by Omidyar as a hobby. However, it gained in popularity to such an extent that his service provider insisted he upgrade to a professional account, with the monthly cost increasing from $30 to $250. He therefore decided that he needed to charge sellers a small fee.[18] And so was born one of the first consumer to consumer (C2C) websites, with the site charging a small fee to post an item and then taking a percentage of the sale price. The transaction took place between the buyer and the seller, with the latter being responsible for arranging delivery. In the early days the site generated huge excitement through the auction process, with bids accelerating as the deadline approached.

In 1996, the first full year of operations, the site hosted 250,000 transactions but such was its growth that in 1997 it had reached that figure by early February.[19] In 1997 10% of trade on the site was in Beanie Babies, a toy craze where collectors would try and complete their collection. The same year the company received its first tranche of venture capital and changed its name. Originally it was to have been called Echo Bay but the domain name was taken so it was shortened to eBay. In September 1998, it became a public company and by 2001 it had become the largest e-commerce site by user base, with 4.5 million items listed on any given day. However growth has not been continuous. In 2014, there were concerns that its growth had stalled, causing a change in direction as explained by its UK marketing director Gareth Jones: 'We don't want to be defined by that online car boot sale reputation anymore. We need to get people to consider eBay in a completely different way. The UK is the petri dish for testing a new approach to rebuilding the brand globally. It is all about a shift away from the marketplace and over to being the ultimate shop.'[20,21]

The strategy worked and the site now has 185 million active users and annual revenue of more than $10 billion; 80% of sales are now new items sold at fixed prices by businesses rather than auctions. It has therefore evolved into primarily a business to consumer (B2C) site with the great advantage that it doesn't handle the goods – they are sent by sellers directly to buyers. All eBay does is facilitate the transaction and take a cut, meaning that its overheads are low and its margins high. The company itself employs 5,000 data scientists and analyses the 50 petabytes of data it generates every day to optimise the user experience.[22] eBay is studied by economists as an example of the perfect market against which their predictive models can be tested. It sells everything within its guidelines: the city of Carlotta in California was sold on the site in 2003, as was one of the tunnel boring machines used to dig the Channel Tunnel. Other sales include a slice of toast half eaten by Justin Timberlake, a single cornflake and the naming rights of an unborn child.

However, most of its sellers are businesses and its impact on the high street is mixed. On the one hand, manufacturers and wholesalers, rather than selling their products through shops or even on Amazon, can sell direct to their customers via eBay, which provides a range of tools including virtual store fronts, search engine optimisation and supply and pricing data. However, this can also be used by high street stores. A small, off-pitch shop with little footfall can become a viable business

GUMTREE

Gumtree is named after the eucalyptus trees that grow in Australia, New Zealand and South Africa. It was established in London in 2000 to carry classified ads for expats from these countries looking to move to London or to establish themselves in the city. It is essentially the digital version of the notices that used to be posted in newsagents windows offering things for sale or just to be given away to a good home. By 2010 it had grown into the largest classified ads site and one of the top 30 websites in the UK, with just under 15 million visits a month.

Unlike other platforms the site tends to be city-based. It started in London and the idea of classified ads is that people can pop around to see the goods before paying for them in person (the site does not handle payments). The site initially expanded to cover cities in the UK and then into Australia, South Africa and New Zealand. In 2004 Gumtree opened a site in Warsaw, Poland, and a year later in Berlin, Milan and Rome. In 2007 it opened in the US, targeting initially expat communities in New York, Boston and Chicago. Its success attracted eBay, who owned the company from 2005 until its sale in 2021 to the classified ads site Adevinta.

The core business of Gumtree is personal listings and as a private seller it is free to post an ad. It has always carried a large number of private car sales but also includes flat rentals, services and jobs. In recent years the company has focussed more on paid company listings, including car dealerships, but also local traders. It is therefore becoming another market for small retailers to sell to a wider public.

by selling via eBay and other online outlets. The purpose of retail is to connect the buyer and seller. In the past that was done by locating shops on busy streets where they were exposed to the maximum number of potential customers. Online sites like eBay potentially create the 'perfect market' by connecting the most niche retailer with customers who would never find their physical shop.

THE INTERNET AS THE SAVIOUR OF THE HIGH STREET?

One of the stories that inspired this book related to the Liverpool Cake Fairy in Garston. In 2013, having been engaged to prepare a strategy for the revival of the high street, we arrived late one winter's afternoon to find that most of the shops were shuttered. It was a gloomy prospect and yet, halfway along the street the lights were on in a shop painted in a shocking shade of pink; behind its brightly lit windows could be seen a hive of activity. The Liverpool Cake Fairy, established by six local women, had taken a unit on the high street because it was cheap. They attracted some walk-in trade, as attested by the queue at the till, but the reason they were able to survive and thrive on a dead high street was the roaring trade they were doing online, catering for children's parties and special occasions. It was like one of those pioneer plants poking through the charred ground after a forest fire.

At the time, the Cake Fairy sold through its own website, taking credit card payments, processing orders, organising deliveries and keeping the takings. Today their website could be built easily and cheaply using online products like Shopify that include not just the website but point-of-sale services, payment processing, marketing, shipping and customer feedback. Today they would also have the option of selling via Etsy or other online stores; they could have set up a shop on Facebook or Instagram and sell via Deliveroo or Just Eat. In doing so, they would have been able to access a market far greater than they could through their own website and vastly larger than was available on Garston High Street, although of course they would no longer be keeping 100% of the takings.

What is true of cupcakes is potentially true of many of the shops that used to populate our high streets. As we have seen, many small traders use eBay, but there are also opportunities for craft, antique and bric-a-brac shops to use Etsy, and many traders also use Gumtree despite its origins as a small ads site. Second-hand record shops can sell via Discogs, while bookshops can sell through Amazon, AbeBooks (although that is now part of Amazon) or use Bookshop.org.

The latter is an online platform for independent bookstores from which you can buy from an individual bookshop or from the general site, with the proceeds being distributed amongst the member bookshops. It was established in the US in a collaboration with the American Booksellers Association and launched in the UK in November 2020 with 130 independent bookstores signed up. Initiatives like this mean that the number of independent bookshops is once more growing in the UK.

The traditional view of the high street has seen online retail as an insurmountable threat; how can traditional retailers possibly compete with Amazon? These initiatives are creating a different narrative. In a paper entitled *The Social Supply Chain and the Future High Street*, Gordon Fletcher and colleagues at Salford University argue that the internet and social media have completely disrupted the relationship between the producers and the consumers of goods.[23] In the past there were two separate fields: supply chain management, which was concerned with how to get goods into the shops, and marketing, which was concerned with how to get customers into those same shops. The 'social supply chain' has now changed all of this – manufacturers can sell direct to customers, and social networks can handle the social interactions that once took place on the high street, while customers have become accustomed to infinite variety and 24-hour availability. There are, however, huge opportunities for physical retailers. They can't compete on price and variety but they can offer experience, character and individuality. The paper suggests that retailers can exploit the social supply chain and harness the internet to combine the best of both worlds:

> 'Retail business models that take up the social supply chain perspective necessarily attend to the construction of a seamless environment for connecting with friends, engaging with the variability and uncertainty provided by independent shops and traditional markets, the provision of sustainable key logistics services and the removal of the many transportation challenges for shoppers, and their shopping, in and out of the future city.'

This is the world of omnichannel retail as we describe in the fashion industry in Chapter 11. In the early days of online retail, purchases were made sitting at home computers but now m-commerce – purchases using mobile devices – accounts for 43% of e-commerce.[24] This makes a huge difference as most customers on the high street have a smartphone in their pocket. Those phones can be used for payment and, of course, m-commerce, allowing customers to compare products from competitors and price match. This is leading to an integration of online and physical retail through initiatives like showrooming. Retailers no longer see their physical stores competing with their own websites as they did until recently, with each controlled by a separate division of the company. A sale is a sale regardless of where it comes from and if you see all retail channels as complementary they can work in tandem. Retailers are now exploiting multiple channels, still selling via their own websites (some like Next incredibly successfully), but they also use online marketplaces and shopfronts on Amazon and eBay, to ensure that their sites are optimised via Google and integrated via social media (which in the case of Facebook now has its own marketplace) and in addition to all of this running their own physical stores.

Physical stores are seen as an essential part of the mix. One of the reasons is the 'halo effect'. A study by ICSC found that a retailer's web traffic is 27% higher in places where they have a physical store.[25] For this reason, many online retailers are opening actual shops. It is happening in the fashion industry and with goods, as well as at the other end of the spectrum with Amazon opening contactless grocery stores, similar to the Alibaba Freshippo stores in China.

At the same time traditional retailers are rethinking their stores. As we will see in Chapter 10 IKEA are rethinking their business model, opening small in-town stores where goods can be displayed but no inventory is kept and sales are in-store, online for home delivery. John Lewis is going through a similar process, having closed a number of stores during lockdown. They are now looking at smaller outlets that display stock, providing advice and consultation in a convivial atmosphere. They have also successfully used click-and-collect to link online sales to store visits.

We might therefore tell a different story of the high street in the age of the internet: there was once a thriving high street but gradually it came to be dominated by a small number of big retailers while being threatened by out-of-town retail parks that offered better value, choice and convenience. Then along came the internet, offering even better value and choice, and the high street was once more under

ETSY

Etsy was founded in 2005 by three friends in Brooklyn, New York. Each was involved in creating handmade goods and frustrated at the difficulty of selling them. It started life in the apartment of one of its founders, Rob Kalin, and is still based nearby. As the company's CEO Chad Dickerson said in 2014, 'We'll remain firmly planted in Brooklyn, where so many independent, creative businesses are flourishing … We'll continue to influence and be influenced by the mix of industries here, from media to fashion to a burgeoning manufacturing renaissance.'[26] It is an example of how the internet can support independent businesses and local traders rather than always being seen as a threat, Etsy's slogan being 'keep commerce human'.

By 2019 the site had 2.5 million sellers including a mix of handcrafted goods and vintage items. Its aim is to be a combination of craft shop, thrift store and bric-a-brac emporium, and it likes to cultivate an indie image, although this has become more and more difficult as it has grown. In 2008, after a major influx of venture capital finance, Rob Kalin posted a clip of himself reading from the children's book *Swimmy*: 'We do not want Etsy itself to be a big tuna fish. Those tuna are the big companies that all us small businesses are teaming up against.'[27]

The tension between the scale of the company and its indie image has been the source of most of its difficulties. Its aim is to create 'a people-powered economy with person-to-person commerce … the feel of a farmer's market instead of a supermarket'.[28] However there was controversy in 2013 when it relaxed the rule that said that all items sold on the site had to be either vintage or made by the seller. This allowed sellers to outsource production and there was a worry that the site would be swamped by cheap goods. There have also been controversies about charging for advertising and prioritising sellers who offer free shipping.

Nevertheless, the site has enabled the creation of hundreds of small businesses with many people turning a hobby into an income and giving up their jobs. According to *Fortune Magazine* 86% of sellers are women and some of the businesses have grown significantly.[29] As the company told the *Entrepreneur*, 'we want to bring the Etsy ethos into the larger retail ecosystem'.[30] The question is therefore whether sites like Etsy are a threat or a boon to the high street.

threat. But this time it was the big retailers who suffered – many did not survive and there were worries that the high street itself couldn't survive. But the retailers that remained, like the mammals that survived the extinction of the dinosaurs, emerged stronger and came to see the internet as an opportunity as much as a threat. The physical and online worlds were merged, allowing businesses to connect with customers, to expand markets and to enhance the experience of shopping in real places. In the end, the internet was not the end of the high street but its saviour. It is a possibility.

9 SOUND AND VISION

As a teenager I (DR) would head into Birmingham with my friends most Saturdays to do the record shops. Having listened to John Peel on Radio 1 all week and read the record reviews in the *New Musical Express*, we would head into town with a list of potential purchases. The trick was to find something that no one else had heard of but which was brilliant, ideally the first release on an independent label of a band that would go on to greater things. This is why I still have the first pressing of 'Gangsters' by The Specials and 'Killing an Arab' by The Cure, unfortunately both badly scratched.

The biggest record shop in Birmingham, at the time, was Virgin Records. This was long before Richard Branson branched out into trains, aeroplanes and space rockets. Back then, Virgin Records was all that Virgin did and it was both a record label and a retailer. Its stores were great matte-black-painted spaces with awesome sound systems and the coolest shop assistants who always seemed to be judging the customers for their choice of record – heaven help you if you asked for something in the charts! We also frequented the much smaller independent Inferno Records, where you were served by the owner who had an encyclopaedic knowledge of music. Then on to Reddingtons Rare Records, squashed into a unit in a subway beneath the Bullring. This was where we got our musical education, searching back through the dog-eared, second-hand albums of the 1960s and 1970s, buying records on the basis of their cover art or just curiosity as to what the New York Dolls, Hawkwind or Bong sounded like (brilliant/disappointing/terrible).

These were the days before streaming, when music outside the charts was still a mystery. You could hear a track on the radio or read a review, and never manage to track it down, which meant you would never hear it again. It is said that punk in the UK was inspired by a review of a single by the band Television in New York, which wasn't available in the UK and therefore no one had actually heard at the time. The Birmingham shops would get a few copies of new records on their release but after that they were gone. Ownership of a rare track on a piece of 7" vinyl was a great source of teenage status because there was nowhere else that your friends could access that piece of music, unless you allowed them to tape it. Despite dramatic posters telling us that 'piracy was killing music', mix tapes were the currency of the time. A curated mix tape of your favourite tracks was a calling card for a new girl or boyfriend to establish your creds and negotiate your common musical territory.

THE OLDEST RECORD STORE

In Cardiff there is a record shop called Spillers Records that lays claim to be the oldest in the world. Established in 1894 by Henry Spiller it specialised in the sale of

Spillers Records in Cardiff: Like an older brother or sister passing on their love of music. Is this the future not just of music retail but of all retail?

wax phonograph cylinders and shellac discs not long after these new technologies were first invented. In the last 30 years, the shop has changed constantly. In the 1990s it was very much like Cardiff's version of Inferno Records, still focussing on vinyl, a place where you could get all the obscure new releases – I (DR) remember buying a single by Cardiff-based band Box of Thumbs, which wasn't very good. Even then, half the store was given over to CDs, although you could tell that their heart wasn't really in it. In the early 2000s, the shop was struggling as its landlord sought to put up its rent and its main business seemed to be second-hand records and CDs, with a poor selection of new releases. It might have disappeared, were it not for a campaign organised by Owen John Thomas, local member of the Welsh Assembly, and supported by the band Manic Street Preachers and Columbia Records.

Spillers moved into a new shop at the heart of the city's arcades and, visiting in 2019, it was thriving and once more focussed on vinyl. Its success mirrors the remarkable revival of the vinyl record bought by punters who have access to everything they need through streaming services, but still want to own the physical product. The British Phonographic Industry projected that vinyl records would outsell CDs in 2021 for the first time since 1987. This is a dramatic turnaround; the sales of vinyl rose by a third in 2020 while CDs fell by a similar amount as people channelled money that would have been spent on gigs into buying records.[1] As reported in the *New Statesman*, such is the global demand for vinyl records that there is a lack of capacity at pressing plants to meet the demand and many smaller artists are being squeezed out.[2] Retailing at anything from £15 to £40, vinyl records have also become a luxury purchase, something that would have been beyond my teenage spending power.

Spillers is now more like a knowledgeable older sibling, passing on their love of music. Many of the records in their racks have a short note outlining the history of the band and why they are so great, the assistants are enthusiastic and knowledgeable, and the shop is a social space where people hang out, listening to new music and enjoying the atmosphere. The music industry is perhaps the best example of a sector that has adjusted to almost complete transfer of its product online and yet has reinvented a role for physical retail spaces. Such is the future of music retail, indeed it is arguable that such is the future of all retail.

THE GREAT NAPSTER PANIC OF 2000

Music retailers faced the online threat much earlier than other sectors. There was, of course, the growth of Amazon as a major retailer of CDs, but what really panicked the industry was Napster. This was a peer-to-peer music sharing network whose users (which at its peak topped 80 million) could share digital music files for free. At the time, some university IT managers reported that up to 60% of their bandwidth was being taken by Napster.[3] The creation of a 17-year-old student, Napster only operated between late 1999 and mid-2001, before being sued by the heavy metal band Metallica and the rap artist Dr Dre, who realised that their entire back catalogue was being circulated online. The end came when the record companies won a court case against Napster causing it to be closed down.

The record companies were however in full panic mode, an industry representative calling 2001 a 'turbulent year' and a 'crisis of monumental proportions'. Napster may have been stopped but other file-sharing sites were appearing and there seemed no way for the music industry to fight back. Then to make matters immeasurably worse, Apple launched the first iPod in October

2001. There had been digital music players before that the record companies had challenged them in the courts, but Apple was a different proposition, particularly since it had also launched iTunes to sell digital music online. The industry had no choice but to come to an accommodation with Apple and by 2006 iTunes had gained 70% of the music streaming market. This was the year that Spotify was founded as a start-up in Sweden by Daniel Ek and Martin Lorentzon. Unlike iTunes, where you had to buy each piece of music, Spotify provided it for free if you were prepared for your listening to be interrupted by adverts, or for £10 a month to listen ad-free.

This put paid to the illegal streaming services, despite the rise of sites like Pirate Bay. By making streaming easy and cheap, most customers started paying for their online music. The problem was that they were not paying very much. Some artists initially boycotted Spotify because the royalties were so low, and Apple wasn't particularly interested in making money from selling music – their interest was in selling iPods. The good news for the music industry was that they started to get some revenue from music streaming; the bad news was that this was a tiny proportion of what they were losing in CD sales. The crisis was greater still for record stores that had expanded on the back of the profits from selling CDs.

It is, however, worth telling the story of Radiohead, who in 2000 were a little-known band from Oxford. Unbeknown to them, their album *Kid A* was pirated months before its release and ended up being downloaded for free millions of times on Napster. Conventional record industry thinking would have suggested that this was a disaster – why would anyone buy the CD when they have had the album digitally for months? Yet this is not what happened. When the album was eventually released, it went straight to number one on the US Billboard charts, despite releasing no singles and having no radio play. It seemed that when people really liked a band, they would purchase a physical product for their collection, be it a CD or, better still, a vinyl record and of course they would also want to see them live. The economic model for the music industry changed, with income coming as much from live music, merchandising and the sales of vinyl rather than from streaming.

The effect was to undermine the power of record companies, allowing independent artists to find an audience, and their music directly via sites like Myspace and more recently Bandcamp to build up a live following. As *Rolling Stone* reported, independent artists generated $1 billion in the US in 2019 and, despite the setback of lockdown, a merchant bank specialising in the music industry was predicting that this would double in the next few years.[4] The question is how can town centres benefit from this?

THE WELSH SOUTH BY SOUTHWEST

FOCUS Wales is a multi-venue festival held in Wrexham as a showcase for the Welsh music industry and emerging talent from across the world. I (DR) first visited in 2018 to see the Welsh artist Euros Childs, who was playing in a large concrete room as part of a modern market. However, over the course of the evening we saw bands from all over the world, particularly small nations like Wales, before ending up in a vacant Sports Direct store for a set by the legendary Manchester DJ, A Guy Called Gerald. Essentially it is a Welsh version of the South by Southwest festival in Austin, Texas, combining live music with a music industry conference, and is a key part of the strategy for the town's revival.

Wrexham is the largest shopping centre in North Wales, although its main competitor Chester is just 16 kilometres away over the border. Like many towns, its strategy has been to attract multiple retailers to improve its position in the retail rankings. It achieved this in 2008 by opening a major new shopping centre called Eagle Meadows anchored by a Debenhams (now closed) and attracting other retailers out of the old high street which started to look a bit run-down as a result.

The Welsh independent music scene has been very strong for some years. It may be known for the Manic Street Preachers, but more recently local musicians have been inspired by bands such as Super Furry Animals and Gorky's Zygotic Mynci, not afraid to sing in Welsh and to promote a very distinctive local sound. This has been continued by bands like Alffa, Gwenno and Adwaith, all singing in Welsh, who are popular way beyond the Welsh border. Wrexham has capitalised on this not only to bring people into the town and revive its evening economy, but also to change its image. Events like FOCUS Wales change how people feel about a place, make it seem 'cool' to younger people, and the spin-off can be seen in the growth of independent shops and bars, as well as the venues.

The most interesting of FOCUS Wales' 14 venues is the concrete market space where we saw Euros Childs. Wrexham has always been a market town, being the place where Welsh farmers traded with English merchants at the point where the Welsh mountains meet the Cheshire Plain. It has three markets: the General Market, the Butchers Market and, on the edge of the town centre, what used to be called the People's Market.

The latter used to occupy a cavernous and unwelcoming space under a multistorey car park. It has recently been refurbished by the council and pulls off the difficult trick of being an art gallery, a music venue and a food hall while retaining the market. Renamed Tŷ Pawb (Everyone's House) it is a cheap-as-chips cultural project, coming in at £4.4 million. The 1980s architecture of the building exterior and the parking decks have been left untouched. The only external sign of the transformation is a diagonal slash of matte black paint with Tŷ Pawb picked out in white lettering. The interior has been stripped back to its concrete essentials, with wire mesh, corrugated sheeting and hanging industrial curtains used to divide up the space. The market stalls are still there, along with a central refectory with communal benches and gallery space that has hosted exhibitions from Grayson Perry and Bridget Riley. There is also a seated performance space in which they also show film screenings. The stallholders were offered pitches in the other market hall while the work took place and some chose not to return. Those that did include a sweet stall, comic books, carpets, textiles, jewellery, clothing and crafts – admittedly the respectable end of the fare that was available in the old People's Market but nevertheless a genuine market. The result, as Rowan Moore wrote in *The Guardian*, is a place that 'feels right for its aspirations. It is welcoming, animated, open, unpretentious and multifarious, while also calm and dignified'.[5] In the long run it is likely to be far more important than the glitzy and pretentiously named Eagles Meadow in securing a sustainable future for the town centre.

RETAIL VIRGINS

Virgin Records started out as a mail order business in 1970, graduating to a small shop in Notting Hill Gate, 'Virgin Records and Tapes', specialising in Krautrock imports. The name 'Virgin' was apparently suggested by one of the early employees Tessa Watts, because they were such innocents in the ways of business. However, Richard Branson always had bigger plans and within a few years the first Virgin Record Shop had opened over a shoe shop at the cheaper end of Oxford Street in

London and by the end of the 1970s, the first Virgin Megastore had opened at the expensive end of the same street.

The Virgin store we frequented in Birmingham wasn't a Megastore – I'm not sure we would have approved. I (DR) am certainly old enough to remember the original Virgin logo on its carrier bags, designed by the science fiction artist Roger Dean. The chain did however expand rapidly, eventually reaching 125 stores in the UK, with a further 35 in France and another 100 or so across the world, from Japan to the US. In the 1990s these stores thrived in the age of the CD, branching out into film and DVDs, computer games and books. At the time the market was driven by an older generation of record owners replacing their vinyl with CDs, with their supposedly better sound quality.

Virgin anticipated the rise of music streaming, launching Virgin Digital in 2005, but this made the fatal mistake of not being compatible with iPods and was soon discontinued. However, for a time, VirginMega was the second most popular music streaming service in France, but it closed down in 2013. By the mid-2000s much of the Virgin Megastore empire had been sold to fund the company's other ventures. The UK stores were subject to an ill-fated management buyout in 2007, on the

SUNDERLAND: DIVERSIFICATION THROUGH MUSIC

When I (DR) was a child my grandmother would take us for lunch in Binns in Sunderland. It was reserved for special occasions because the store, with its four restaurants and spiral staircase, was one of the grandest department stores in the north.

Founded in 1807, Binns had outlets across the north before becoming part of House of Fraser. But it started in Sunderland and had its headquarters there. It was a huge blow in 1993 when competition from the Metrocentre led to the closure of the Sunderland store. The main Binns store has been reused as a library and gallery but its original building in the city has just opened as 'Pop Recs', a record shop and venue. Music is one of the things that Sunderland does well, as the home of acclaimed bands like the Futureheads and Field Music, who played, along with other local bands, at the launch of the new venue.

The last retail assessment in Sunderland in 2016 concluded that the covered shopping centre was doing well but the shopping streets were struggling. There were 68 vacant units (16.2%), well above the national average, and the centre was 'dominated by mid-market and down-market shops'.[6] Our data shows that the vacancy rate had risen to 21.1% pre-pandemic and to 23.2% in 2022 following the closure of the Debenhams and Arcadia stores. Sunderland was therefore in a very vulnerable position and, as the 2016 report recommended, in desperate need of diversification.

In doing this, the city's musical heritage is a major asset. Sunderland College, where many of the local bands started, is building a new city centre campus and the western part of the centre has been designated as the Music, Arts and Culture (MAC) Quarter. This includes the city's huge Empire Theatre, along with the historic Dun Cow and Peacock pubs, the latter owned by the Futureheads frontman Barry Hyde and includes a 220 capacity venue. Next door the MAC Trust has completed the £7 million refurbishment of the former fire station as a cultural venue and there are plans for an even larger 450 capacity (800 standing) music venue.

Meanwhile, Pop Recs in the former Binns store is a good old-fashioned record shop, together with another venue, a café, a training kitchen for young people and a teenage market where young people can try out business ideas. The conversion was undertaken by the Tyne & Wear Building Preservation Trust and Martin Hulse of the Trust told *The Guardian*: 'The returns on social outcomes of community engagement, improving security of the area and bringing footfall and making it a nicer place to live, are really difficult things to monetise but that is what we are delivering – huge change for the area. You now see people on the streets at night.'[7]

Popular music is a powerful economic tool in these circumstances, far beyond the sale of records or gig tickets. Music generates activity throughout the day and evening and also has a positive effect on the city's image, especially amongst young people and students. Dare we say, it makes the city 'cool', which is a powerful force for regeneration.

eve of the financial crisis. The stores were rebranded as Zavvi but lasted less than two years. What did for them was not so much falling demand, but the collapse of Woolworths which, through its wholesale arm Entertainment UK, had been Zavvi's major supplier.

HIS MASTER'S VOICE

Back in the 1970s, HMV was not on our radar, seen as the place where our parents bought their 'easy listening' records. However, it now is the last remaining major record store chain in the UK with 107 stores. In 2021, it reached its 100th anniversary, something that had seemed unlikely when it was placed into administration in January 2013 and again in February 2019. Successive owners tried and failed to ride out the changing music market, together with the effects of the credit crunch and the retail crisis. Now, however, it is back in profit under the ownership of Sunrise Records and its Canadian owner, Doug Putnam, riding the same trends that saved Spillers Records.

Like Spillers, HMV's history stretches back to the invention of the record, although initially it was a record manufacturer rather than retailer. Its first record shop opened in 1921 on Oxford Street in London, with a special guest appearance from the composer Edward Elgar. In the 1930s it was instrumental in setting up Electric and Musical Industries Ltd (EMI Records) and was also a major manufacturer of TVs, radios and record players. HMV stands for 'His Master's Voice', illustrated by a logo showing a dog looking into the horn of a gramophone having recognised the voice of his master, the sound quality being that good.

Its retail expansion started in the 1960s and through the 1970s it went head-to-head with Virgin Megastore and Our Price (the other major record retailer at the time). By the 1990s, HMV had achieved a dominant position with 320 stores, also acquiring Dillons book stores and later Waterstones, so becoming the largest book retailer on the high street.

HMV may have transformed its easy listening image to appeal to a younger market but it never quite captured the 'indie' music market. With this in mind, it bought the record store Fopp out of administration in 2007. Fopp had started as a market stall in Glasgow in 1981 but grew into a chain of almost 100 stores before overextending itself and falling into administration. HMV only retained a few profitable stores, mostly in big cities where they worked hard to create the atmosphere of an independent record store. It worked; it was a few years before many realised that Fopp stores were part of HMV.

Following its collapse in 2013, HMV itself was purchased out of administration by Hilco, who briefly brought it back into profit. However, by the beginning of 2019, it was in receivership once more, the then chief executive telling the BBC: 'Even an exceptionally well-run and much-loved business such as HMV cannot withstand the tsunami of challenges facing UK retailers over the last 12 months on top of such a dramatic change in consumer behaviour in the entertainment market.'[8] By the time of its second administration HMV was selling 31% of all 'physical music' (CDs) in the UK and 23% of all DVDs and Blu-rays. It even overtook Amazon in these sectors, but while its market share may have been growing, the market was disappearing. The CD market in the US shrank by 96.6% between 2000 and 2020 and the UK wasn't far behind.

It is therefore remarkable that despite COVID, HMV is once more in profit, helped by a boost in online sales through lockdown. Its new owner, Doug Putnam, started out in toys and turned to music in 2014 when he bought the Canadian chain Sunrise Records. His formula to turn around HMV is similar to Spillers Records but on a much bigger scale. The focus is on vinyl, as Putnam told *Retail Week*: 'We are trying to encourage people to try vinyl who haven't, to get the enjoyment of collecting it, the enjoyment of the sound ... You hear a lot of people saying: "vinyl is going to come and go", but they were saying that four years ago and it's just gotten stronger. I think we are going to grow that base of people that want something that isn't just digital.'[9]

He also believes in physical stores, seeking to grow the chain to around 150 stores. The model for these is the HMV Vault store in Birmingham, a cavernous space under a multistorey car park, painted matte black, with cool shop assistants and graffiti on the outside walls. The space has acres of vinyl but also CDs and Blu-rays as well as a permanent stage. It hosts artist signings and live acoustic sets and aims to recreate the excitement that I experienced back in Birmingham in the 1970s. The record shop has survived against all the odds and HMV has survived by learning from the independents. This was not at all inevitable, as can be seen from the parallel history of the video shop.

BLOCKBUSTER

Sony released their first commercially available video recorder in 1975, so the history of video shops is much shorter than that of record shops. Nevertheless, for 30 years the video shop became a staple of our high streets, far more numerous than record shops, but following a similar pattern with small independents, specialists and large chains, which turned into one huge chain called Blockbuster.

Back in the 1970s, the film companies tried to block the sale of VCR machines and the rental of movies, seeing them as a threat to the industry. The court case in the US was not resolved until 1984, but after that video rental took off. It started in record shops and even grocers, but soon specialist shops grew up stocking Betamax, VHS and later DVDs and Blu-ray Discs.

The biggest company by far was Blockbuster, which at one time was earning $800 million in the US from late fees alone.[10] The first store opened in Dallas in 1985, its success based on an innovative barcode tracking system that allowed each outlet to stock thousands of titles, whereas previously stores had only been able to deal with a few hundred. Huge distribution centres and franchising allowed the chain to grow rapidly, arriving in the UK in 1989, where it grew to 800 outlets at its peak. By that time, the company was the largest video store in the US and in 1994 was bought by Viacom for $8 billion.

In 1997, a Blockbuster customer called Reed Hastings, annoyed at being charged $40 in late fees, decided to open a DVD by mail business. You paid a monthly subscription and could keep the DVDs for as long as you wanted, with prepaid return envelopes. Two years later Blockbuster turned down the chance to buy the company that Hastings had called Netflix for $50 million. It decided instead to build its own video on demand services, which it abandoned in 2001. By 2013, the Blockbuster chain, which at one time had 9,000 outlets, had largely collapsed. As *Business Insider* wrote: 'They were too busy making money in their video stores to imagine a time when people would no longer want or need them.'[11]

Meanwhile in Liverpool after lockdown, Andy Johnson opened VideOdyssey in Toxteth, a new independent video shop based on his huge collection of old VHS tapes.[12] He is trying to do for the video shop what vinyl has done for the record shop

SPOTIFY

The first album I (VP) bought was *Spiceworld* by the Spice Girls. It was 1997, I was nine. I purchased the cassette in the Llandudno Woolworths with money from my parents. I can listen to that same album today, 24 years later, on my iPhone, sitting at my grown-up desk doing my grown-up job. The cover art is the same, the sound quality is better (bye-bye magnetic tape!), and I still haven't paid for it myself as I am listening on my sister's Spotify Premium account.

Spotify, though modern compared to my Spiceworld cassette, has been around since 2006. It was created as part of the response to online piracy. The Napster panic in 1999–2001 introduced the music-listening public to the benefits of being able to access a world of music beyond their CD collections. It also caused the record industry to fear for its very existence. So, whereas in the 1990s the music industry had fought to prevent digital music streaming, after Napster they decided that it was better to generate at least some revenue from streaming rather than having it pirated.

Apple was first off the mark with iTunes, which had gained 70% of the music streaming market by 2006. This was the year that Spotify was founded as a start-up in Sweden by Daniel Ek and Martin Lorentzon. Unlike iTunes, where customers had to buy each piece of music, Spotify provided it for free if you were prepared for your listening to be interrupted by adverts, or for £10 a month to listen ad-free.

With Spotify and iTunes, streaming was easy and cheap and most customers were happy to pay for their online music. The problem was that they were not paying very much (artists were getting as little as $0.000029 per play), causing some artists to boycott the platform. And yet unlimited access to music has also had a positive effect on the music industry, with people being able to find their new favourite bands without having to shell out on an expensive CD – then, having found them, being willing to spend on concert tickets and vinyl. The rise of Spotify has therefore been accompanied by the revival of the record shop.

Meanwhile, Spotify goes from strength to strength. It achieved its first million paying subscribers in 2011 and today has 133 million. Despite controversy over royalties, the most serious threat to its business model has come from its decision to host the far-right Joe Rogan, which has led to further boycotts and a 26% year-on-year drop in its share value ($6.7 billion) in 2022.

So while Spotify together with the other two main streaming services, iTunes and Amazon Music, might now determine who tops the charts, it does not have the romance or appeal of the record shop. In 20 years' time will anyone remember their first stream?

Humber Street in the Fruit Market in Hull where there is a stage for live music in one of the shopfronts. Music is a powerful tool for regeneration.

and is attracting customers from across the world. Whether this is the start of a trend with the potential to revive the industry, however, is doubtful.

The story of the video shop illustrates the volatility of the high street. An entire category of stores can come into existence, dominate the high street, fail to innovate and disappear within a few decades, leaving thousands of empty stores and tens of thousands of lost jobs. Yet the high street moves on and heals itself.

10 HOME AND GARDEN

O f the three waves of out-of-town retail that we described in Chapter 3, the first involved the supermarkets, while the third was the advent of regional shopping malls. In between the two came retail parks, and initially planners only allowed them because of the home and garden sector. The argument was that there was no room for them in town centres so that retail parks were needed to accommodate these bulky goods. DIY stores, furniture showrooms and garden centres therefore arrived like the horsemen of the apocalypse, opening the door for a massive expansion in out-of-town retailing that would soon be exploited by other retail sectors. As a result, the home and garden sector was of limited relevance to town centres, but this is changing as the sector evolves and is starting to look once more at town centre locations.

DO IT YOURSELF

The 'home-owning democracy' promoted by the Conservative government of the 1980s created a huge market for DIY retailers. As more people owned their homes, including council tenants who had been given the 'right to buy', there was a boom in home improvements. There had been hardware stores in towns for many years, but it was the builders' merchants that saw the opportunity to exploit a huge new market fuelled by TV makeover shows. The new format demanded enormous spaces, capable of holding the sort of building materials, tools and products previously only sold to the trade. Size was pretty much all that mattered – the buildings created to house this new form of retail were so basic in both their function and construction that architects referred to them as 'sheds'. Planners were forced to accept that the scale of these units dictated that they had be out-of-town, as existing urban centres would never be able to provide plots large enough. And so new typology was born – warehouse-style retail units with merchants' yards to the rear and a sea of car parking out front, all built a convenient driving distance from urban centres.

The lead player in this new sector was B&Q (originally Block & Quayle) who, anticipating the forthcoming trend for home improvement, converted a disused cinema in Southampton to create their first store in 1969. In the 1990s, they started to open the types of stores B&Q are now synonymous with, terming them 'B&Q depots' to begin with, and then 'B&Q warehouses'. Such was the scale of their success that they expanded overseas to Taiwan, Poland and France, then later China and Hong Kong. Whilst not all their overseas ventures have endured, B&Q continue to be the market leader in the UK DIY sector with over 300 UK stores. They were joined by others, including Homebase (which was originally started by Sainsbury's), Texas Homecare, Focus Do it All and Wickes. These companies have a tangled corporate

Ikea: The company experimented with a new format of multi storey stores in town centres. Unfortunately the store in Coventry was not a success and has since closed.

TRENTHAM LAKES

'How is it possible', we were once asked by a retail agent, 'to erect a set of timber cabins, costing next to nothing, on the edge of Stoke – a town with more than its fair share of struggling shopping centres – and attract 3 million people a year?' Trentham Lakes Shopping Village, which opened in 2004, is a curious mix of garden centre, outlet clothing shops and homeware. The cabins contain 80 retail units arranged informally along a village street, surrounded by a huge car park; for much of the year, it is packed with shoppers.

The Trentham Estate was the seat of the Duke of Sutherland, who tried to donate it to the council when the industrialisation of the surrounding area made the house virtually uninhabitable. The council declined and in the years that followed the house was demolished and the grounds (designed by both Capability Brown and Charles Barry) were turned into an amusement park. By 1996, when it was bought by the developer St Modwen, it was abandoned and derelict. Their initial plans were to rebuild the house as a luxury hotel. That didn't work, but they did restore the gardens as a tourist attraction. The commercial element of the scheme was a large garden centre on the main road frontage and from this grew the idea of a shopping village. Initially this was an expanded version of 'exit through the gift shop', but soon the shopping village became an attraction in its own right.

Factory shops have a long history in the Potteries and many of the ceramics manufacturers had shops where they sold seconds. Some, like Wedgwood, had become major tourist attractions. The initial idea at Trentham was to bring these factory shops together in one place and Portmeirion and Emma Bridgewater were early tenants. However, the range of retailers has since expanded, with designer outdoor clothing alongside homeware and food and leisure outlets plus, of course, an enormous garden centre.

This is shopping not as necessity but as leisure, buying things that you didn't know you wanted, making a day of it. As the lockdowns were lifted the shopping village once more filled with people at a time when the traditional shopping centres of Stoke continued to struggle.

history with a series of mergers and demergers; Texas was bought by Homebase, Focus went into administration in 2011 and Homebase, having been bought by the Australian DIY chain Bunnings, was sold for £1 in 2018 and subsequently entered a company voluntary arrangement to allow 42 stores to be closed. The DIY industry received a COVID boost as people took the opportunity to do some lockdown home improvements, but peak DIY has probably passed and the long term trend of reducing home ownership will probably see the sector contract. Nevertheless, the sector changed retailing for ever as the vanguard for the out-of-town revolution.

HOMEWARE – THE STORY OF IKEA

Furniture retailers were also part of the original out-of-town wave. Companies like MFI came to dominate the market, selling flat-pack furniture and riding the same wave in home ownership as the DIY warehouses. According to *The Guardian* there was a point when 60% of British children were being conceived on an MFI bed.[1] However the company failed to innovate and collapsed in 2008, having lost out to a Swedish company that would come to dominate the sector.

With over 460 stores in 63 countries and an average store size of 300,000ft^2 (28,000m^2) – the equivalent of five football pitches or two and a half Trafalgar Squares – IKEA took the 'big box' retail model to another level. It was founded in 1943 by Ingvar Kamprad who, by the time of his death in 2018, had become the 8th richest person in the world thanks to his flat-pack empire. It started out as a mail order business (a precursor of the threat to high street retailing posed by online shopping today). The annual catalogue remains central to the business despite the dominance of online retail, with more than 200 million hard copies printed every year, in 29 languages.

But the flat-pack mail order model was plagued by a persistent flaw – damage to the products during the delivery process. The solution was to create physical IKEA shops where customers could see and try the assembled products and then collect and take home the flat-packs themselves. The model created is so phenomenally successful across the globe that it has arguably become a cultural institution. The first store opened in Sweden in 1958, followed by other parts of Scandinavia in the 1960s. It then spread across Europe, Japan and the US in the 1970s and early 1980s. The UK was late to the game, with the first IKEA store opening in Warrington in 1987 (they had wanted to build in London but the New Town Development Corporation provided a package of benefits that they couldn't resist).

Selling furniture for customers to take away there and then meant keeping stock on site, and even in its flat-packed form it required an entirely new scale of retail unit. The size of these stores led to the invention of an ingenious spatial sales tactic – 'the long natural way'. This is at the heart of the IKEA experience and means that whilst you may only be there to buy a particular item, you are forced to follow a set path that takes you through every part of the store, being tempted on the way by lots of things that you hadn't realised you needed. Some items can go directly into your trolley while others are written on chits to be collected from the warehouse that you pass through just before the checkouts, with their queues of customers laden with far more than they came for.

DISCRETIONARY PURCHASE

DIY and furniture stores illustrate the ways in which the home and garden sector is particularly susceptible to changing consumer trends, making it difficult to predict the future. Garden sales are, unsurprisingly, seasonal and sensitive to the weather, but the most important factor across the home and garden sector is that sales are primarily discretionary items and therefore sensitive to economic expansion and contraction. We can see this in the squeeze on the sales of furniture and household goods that took place following the 2008 financial crash, as people cut back or deferred large purchases. As well as MFI, the credit crunch saw off Habitat, which went into administration in 2009. Habitat was in many respects the UK version of IKEA; set up in 1964 by the designer Terence Conran it went through a number of ownerships, including for a time being owned by Ikano (part of IKEA). But it collapsed in 2011 with the closure of all of its stores except for the three in London. The brand is now owned by Sainsbury's.

The exception to the discretionary nature of home and garden purchases are the 'distressed' purchases, which could reasonably have earned this name because of the state people are in when they have to make them, but refers to essential household items that expire. We're talking about panicked replacement of the washing machine that let you down, the freezer that packed up or the toaster that caught fire. In this arena, the retailers who win out are not those with strategically located stores or even the best prices – the winners are those who offer fast delivery.

During the COVID pandemic a shift occurred in spending patterns across the home and garden sector. With a large proportion of the population in lockdown, those with disposable income that might usually have been spent on holidays, restaurants and entertainment, instead prioritised improvements to the homes where they were suddenly spending so much time. The increased spending on discretionary home and garden items saw a year-on-year growth that peaked at 150% across the sector. In one month alone, garden sales leapt by over 800% – thanks to an additional three million gardeners that were created by the lockdown experience. Furniture continued to trade at more typical levels, probably because these items tend to be much higher priced and the pandemic also brought financial uncertainty to many households.

The pandemic bonanza came to an abrupt end, with sales falling 30% in the month following the first lockdown. Since then, sales have fallen further and are now down on pre-COVID levels, compounded in 2022 by the cost of living crisis. Having struggled to keep up with demand earlier in the pandemic, due to supply chain issues and protracted lead times, retailers were forced to do some long-range forecasting and many got it very wrong. They ended up with an oversupply of stock that, with the economic downturn and the return to pre-pandemic lifestyles, they just cannot shift. As we write, online furniture retailer Made has seen its share price fall by 98% since its flotation just over 12 months ago (it has since collapsed) while Kingfisher, owners of B&Q, announced a 30% fall in profits.[2,3]

The worry is that the boom and bust of COVID conceals deeper trends affecting the home and garden sector. Retailers have traditionally segmented their market in terms of life stages: student, single professional, homebuyers, young parents and retirement. These are the life stages when we move house and look to do up, furnish and sort out the garden of a new property. It is not therefore good news that home ownership rates have fallen dramatically in the UK, with the proportion of 25–34-year-olds on middle incomes owning their home falling from 59% to just 41% since 2003.[4] Over the same period, median house prices have risen from 5.1 times average income to 7.8 times, far more in London, while mortgage lenders have demanded large deposits. People are therefore renting or living with family for longer (or indeed permanently) and spending far less on furniture and DIY. Restrictions on what tenants can do to a rental property and uncertainty over the duration of their tenancy mean they are disinclined to acquire large, hard-to-move items of furniture – impacting both DIY and furniture sales.

Nevertheless, as recently as autumn 2021, GlobalData were predicting that online homeware sales would rise by 90% to £8.9 billion by 2024, while high street sales would fall by 1 billion.[5] Only 12 months later the opposite appears to be happening. The retailers who are proving most agile are those with physical stores. In these settings, even where consumers go to shop for something specific, additional small impulse purchases are more likely. Savvy operators in the home and garden sector know this and are pivoting to smaller purchase items (candles, plant pots, photo frames and so on), sales of which are still fairly consistent even when wallets are squeezed. Those who lack agility are the retailers whose entire brand is built on one high-price item and trade solely online. In addition to the problems at Made, mattress specialist Eve was put up for sale in 2022, having seen its shares slump by 90%. Analysts are also warning of problems at Wayfair, which is losing market share, in part because of its 'dearth of stores'.[6] Meanwhile, physical retailers have expanded their homeware ranges, including M&S, John Lewis, Next and H&M, which has opened 28 'home' stores since 2019, and even Zara, which has opened eight homeware stores.

This only proves the uncertainty of predicting anything in the world of retailing. In the home and garden sector, there is still value in being able to visit a shop and touch and feel the quality of the product. Customers still prefer to shop in person for bigger items like beds and sofas that are difficult to send back if they're not right. Even when the purchase is made online, it is often preceded by a trip to a physical store. There are also trends in car ownership rates, which have fallen dramatically in younger demographics – a problem for the car-dependent out-of-town retail model that has served home and garden retailers well for several decades. As a result, the 'big box' model traditionally favoured by the sector has been called into question, and retailers are seriously rethinking their physical retail formats.

BACK TO THE HIGH STREET

So, what does this mean for the high street? After COVID, many in the industry had predicted a permanent shift online as shopping habits changed, but the difficulties being experienced by online retailers suggest this was premature. As with many other sectors, what appears to be evolving is a hybrid model where online sales are combined with physical stores. The question is where those physical stores are located and what format they should take.

This is a question that IKEA has been struggling with for some time. Back in the mid-2000s, the company started experimenting with urban stores. They built prototypes in Southampton, Coventry and Ashton, east of Manchester (see image at the start of this chapter). The stores maintained the 'long winding way', with just under 350,000ft^2 (32,000sqm) of space over seven storeys, with parking on the top two floors, the store on the middle floors and the warehouse on the ground floor. This meant that they could be located on tight town centre sites, a reaction (according to IKEA) to the restrictive planning regime in the UK and the increasing number of customers without access to a car. The Coventry store, which had opened to queues so large that the police had to be called, closed in 2020, having never made a profit. The format was shelved because customers preferred the out-of-town sites and were buying more online, so that the higher costs and rates bill of the urban stores couldn't be justified.

The press lumped together the Coventry store closure with all the other stories relating to the crisis on the high street and it was certainly very bad news for Coventry, not least because the city lost £1 million in business rates. But it wasn't a sign of a crisis at IKEA as the retailer continues to experiment with different formats to respond to global trends. The nature of experiments is that some don't work. The company had already experimented with 'midi' or boutique city centre stores (less than $100,000ft^2$) in Canada, the Netherlands and New York. These were stripped-back versions of the big stores and, while the company was pleased with their consumer uptake, the high costs meant that profits were also disappointing.

The company therefore started to experiment with 'order and collection', opening stores in Aberdeen, Norwich and within the Westfield Shopping Centre in London. IKEA have also opened 'planning studios', the first of which opened on Tottenham Court Road followed by a second in Bromley. These are much smaller $5,000ft^2$ high street units where customers have one-to-one consultations and then order items for delivery. Then in late 2019, IKEA bought the Kings Mall in West London, one of 44 malls the company own worldwide. Each is anchored by a small IKEA store (carrying about 2,000 lines) with the other units being let to complementary retailers from whom IKEA takes rent.

But the watershed moment came when IKEA took over the former Topshop flagship store on Oxford Street by Piccadilly Circus in 2021. This is arguably the most iconic retail unit in the UK and to have it occupied by a retailer whose model has so successfully been massive out-of-town sheds really exemplifies the transition of the furniture sector from the retail park to the high street. The home and garden sector is ideally suited to the hybrid retail model in which physical stores and online purchases work hand in hand. It is a hopeful trend for the high street but a worrying one for out-of-town retail parks particularly with profits warnings from the likes of DFS, ProCook, Kingfisher and Wickes. We are not suggesting the end of retail parks, particularly since they were so recently doing well with customers worried about social distancing. We are not dismissing the online home and garden sector, which was doing well until recently. However, it does seem that both current and longer-term trends mean that we shouldn't write off the high street once more playing an important role in the sector.

11 FASHION AND BEAUTY

F or a certain age group, in a certain generation, on a certain student budget, there was nothing quite like a Topshop sale. Maybe you remember the thrill yourself. Long rails crammed with denim, sparkle and lace. Pink price stickers on black and white tags. The screech of hangers and the heft of garments parted for careful consideration. Forearms aching on the walk to the changing room. Victory over the rails meant acquiring a garment within your size and budget that you had previously lusted after in the main store. Non-sale visits were always, by dint of a limited bank balance, purely experiential in nature; look at it, try it on, put it back.

But what an experience it was, even when you couldn't afford the clothes. At one time, walking into the Topshop in Manchester's Arndale Centre, you might have been greeted by the thumping bass of a live DJ, while a pop-up piercing shop punctured young ears, noses and belly buttons behind a photobooth curtain, all amidst clusters of the coolest, most desirable clothes imaginable. Kate Moss had a Topshop collection, their clothes were featured in *Vogue*. All this speaks to a high street retail brand at the very top of its game.

THE GOLDEN AGE

Topshop may have been the jewel in the crown of UK high street fashion in the 2000s, but the rest of the crown was also pretty bedazzling. Other retailers such as River Island, New Look and H&M formed a coterie of brands in their heyday, bringing the British public relatively affordable access to the latest fashion trends. Where previously high street retailers would take a season to emulate catwalk looks, the internet disseminated once closely guarded runway images quickly, allowing the high street to serve up adulterated versions to ravenous shoppers.

According to Euromonitor, the UK apparel retail industry had a compound annual growth rate of 1.9% for the period spanning 2005–9.[1] During that time the market grew by 6%, but the actual volume of clothes purchased grew even more – the prices were just lower. From 1995 to 2013 Swedish brand H&M's sales grew through an explosion of new stores. By 2014 there were 3,132 H&M stores in 53 countries, although over half of their sales came from just six of them, including the UK. London-headquartered River Island did similarly well on home turf, having a bit of a wobble between 2010 and 2012, but coming back fighting with a 2013 collaboration with Rihanna, after which turnover increased consistently for the following three years.

The Centre MK: Fashion has always been at the heart of the retail experience in town and city centres.

Topshop, however, led the field. As we saw in the Introduction, it started in 1964 as the fashion department on the top floor of the Peter Jones department store in Sheffield. In 1994 it had grown to such an extent that the 90,000ft^2 (8,361m^2) Peter Jones flagship Oxford Street store was taken over entirely by Topshop. By the 2000s, it was reporting record sales and profits, with plans to increase its trading space in the UK by a further 210,000ft^2. Tony Colman, a leading backbencher during the Labour government from 1997 to 2005, when he was chair of the All Party Group on Retail, is also credited with creating Topshop when he was a merchandise manager at the Peter Jones store in Sheffield.[2] He went on to become a board director of the Burton Group after it acquired Topshop before it, in turn, was bought by Philip Green and became Arcadia.

He described to us the lengths that Topshop would go to, to ensure their relevance to the young fashion-buying public. The company would completely revamp their look and the design of their stores every two years, using leading designers. They would show at London Fashion Week alongside designer brands. Like many retailers they offshored the manufacture of their main lines. However, they would use manufacturers in the UK to supplement the best-selling lines. Tony Colman describes how he would sit next to the tills, monitoring what was selling and spotting trends as they emerged. For a time, Topshop was the most innovative

Reading: The town centre has four shopping centres the backbone of its retail appeal being a full range of fashion retailers even if this range is smaller than it was post-pandemic.

fashion retailer on the high street – the first, for example, to introduce a store credit card.

When the bubble burst it did so for several reasons, some specific to Topshop, others more wide-ranging. As we described in Chapter 4, Green's acquisition of Arcadia was funded by borrowing that was repaid by selling and leasing back the stores with upwards-only rent reviews. This – combined with inflexible business rates that disproportionately affect bricks and mortar stores – made it difficult to respond to the emerging threat of online fashion retailers. Topshop also suffered as Green's and Arcadia's reputation plummeted when stories of harassment, bullying, tax avoidance, pensions deficits and poor working conditions emerged. Turnover in 2017 at Arcadia Group – which in addition to Topshop included Dorothy Perkins, Miss Selfridge, Evans, Wallis and Burton – had fallen by £113 million, or 5.6%, on the previous year. Topshop had long abandoned the idea of regular shop refurbishments and collaboration with top designers. In the words of a shopper quoted in *Grazia* magazine: 'They started doing a lot of sales, and I guess it devalued the brand and looked a little embarrassing … They slipped into the ways of BHS and didn't innovate through experimentation.'[3] The stores were out of touch and tired, not a good look when seeking to appeal to a young fashion market whose head had been turned by the low prices, instant availability and endless variety of Missguided or Nasty Gal.

Arcadia collapsed in November 2020 with the loss of 13,000 jobs and the closure of its 450 UK stores along with many concessions in department stores. It was also the nail in the coffin for Debenhams, which couldn't survive without the Arcadia concessions. The Topshop brand was bought by online retailer ASOS while Dorothy Perkins, Wallis and Burton went to Boohoo, raising questions about the future of physical fashion retail. Between 2019 and 2020 there was a 24% drop in clothing sales of £9.6 billion, but within that figure was an increase in online sales of £2.7 billion.[4] Pretty Little Thing reported an annual revenue increase of 38% in 2020,[5] while parent company Boohoo's sales increased by 41% during the pandemic to £1.7 billion.[6]

As Jane Shepherdson, once the most powerful woman in British retail as brand director of Topshop, told *The Guardian* in 2021, 'People are going to be shocked when they return to the high street and find that a huge number of fashion retailers have gone.' The reduction in the number of physical fashion outlets means that fashion can't bounce back to where it was post-pandemic. GlobalData predict that the percentage of online fashion sales is unlikely to drop below 40%.[7]

BOOHOO

When the first UK lockdown was announced in March 2020, the fashion retailer Boohoo changed its entire inventory in less than two weeks. Out went the partywear and those sparkly dresses for a big night out and in came knitted loungewear and loose-fitting binge PJs. Something that would take traditional fashion retailers months to achieve – designing new lines, reconfiguring production lines, setting up contracts and supply chains, fashion shoots and advertising campaigns – had been done virtually overnight.

In the months that followed, Boohoo was seen by the market as one of the winners of lockdown. As traditional retailers saw their stores closed, Boohoo increased its sales, announced a 54% increase in profits to £92 million and saw its stock market valuation rise to £5 billion, eclipsing that of Marks & Spencer. It added to its existing stable of brands, including the American brands Nasty Gal, Misspapp and Pretty Little Thing, spent £200 million buying the Oasis and Warehouse brands out of receivership, adding to Karen Millen and Coast, bought the previous year, and then at the end of 2020 buying Debenhams, and the rump of the Arcadia brands, Burton, Dorothy Perkins and Wallis. The strategy was to diversify the company away from the disposable teen fashion business into higher-spending markets, but in doing so it seemed to have eaten the high street.

Yet in 2022, Boohoo's share price has lost 80% of its value and the company has issued two profits warnings. Meanwhile, its great competitor Missguided has collapsed under the weight of supply chain problems, weak sales, high levels of returns and the reopening of the high street. As Nils Pratley wrote in *The Guardian* in early 2022: 'The online clothing game is a fiddly business and requires a lot of things to run perfectly. Over at Primark, which resolutely sticks to fuddy-duddy physical shops, life looks easier.'[8]

The Boohoo story starts with the arrival in Manchester of Abdullah Kamani, fleeing the war in Kenya in the 1960s. He started off selling handbags on a market stall before setting up a wholesale business called Pinstripe, buying from Indian suppliers and selling to high street retailers like Primark. His son Mahmud began working on the stall before graduating to delivery driver for the wholesale business. In 1993, the business hired a twenty-something fashion designer called Carol Kane who set up a design office within the business to create their own clothes. In 2006 she and Mahmud Kamani left to set up Boohoo with three staff.

Six years later Mahmud's sons Umar and Adam set up Pretty Little Thing, initially selling accessories but soon branching out into teen fashion and beauty products. Using celebrity endorsements, it opened up markets in the US, Australia and France. By 2017, it was ranked as the fastest growing fashion brand on the internet, beating Gucci following the launch of its mobile phone app. The brothers subsequently sold the company to their father to become part of the Boohoo group.

The idea behind Boohoo was to design and manufacture their own clothes and then sell direct to the customer, in other words to become manufacturer, wholesaler and retailer by tapping into what in 2006 was still the emerging potential of online retail. The Kamani family were well placed to do this because of their connections with the textile industry that still exists in places like Manchester and Leicester, owned by the Asian community. Other retailers have been criticised for the working conditions of their supply chain in places like Bangladesh, but the Boohoo approach required something much more local. Their model is to design a large number of lines that are initially manufactured in small batches of a few hundred items, then publicised on social media through 'influencers'. The designs that sell are then manufactured in quantity, those that don't are quickly dropped. The turnover of products is huge and the company boasts that it can get a new product to market in as little as 48 hours.

The price point is also incredibly low, with dresses for £5, jeans for £10, and famously Boohoo's great rival, the now collapsed Missguided, produced the £1 bikini – as seen on 'Love Island'. Young people wanted to buy the clothes they saw being worn by celebrities on reality shows and social media and they wanted them now, for as little as possible (what Boohoo calls 'aspirational thrift').[9] This is disposable fashion, bought on an impulse, often through a phone app, worn once and thrown away. It contrasts with the traditional fashion approach of developing a line of clothing each season, lining up manufacturers on the other side of the world

Boohoo: The company's office remains in a former textile warehouse on Manchester's Northern Quarter.

and hoping you have read the trends correctly. Boohoo's business model means that they can't be waiting a month for a container of the new lines to arrive from an overseas manufacturer – they need to manufacture locally. This very nearly was their downfall.

In July 2020, the city of Leicester became the first place in the UK to be put into a local lockdown after a spike of COVID cases. In the weeks that followed, a scandal broke after *The Sunday Times* sent an undercover reporter to work in one of the Leicester factories allegedly supplying Boohoo.[10] Not only were they offered less than half the statutory minimum wage, but they were also expected to work in cramped conditions through lockdown. No wonder the city had the highest COVID infection rate in the country. This, it appeared, was how Boohoo were able to churn out the new lockdown lines so quickly and at such low prices. The revelations knocked £1.5 billion off Boohoo's share value in the first week of July 2020 as retailers like Next, ASOS and Amazon pulled Boohoo clothing from sale.[11]

Boohoo denied the allegations, saying in a statement that it was 'shocked and appalled' by the allegations and committed to rebuilding the reputation of textile manufacturing in Leicester.[12] It appointed Alison Levitt QC to undertake an independent review, which uncovered failings that the company undertook to address. Its share price recovered, and with the acquisition of household names like Debenhams, it will hope that the scandal is behind it. The current dip in share price is more to do with supply chain issues and the volumes of goods returned. This, together with the ongoing impact of the scandal, means that Boohoo is no longer the darling of the markets and the fundamental question remains – in a world of disposable fashion how do you responsibly manufacture a £5 dress and make a profit?

ONSHORING

In a 2011 article entitled 'Long Live the Industrial City', Tom Vanderbilt examined the extraordinary resilience of the garment district in New York, where small-scale, scruffy factories survive amidst some of the most expensive real estate in the world.[13] This at a time when clothing retailers were offshoring their supply chains to places like Bangladesh and Sri Lanka, 'chasing cheap needle around the planet'. The reason was that New York's fashion industry needed access to small specialist garment manufacturers that could turn a job around in days or even hours and were willing to pay good money for this. In a world where the consumer was demanding endless variety, Vanderbilt argued that onshoring was the future not just of fashion but of many industries.

Back in the UK, Leicester has a long history of textile manufacture. In the 1980s its factories supplied mainstream retailers like British Home Stores under the motto 'Leicester clothes the world'. The largest company Corah employed more than 6,000, bringing in skilled labour from India and with a good reputation for working conditions and wages. However, Leicester's factories couldn't compete with the offshoring of manufacturing to the Far East. Some companies survived by supplying wholesalers and value retailers when they needed a quick turnaround, but to compete wages were squeezed and conditions worsened.

With the advent of online retail, the fashion industry changed again. In order to be responsive to the fast-moving online market, retailers turned once more to UK manufacturers, although they still demanded low prices. So, while Leicester's manufacturing sector recovered, the conditions in the city's factories worsened. A University of Leicester study suggested that there were now around 1,000 textile factories in the city, the average size being 10 employees, sometimes with scores of factories housed in a single building.[14] The researchers concluded that the 'onshoring' of manufacturing by British retailers presented a considerable opportunity for the city. However, they also highlight 'anecdotal' concerns over working conditions in factories operating behind closed doors with a mostly Gujarati workforce, often with limited English.

These concerns have been around for a number of years, as highlighted by the campaigning group Labour Behind the Label. Thulsi Narayanasamy at the Business and Human Rights Centre was quoted in a *Guardian* article saying, 'I've been inside garment factories in Bangladesh, China and Sri Lanka, and I can honestly say that what I saw in the middle of the UK was worse than anything I've witnessed overseas.' In the same article an analyst is quoted as saying, 'There is simply no way that they can be buying things at the prices that they are and getting them at the pace that they are while ensuring adherence to ethical conditions and pay.'[15]

As a result, many retailers have stopped using factories in Leicester. When Anders Kristiansen took over as CEO of New Look, he was quoted as saying, 'When I came to the UK and I discovered what was going on in Leicester, it was mind-blowing.'[16] Missguided once manufactured half of its stock in the city but stopped because of concerns over working conditions. The Leicester industry is left with Boohoo, which sources about 40% of its garments from the city, accounting for 75–80% of its output. Online may be more efficient and fleet-footed than traditional retailers, but the real reason that online fashion retailers did so much damage to the high street was that they invented a new business model, one that may not stand up to the scrutiny that it is now receiving.

FAST FASHION

This is not the image that online fashion wants to project. On the surface its bright and flawless Instagram posts feature trending influencers and celebrities, promising an aspirational aesthetic at an attainable price point. But beneath the veneer lies disappointment, exploitation and waste. The clothes are made to be disposable – good for a few wears, if that. They are of such low quality that charity shops are often unable or unwilling to resell them. Around 300,000 tonnes of clothes are burned or buried in landfill in the UK each year – some of it never worn, some of it never even sold.[17] The success of the sector was partly based on price. Items can often be purchased for under £5 and services like Klarna allow easy credit. This is not to demonise the consumer, for whom low-cost clothing and split payments are one of only a limited range of options available to them, but the rise of fast fashion is driven by far more than necessity.

Advertising is another key driver. Instead of becoming excellent at making clothes, fast fashion companies have become excellent at selling clothes. In 2019 Boohoo spent £90 million on advertising campaigns, which is 9% of its annual sales.[18] In 2020 Pretty Little Thing worked with a company called Epsilon, which creates highly targeted, highly personalised advertising. Their AI platform uses in-depth consumer data to decide when and where to show consumers one of the 'unlimited creative iterations of an ad'. So, if you're scrolling late at night, the hangxiety already creeping in from an evening of disappointing cocktails, they're ready for you. We've come a long way from seductive window displays.

You don't buy these clothes on a breezy Saturday morning on your local high street. Fashion has never been about clothing. It holds out the opportunity to be more like the celebrities and influencers who model the clothes, the promise that you will be more attractive, interesting and successful if you just buy that dress. This is all the more powerful in the privacy of your own home, in the privacy of your own device.

It's easy to demonise fast fashion as vampiric, sucking the lifeblood of high streets, draining the dignity of garment workers and emptying the wallets of consumers. The question is whether they are the future of fashion retail. If they are then the high street will have to survive without the fashion retailers that have been such an important part of its offer for years. However, before we accept the death of high street fashion it is worth considering a couple of counter-trends.

TO SEE AND BE SEEN

If you were out shopping in Liverpool City Centre at the weekend in the mid-2010s, you may have noticed an unusual piece of headwear: rollers. Yes, in the unofficial 'glamour capital of the UK' it's acceptable, nay encouraged, to spend Saturday morning browsing the shops with a full head of rollers, ensuring gorgeous, bouncing, voluminous hair upon removal, ready for that big night out. In 2015, retailer House of Bath announced that sales of hairnets had risen for the first time in more than 50 years, with 64% of sales originating from Liverpool.[19] Far from being a practical abandonment of vanity, the phenomenon is a trend in itself, seen on famous Liverpudlians like Abbey Clancy and Coleen Rooney. It is an example of something Liverpool excels at: the theatre of the high street – the drama and pageantry of seeing and being seen – that might hold the key to the future of physical fashion retail.

Liverpool ONE, one of the largest shopping centres in the UK, provides the perfect stage for such performance. Opened in May 2008, it doesn't feel like a conventional shopping centre. It is open to the elements, with no doors and minimal branding, and it is hard to tell where the 42 acre (17ha) scheme ends and the rest of the town centre begins, although the sanitised nature of the space is a slight giveaway: no love padlocks, posters, protests or unsanctioned loitering. But in opening up, putting the conspicuous into conspicuous consumption, it is now seen as a part of the city centre. It provides what anthropologist Rebecca Toop describes as 'a stage for people to explore ideas about their identity all while buying into a sense of community'.[20]

Liverpool ONE was developed as a partnership between Liverpool City Council and their chosen development partners Grosvenor, appointed in 2000. The completed scheme has 2.5 million ft^2 of space (232,000m^2) and is anchored by a John Lewis and a Debenhams together with 200 shops, 25 restaurants, 700 apartments, a 14-screen cinema and 2,000 parking spaces. It operates on

Liverpool One: The city's main shopping centre opened just before the 2008 financial crisis and has reimagined fashion retail as theatre where people can see and be seen.

three levels and includes the 5.5 acre Chavasse Park, built from a mountain of polystyrene blocks, over the car park.

Whether you see it as positive or negative that transactional commercial spaces are providing the kind of fulfilment that Toop describes, Liverpool ONE has certainly been successful. Pre-pandemic, it was attracting 29 million visitors annually. Some will be tourists and others will be locals, searching for that perfect outfit for the night ahead. The key to the centre's success is the way it has become part of the city; it reinstates the old street pattern and its place names reflect the local heritage – it is built on the site of the original Liver (muddy) pool, the city's first dock. It retains a number of historic buildings and is organised into a series of quarters, each with its own identity and retail niche. Its 36 buildings were designed by 26 different architects within a masterplan created by BDP. Most importantly, it doesn't have a roof. As a Norwegian visitor told Rebecca Toop, 'it is strange that they made the shopping centre outside, with all the bad weather'. Another local is quoted as saying, 'well this will never catch on, the roof doesn't go right across' before admitting: 'We were wrong obviously, because you don't think twice about it … it makes it more airy … welcoming'. Liverpool ONE is a mall that doesn't look or feel like a mall. In the same way Topshop fought to provide a superlative store experience, Liverpool ONE endeavours to lure shoppers into a sparkling city centre playground of retail, food and leisure and in doing so might just give the online fashion retailers a run for their money.

IN THE EYE OF THE BEHOLDER

Many high street fashion retailers may have been killed off by more agile, less scrupulous online competitors. But this doesn't necessarily mean that high street fashion is dead, as demonstrated by the beauty and cosmetics sector. A symbiotic model is emerging that has seen bricks and mortar stores develop a mutually reinforcing relationship with online disruptors. Instead of raising the battlements and defending themselves, stores like Superdrug and Boots have opened the gate and offered up a seat at the table, enticing customers in the process.

A good example is The Ordinary. Like the fast fashion retailers, The Ordinary (part of Canadian parent company DECIEM) sought to provide consumers with affordable skincare. But where fast fashion is often judged for cutting corners, The Ordinary focussed on science-based, transparent business practices to bring consumers affordable, single ingredient products. UK customers out of reach of the single Covent Garden store could shop online, purchasing whole bottles of active ingredients for less than they might spend on a formulated face cream containing a fraction of the amount.

An influencer-backed, scientifically credible, wallet-friendly skincare brand might seem like a mortal enemy to a retailer like Boots, stuffed to the gills as it is with exactly the kind of high-price, low-reward products that The Ordinary could supplant. So, Boots decided to bring them on board; from July 2019, The Ordinary was stocked in selected stores and on the Boots website. And it wasn't the only one. Boots launched 36 brands that year, including Rihanna's Fenty and cult brand Huda Beauty, founded by beauty blogger Huda Kattan.

The ability of high street beauty retailers to bring competitors 'in-house' is a potential source of resilience for the post-COVID high street. Global cosmetics markets contracted during the pandemic as consumers declined to primp for yet another day at home, or focussed on more practical expenditure.[21] Boots was not immune and its UK annual report showed losses of £258 million up to August 2020. Things are however looking up in 2022, and experiential beauty shopping may be playing a role. Seb James, Managing Director of Boots UK & Republic of Ireland, cited a 'strong performance' in the first quarter of the year, with 'beauty performing particularly well'.[22] The strategy is part of a wider 'Beauty Reinvention' plan, a multi-format store strategy aiming to attract in-person customers with the world's leading beauty brands.

In late 2021, Boots launched 30 new 'beauty halls' in addition to the 60 already situated within Boots flagship stores. The halls will feature 'trending zones', 'discovery areas' and that thing that is so hard to replicate online: in-person consultation spaces. The new halls will feature in smaller towns like Burton-on-Trent, Carlisle and Sevenoaks that have historically fallen foul of major retail closure strategies. Boots bringing the kind of playful shopping environment usually reserved for city centre flagships to smaller centres could provide footfall, and hope for local high streets.

Beauty halls, with their immaculately made-up shop assistants and concoction of exotic scents, were always placed at the entrances to department stores. They offered a sense of glamour mixed with practical advice that is hard to replicate online. Following the collapse of Debenhams, five of its former beauty halls have been taken over by Next to create a new concept, The Beauty Hall, which the company describes as a 'new force in beauty retailing'.[23] Meanwhile, Boohoo have opened their first physical store in Manchester's Arndale Centre under the Debenhams brand and focussing entirely on beauty products. Their aim is to create a 'destination that is a fresh, modern and unique space where customers can experience the latest in beauty ... merging digital and physical elements'.[24] This may provide a wider model for online retailing, combining the value for money and convenience of the internet with the excitement and hands-on satisfaction of a physical shopping experience.

OMNICHANNEL FASHION

In a survey of US and Canadian consumers spanning four generations, the Kearney Consumer Institute found that Gen Z (born between 1995 and 2010) were the most amenable to physical retail. More than 80% of those surveyed liked to shop in-store and 74% agreed that a 'well curated store experience focussed on a limited number of products' was important, seeing shopping as a way to escape from social media. Before the pandemic, *Insider Trends* listed 45 online retailers who had opened physical stores.[25] Missguided had a concession in Selfridges and opened a physical store in the Bluewater Shopping Centre. Other fashion brands like Snowe, Allbirds, Bonobos, Man Repeller and Blaiz have opened physical stores, although they don't look much like the fashion shops of the past. A good example is MatchesFashion.com that has opened its London townhouse concept 'brimming with installations, talks, dinners and, of course, products'. Customers can browse, try on, get advice or just hang out and then purchases are made through online touchpoints.

The hybrid approach also works for smaller companies, such as the Barnsley-based designer dungarees retailer Lucy & Yak, which started online but has now opened a physical store in Brighton's North Laine. Many other online companies have experimented with physical stores and pop-up units. Meanwhile, many independent fashion retailers also sell online either via their own website or sites such as Etsy. This extends their reach and customer base far beyond their hometown, enabling shops to be viable even in locations where there is insufficient local fashion trade.

This crossover has the potential to reinvigorate physical fashion retail. In 2020, Unibail-Rodamco-Westfield, the owner of Westfield, Stratford, produced a report called 'How We Shop: The Next Decade', predicting that more than half of retail space would be dedicated to providing customer experiences, turning the retail model on its head. The report talks about 'anti-prescription, self-sustaining stores, retail surgeries and locally morphed retail'.[26] Behind the jargon, it boils down to something similar to MatchesFashion.com's London townhouse. In summer 2021 they launched Side Hustle Heroes to provide shop windows to six online start-up businesses. The brands were a mix of fashion, homeware, beauty and a bespoke tie-dye clothing business, each with a QR code on the store window that could be scanned as a gateway into each company's social media and digital online store.

The crossover between online and physical retailing also has the potential to revive established fashion retailers. Perhaps the best example of this is Next, now the largest clothing retailer in the UK. The company started out as Hepworth, a men's tailors founded in 1864 in Leeds. In 1981 it bought the womenswear retailer Kendall and Sons with the idea of opening a women's fashion chain. However, it decided to rebrand the chain as Next and later to convert all the Hepworth stores to the Next format. In 1987 the group acquired the Grattan Catalogue Company, allowing it to launch Next Directory as a home shopping service. The company has not been without its problems and came close to collapse in the late 1980s after 'suicidal' overexpansion.[27] Its structure is however ideally suited to omnichannel retailing with 550 branches in the UK, 180 stores elsewhere in the world and a website with 3 million active users. Its experience with catalogue shopping has fed directly into its online retail operation and it also runs Lipsy, an online fashion brand for younger women, as well as managing e-commerce for other retailers like Gap.

As people returned to the high street post-lockdown, it was indeed a shock to see that so many familiar fashion retailers had disappeared. It is tempting to think that high street fashion cannot possibly survive in the face of online fashion retailers in terms of price, range and responsiveness to rapidly changing trends. However, physical fashion retail also has advantages – it engages touch and sight, the chance to try things on and ask your friend or partner how it looks. Online fast fashion serves a value-conscious market but there will always be a demand for physical fashion retail in a world where people are drawn to the experience and theatre of shopping.

Doncaster has struggled with the loss of all its departments stores but has a strong independent and creative community seeking to reimagine the town.

PART 3

FUTURE HIGH STREET

What do these trends mean for the future high street, for cities, towns and local centres? What indeed do these trends mean for malls and out-of-town shopping? Drawing on a series of case studies we use this final section to explore how town centres might evolve in the future.

12 THE CITY

Finally getting a table at that brunch spot everyone is talking about. Clocking off on 'thirsty Thursday' into an after-work playground with fellow under-stimulated office workers. Renting an apartment that's 'just a base' (you'll be out all the time anyway), your decision, influenced more than you'd care to admit by TV shows like 'Sex and the City' and 'Friends'. Getting indigestion, shovelling down a sandwich after attempting to buy a new outfit on your lunchbreak. Becoming so familiar with the body odours of your fellow commuters that you could pick them out of an olfactory line-up. For many this was the pre-pandemic city. The cost, the noise, the lack of space, the air quality, all unimportant because the city was the place to be – a hive of opportunity, creativity, consumption and entertainment.

In his book *City Economics*, Brendan O'Flaherty writes that: 'Cities could persist – as they have for thousands of years – only if their advantages offset the disadvantages.'[1] In other words, there are downsides to being in a city, it's just that if you are a city dweller you can't imagine being anywhere else. At least that was the case before COVID. The pandemic temporarily erased the advantages of city life, leaving people to contemplate only the disadvantages. For a while shops, restaurants, bars, galleries and events spaces were all held in suspended animation. When city dwellers were finally able to return they were left to question their commute, the quality of their homes in relation to their cost, the availability of green space, the opportunities to do things that don't involve spending money.

For these reasons, city centres were the places worst hit by the pandemic. Lockdowns were bad enough, but as homeworking persisted after lockdown was lifted, concerns about social distancing remained and restrictions on travel caused tourism to disappear, cities found themselves exposed. The Centre for Cities recovery tracker showed that most of the worst-performing centres immediately post-pandemic were big cities, and most of the best-performing ones were suburban centres.[2] This caused some to question whether the growth of urban areas, which has been a feature of the last few decades might be thrown into reverse. However, cities have been with us for millennia and a longer perspective would suggest that it is too early to write them off. Their death has been predicted before, including in the quite recent past. As the Centre for Cities argues in their report 'Why cities will become our main job creators post-COVID', the city is changing, yes, but it is not dead.[3]

Princes Street in Edinburgh: A street that has lost most of its department stores and has been through a torrid phase of transition but is already showing signs of recovery.

BROADMARSH, NOTTINGHAM

Peak retail in Nottingham was 2013. That was the year in which the city reached number three in Experian's retail rankings, ahead of Leeds, Birmingham and Manchester. Given Nottingham's smaller population, this was punching well above its weight and it is a good place to start when looking at the future of retailing in cities.

Nottingham has 1,659 retail units and 5.5 million ft^2 of space, making it the third largest centre in our case studies after London's West End and Manchester. The reason for its success, according to Paul Whysall writing in *The Town Planning Review*, was that it had two major covered shopping centres and multiple retailers often opened branches in both of them.[4] The two shopping centres, Broadmarsh and the Victoria Centre, sat at either end of Nottingham's main retail drag, forming a classic dumbbell arrangement, something seen by retail analysts as giving it a huge advantage over other cities.

However, this analysis is thrown into question by the fact that the Broadmarsh Centre was already in steep decline in 2013 when the city peaked in the retail rankings. Nottingham has consistently had a higher vacancy rate than most of our case studies, peaking at 19.6% in 2012. While the rate has since fallen, this is largely because Broadmarsh closed for refurbishment and was no longer being counted. Then, halfway through refurbishment works, Intu, the owner of both Nottingham's shopping centres, fell into administration and the work on Broadmarsh was halted. The City Council took ownership of the centre and spent the next 18 months considering what to do with it, a process that also involved rethinking the city centre's role in a post-retail age.

As part of our research for this book, we were asked by the city to sit on an advisory group considering the future for the Broadmarsh Centre. The group oversaw the appointment of the designer Thomas Heatherwick, whose radical suggestion was to strip back the part-refurbished shopping centre to its concrete frame and to populate that frame with a huge variety of uses, from independent shops and restaurants to community spaces, playgrounds and gardens.[5] The 'frame' is part of a wider masterplan that includes a new park (the public's first choice in the 'big conversation' consultation exercise organised as part of the process).[6] It is a vision of a city centre with fewer multiple retailers but a profusion of other stuff, a laboratory in which ideas can be tried and experimentation can happen. In many respects it is a return to the city as it was before it was taken over by mainstream retail.

Back in the 1960s, the original plans for Broadmarsh were also promoted by the council, the City Planning Officer writing in a 1964 report that 'it would be quite wrong to allow it to be developed by a series of piecemeal buildings each unrelated to a comprehensive plan'.[7] Their scheme was very much of its time, a brutalist structure built across the main routes from the station into town. The same report noted that the council had also received an approach from developers looking at the soon to be vacated Victoria Station site. They were also planning a retail scheme 'whose size and nature could make it one of the most important schemes on fully comprehensive lines to be carried out in any provincial city'. The plans for the Victoria Centre were published a few months later, with 2.7 million ft^2 of space (including 650,000ft^2 of retailing), about a quarter of the size of the entire city centre. The officers described the scheme as having 'great merit and advantage' but worried that its size would undermine the viability of their own Broadmarsh scheme. In the end, a reduced Victoria Centre was approved in June 1965, with 385,000ft^2 of retailing, and later that year consent was granted for the Broadmarsh redevelopment with 210,000ft^2 of retailing, along with a bus station, two car parks and three blocks of flats (that were never built).

The planning officers maintained that the combined retail floor space in the two centres would not exceed the total that the city could absorb. This may have been true, until the council agreed proposals to expand the Victoria Centre to accommodate a Jessops department store (part of the John Lewis Partnership),

Nottingham City Centre: The city has long punched above its weight when it comes to retailing but is now having to rethink its retail role following the closure of one of its shopping centres.

pushing the floor area back up to 622,000ft², making it the UK's largest shopping centre when it opened its doors in June 1972. Broadmarsh opened in November the following year but was already playing catch-up.

The north/south retail spine between the two centres, from Clumber Street to Bridlesmith Gate, was pedestrianised in the 1970s and its retail footfall increased by 88%.[8] Before long, the increased attraction of Nottingham's two modern shopping centres had lifted the whole city. However, Broadmarsh was always the weaker of the two centres. It was smaller, had less strong anchor stores (originally a Co-op department store) and from the start its layout was inefficient and confusing. As early as the 1980s a contrast was being drawn between 'the advanced retail concept which the Victoria Centre symbolises' and the less 'ostentatious Broadmarsh Centre'.[9] In 2002, when Broadmarsh was being refurbished, the *Estates Gazette* headline ran 'ugly sister gets a facelift' and the *New Statesman* wrote that 'the Broadmarsh Centre sounds unfortunately like a high security mental hospital and doesn't do much to dispel that impression once you are in there'.[10,11]

GOAD data quoted by Paul Whysall shows that the Broadmarsh Centre's problems date back to the closure of the Allders department store in 2003. By 2011 the centre had a 40% vacancy rate and shoppers were telling its then owners Westfield that the centre was 'shabby, outdated, and that few people really enjoyed shopping there'. Soon after, Westfield was sold to Capital Shopping Centres (who also owned the Victoria Centre and would later rebrand as Intu), prompting an Office of Fair Trading enquiry. The enquiry concluded that the two centres were now serving such different markets that there was unlikely to be a loss of competition.[12]

Plans to redevelop Broadmarsh date back to the 1990s. Planning consent was granted in 2002 for a £400 million scheme that would have tripled the size of the centre, with two department stores and three levels of retailing. Progress was slow and the 2008 financial crisis rendered the plans unviable. However, the council were insistent that something should happen, the deputy council leader Graham Chapman warning, 'We need to see bulldozers going into the Broadmarsh Centre, not just on paper' before they would agree to any investment in the Victoria Centre.[13] A deal was agreed in November 2013 by which Intu would spend £390 million to refurbish both centres, with the council contributing £50 million to Broadmarsh. The revised plans for Broadmarsh were approved in June 2015, reducing the amount of retailing but including restaurants, cafés and a cinema. At the same time, the council was progressing plans for the redevelopment of the adjacent bus station and car park, the development of a new central library and the pedestrianisation of Collin Street as a linear park. Contractors were appointed and work started on the new Broadmarsh in 2019, only to be halted by the first COVID lockdown. Before work could recommence, Intu had got into difficulties and collapsed. The site therefore reverted back to council ownership and the question is, as it was back in 1964, what do we do with it?

This leaves us with the conundrum of why Nottingham's retailing has remained so strong despite the long-term decline of one of its two shopping centres. Its classic 'dumbbell' layout may have played a role in the 1980s and 1990s, but this has not been the case for a long time. It is even questionable whether the dumbbell concept – which refers to the layout of shopping centres with a department store at either end – can really be applied to a city centre with a shopping centre at either end. Shopping centres are after all designed to retain customers within their malls and to prevent them 'leaking' out to enliven surrounding streets. The answer to the conundrum probably lies with the Nottingham designer Paul Smith, who opened his flagship store on Low Pavement at the end of Bridlesmith Gate in 2004. This became the focus for a cluster of high-end fashion retailers including American Apparel, Jack Wills, Ted Baker, Diesel, Fred Perry, Kurt Geiger, Hugo Boss, Reiss and Lacoste. Not all of these have survived the current retail crisis, but what they have done is to replace Broadmarsh as the anchor at the southern end of the retail spine. This fashion cluster was not planned and provides a counter to those who argue that traditional multi-ownership town centres cannot compete with the coordinated management of a shopping centre. While the management of Broadmarsh has vacillated, the surrounding streets have self-organised and regenerated, rendering the shopping centre irrelevant. This provides a huge opportunity for the city to redevelop the Broadmarsh Centre for something other than mainstream retailing.

This brings us back to Thomas Heatherwick's plans to populate the frame of the Broadmarsh Centre with a raft of activities rather than mainstream retail and to surround it with housing and workspaces. Crucially, the plan is to reinstate the street network obliterated by the original proposals. As Greg Nugent of the Nottingham Project told *Nottinghamshire Live*: 'We are proposing bringing back so many of the streets and routes around the city because actually they used to work really well.

This is why New York and even Glasgow work, the streets connect with each other. It is a brilliant opportunity to reconnect the city.'[14]

For all the arresting visuals by Heatherwick and received with great enthusiasm by the people of Nottingham, the key point is not the specifics but the opportunity for the city to self-organise and evolve. By creating the conditions for different things to happen, the plan makes space for a future Paul Smith to transform the city in a way that we can't currently imagine. This is why cities are different – it is not just that they are bigger than other centres, but that the scale and diversity of their population and business communities mean that they are greater than the sum of their parts. They will always have the potential to regenerate themselves.

The question in Nottingham is the viability of creating the Frame. With a few exceptions, the activities that will fill the frame will not pay high rents and will not generate capital value. How then is the cost of creating the frame to be funded? As we will come back to in the concluding chapter, the economic model on which retail development has been based needs to be rethought. Reinventing this economic model is a much more pressing task than the physical reconfiguration of city centres.

FUTURE OF WORK

In April 2022 Jacob Rees-Mogg became a talisman for the 'back to the office' movement. In the honourable tradition of British passive aggression, he left a note at the unmanned desk of a civil servant. Emblazoned with the Royal coat of arms, the serif typeface read: 'Sorry you were out when I visited. I look forward to seeing you in the office very soon.' Of all the changes that have befallen cities in the wake of the pandemic, the location of white-collar employees has attracted the most attention. It is often reductively characterised as a binary choice between a return to the old ways of the office or a future based almost entirely from home.

Rees-Mogg is not alone in yearning to be surrounded once more by warm bodies in inoffensive clothing, soothed by the clattering of keyboards, muted footsteps on gently ageing carpet tiles and the smell of over-brewed coffee. Across the world, some of the biggest companies are pushing for a return to the office. As reported in the *Financial Times*, Goldman Sachs boss David Solomon described homeworking as 'an aberration', Tesla's Elon Musk wants employees at their desks 40 hours a week, and both Apple and Peloton are pushing for at least three days a week.[15]

Surprisingly, given all the attention working from home has garnered, the number of people who are actually able to work from home is overstated. The Centre for Cities report 'How will Coronavirus affect jobs in different parts of the country?' suggests that people able to work from home are a minority in every single city and large town in the UK. There are also significant regional differences, with higher working from home capability in London (up to 50%) and the Greater South East than in some northern cities (around 20% in Barnsley, Burnley and Stoke), although Manchester, Leeds, Warrington and Newcastle have a slightly higher share than other northern cities.[16]

Part of the reason for increased attention given to working from home, is the spending power of the office worker. In their September 2020 report 'The Economic Impact of Returning to the Office' PwC looked at three key channels of economic impact in the periods before, during and after the March to July 2020 lockdown. These were 'consumption' (pure spending), 'agglomeration' (the economic benefits derived from the clustering of workers in a particular place) and 'productivity' (the value generated through work).[17] For the high street, consumption and agglomeration are the most relevant.

PwC found that working from home lowered consumption across the board, but especially in retail, hospitality and leisure. They estimated that lowered spending could amount to £12 billion each year. This is a double loss for the city. Not only is overall spending down, but also the spending that is taking place is less likely to be taking place in city centres. The geographical shift creates a real problem for cities in terms of agglomeration; PwC note that workers bring a variety of economic benefits to the places where they work. In addition to spending money in local shops they collaborate with each other, exchange ideas, generate new businesses and attract investment. This is what Andy Haldane, former Chief Economist at the Bank of England, called the 'Medici Effect' in the 'Levelling-up White Paper'.[18] This is the force that will inevitably regenerate Nottingham – the notion that the agglomeration of economic activity in certain geographical areas, economies of scale and a density of diverse people and ideas drives economic growth. In this respect size matters, and agglomeration creates something that is greater than the sum of its parts, as PwC write:

> 'The total value of agglomeration can rise or fall as economic activity moves from one place to another. Workers who used to purchase lunch in a city centre might instead buy locally in their suburban or rural home. While the value of spending is the same, agglomeration may be lower if the supply chain in the city is larger. The fall in value of a worker no longer collaborating in a city may also be greater than the gain to a suburban or rural area of that worker sharing ideas there.'

PwC estimate that sustained working from home could decrease agglomeration by more than 4%, with a net cost of around £3.2 billion GDP. For city high streets the proportional impact will, once more, be higher. For well-connected places with highly integrated supply chains, a reduction in spending will have a larger knock-on effect than a similar increase in spending in a rural area. Essentially, cities have the most to lose from this shift.

Whether this shift to homeworking is permanent remains unclear. In late 2022 *The Spectator* was speculating that rising energy costs will push people back to the office.[19] Why pay to heat your home during the day when you can work in a warm office? However, for every employer pushing for a return to the office, there is another taking the opportunity to reduce their office space, which suggests that they think that a change to hybrid working is more permanent. Over half the major UK employers surveyed by PwC in February to March 2021 expected to reduce the size of their property portfolio, with one-third believing they will reduce their office footprint by more than 30%.[20]

Borrowing from Buddhist tradition, the future of offices will likely find a 'Middle Way' – a combination of homeworking and office working in any number of configurations. For this arrangement, a different type of workspace is required, one that can benefit the high street. Co-working spaces allow office workers from different companies to share a building, allowing for cost savings and convenience. More than half of UK co-working spaces provide fewer than 50 desks and an area of less than 5,000ft^2.[21] This smaller floor area means that they can integrate more comfortably in a high street ecosystem, drawing the economic advantages of office

Manchester City Centre: The retail role of the city has been transformed as a result of the wider transformation of the city centre and the development of city centre apartments.

workers closer, rather than relying on trips from business districts and footfall from commuter routes.

CITY LIVING

If cities can't rely on the return of office workers to pre-pandemic levels, where else can they look for prospective customers? One potential avenue is to further grow their residential population. After all, the smaller towns and suburban centres that did best out of lockdown, did so because of their residents. Before COVID, the received wisdom was that city centre housing had only a limited impact on retailing and other city centre uses. People, after all, were out at work during the day and their shopping and leisure habits were tied more to their place of work than their place of residence. Homeworking changes this equation. With people working at least partly from home, residential development can contribute to footfall in cities. There has been a huge increase in town centre living in the last two decades, particularly in the largest cities.

However, the impact of this will be limited if, as we suggested earlier in this chapter, the pandemic has caused more people to sell up, leaving the metropolis to live the good life in the country. The Economic Statistics Centre of Excellence in January 2021 suggested that 700,000 people had left London over the previous 12 months causing its population to fall for the first time since the 1980s.[22] This is not a new trend and the fall was more likely a result of Brexit rather than COVID. However a YouGov survey in November 2021 found that 52% of Londoners wanted to leave the city.[23] Even before the pandemic Yolande Barnes at UCL Bartlett Real Estate Institute was pointing to a net out-migration from London in all age groups, driven by the high house prices in the city and the impossibility for many of ever buying a home.[24]

The difference, since the pandemic, is that people have been leaving London and other cities to live more remotely, whereas previously provincial cities had benefited from London's exodus. In the summer of 2020 data from Rightmove showed a 126% increase in enquiries from city residents about village homes. It is easy to overstate these trends. Internal migration data from the Office for National Statistics shows that there has always been an outflow of people from cities and London in particular. The 700,000 figure needs to be seen in the context of 500,000 people leaving London every year. The question is how this compares to the numbers arriving. For a long time, the equation in British cities was negative – until the 1990s most cities were losing more people than they were attracting. However, in the last 20 years the situation has reversed and, more than anything else, this population growth lies behind the economic renaissance of cities and the success of their city centres. If the pandemic was to change this then the effect on city centres would be profound.

OXFORD STREET – THE ETERNAL HIGH STREET

All these issues come together on Oxford Street in London, described by some as 'the nation's high street'. We described the history of Oxford Street in Chapter 1 – its quarter of a billion annual visitors make it Europe's busiest shopping street. And yet COVID saw its footfall drop by 90% and the Centre for Cities *High Street Recovery Tracker* consistently showed London's West End as the UK's most severely COVID-impacted retail area through 2020 and 2021.[25] This continued after lockdowns were lifted with its 2020 Christmas footfall down 68% year on year.[26]

If you look at a Space Syntax map of London the reason for Oxford Street's prominence becomes clear. The map shows cul-de-sacs in dark blue, a side street with a couple of connecting streets light blue, upwards in connectivity through green, yellow and orange. The map is a kaleidoscope of colour. Cutting across it, running broadly east to west, is a distinct red line, the only one on the map. That red line is Oxford Street, London's best connected street, which is why the shops are there.

Experian's data covers the whole of the West End, which extends well beyond Oxford Street to include Regent Street, Carnaby Street and Marylebone High Street. The area includes 9,000 outlets and 22.6 million ft^2 of space. The data shows that the vacancy rate hovered between 5 and 6% for much of the 2010s, rising to 8.3% in 2020 and 9.7% in 2021. While this is lower than the average for our case studies, it has been a cause for concern in the area. In January 2021, the Local Data Company showed that there were 24 vacancies on the street, the highest for a decade and this was before the closure of its Debenhams and flagship Topshop stores.[27] But this is only part of the story. Retail analyst Jonathan De Mello is

Oxford Street in London: 'disliked and even disdained' and yet still a 'howling success'.

quoted in *Retail Week* as saying that it's not just about empty stores but the fact that many once prime locations are now occupied by 'tourist tat'.[28] The most recent press stories have been about the proliferation of American candy shops (there are apparently 30 on the street).[29]

The problems run deeper than COVID. One of the fundamental issues is business rates, which often cost businesses three or four times more than their rent. The Selfridges store pays just over £17 million a year in rates while JD Sports reports that its Oxford Street store is the worst performing in its portfolio. Even

Starbucks found that it couldn't sell enough cups of coffee to pay its rates bill. Business rates were suspended during COVID but as Jace Tyrrell, Chief Executive of the New West End Company, told *Retail Gazette*: 'I know that there are hundreds of businesses in the West End that are going to decide whether to stay or leave depending on what happens to business rates.'[30]

In an ill-fated attempt to revive Oxford Street, Westminster Council promoted the Marble Arch Mound.[31] This was a 25m high artificial hill built to provide a viewing platform down the street, in order to attract visitors post-lockdown. Designed by the iconic Dutch Architects MVRDV, the mound ended up costing almost twice its projected budget of £3.3 million and failed to deliver on the promise of a lush green hill with mature trees and a view down Oxford Street. The initial entry fee of £4.50 to £8 was soon waived but still visitors failed to come and the Mound was dismantled in early 2022. The controversy was cited as one of the reasons that the Conservatives lost control of Westminster Council for the first time ever.

The project was part of a £150 million package from the council to revive Oxford Street. The small-scale interventions were more successful – widening pavements and planting trees – even if they didn't manage to resolve the age-old conundrum of pedestrianisation. While cars have long been excluded, the street remains London's busiest east/west bus route, with 300 buses an hour as well as black cabs. The problem with pedestrianisation is that there is no obvious alternative route for the buses despite suggestions in the past that the street should be decked or even an idea to run mini cars on air cushions along the centre of the street. All these plans were seen off by the power of the retailers and one suspects that they will also see off the pedestrianisation plans that were a manifesto promise of the current mayor Sadiq Khan.

And yet for all these problems and predictions of doom, Oxford Street is bouncing back. It may be, as the planner Colin Buchanan described it in the 1960s, 'the most uncivilised street in Europe', but as Andrew Saint writes in his 'Survey of London', despite being 'widely disliked and even disdained ... Oxford Street flourishes ... indeed is a howling success'.[32] As Simon Jenkins concludes: 'For all its ugliness, Oxford Street's longevity is astonishing ... The street may have lost its looks, drifting from style and fashion to tackiness and bling ... But it has survival in its genes. It will outlive us all.'[33]

As with other cities, the fundamentals will always cause Oxford Street to bounce back regardless of short-term trends or even regeneration initiatives. The retail analyst Jonathan De Mello points out that an Oxford Street store is a must for any brand that wants to be taken seriously: 'I know five or six brands that are looking at an Oxford Street store in the same way as they would look at an advertising campaign on TV ... Taking the budget from marketing rather than the property team.'[34] IKEA have recently taken on the flagship Topshop store and it is even rumoured that Amazon is looking for a store. It is far too early to write off Oxford Street as the nation's high street despite all of its problems.

There has been a great deal of speculation since the pandemic that cities will be the places most impacted, that the persistence of homeworking and the trend of people living more remotely will impact city centres to a greater extent than smaller towns and suburban centres. But this ignores the fundamental fact about cities, which is that they are big, and for any customer-facing operation big is most definitely best. One of the figures that retailers are most concerned about is catchment population

– how many potential customers are available to them in a particular location. Cities win on a number of counts in this respect – they have large populations, a lot of people work there and they lie at the centre of transport networks that make them easy to reach for people living in surrounding areas. Homeworking and population trends may have an effect at the margins but do not affect this fundamental fact.

Because of this, cities are a focus for uses that need access to large numbers of people – the largest department stores, the best restaurants and nightclubs, theatres and other cultural institutions, libraries, concert venues, sports stadia and so on. They are also the best place for specialist shops to locate – if you only appeal to a small proportion of the population you have the largest possible pool of people to draw from. Retailers looking to create a national chain will concentrate on the cities first and those looking to cut back will close their city stores last of all.

This, together with the forces of agglomeration and the Medici effect described earlier, will bolster the success of city centres, reversing lockdown trends. These trends also give cities an advantage over the large out-of-town malls that are also designed to serve the largest possible catchment area but lack the diversity of uses and the intensity of people coming for a variety of reasons rather than just to shop. The UK, having only rediscovered the power of its cities relatively recently, is not likely to see them fall once more into decline.

13   THE MALL

I t is fair to say that urbanists are not keen on malls. Malls, or shopping centres, as they are called in the UK, are introspective and monofunctional, those in town centres fail to address the street or contribute to the life of the town, those built out-of-town undermine the viability of town centres, are unsustainable and car-dependent. Malls are by their nature anti-urban. The caveat to this rule are the Victorian and Edwardian shopping arcades, which are similar to malls in many ways, but have the benefit of age, have a greater variety of independent retailers and are better knitted into the urban fabric. By contrast modern malls are typically massive standalone 'objects' with an expanse of dead frontage (the Arndale Centre in Manchester was described by *The Guardian* as 'the longest lavatory wall in Europe'), while inside they are an expanse of marbled, air-conditioned space filled with fake palm trees and identikit retailers.

THE MALL IS DEAD – LONG LIVE THE MALL

There are two types of mall – vast out-of-town complexes surrounded by thousands of car parking spaces and in-town shopping centres sitting like alien spaceships that have landed on existing towns and cities. Both face an uncertain future because they are built to cater for the multiple retailers that have been so badly hit by the current retail crisis. However, it wasn't so long ago that a very different story was being told. As we saw in Chapter 3, in the 1990s the development of regional shopping centres and retail parks precipitated a full-scale crisis on the UK high street as town and city centres struggled to compete. Our case studies include just four large out-of-town malls: Meadowhall, Westfield Stratford, the Metrocentre and the Trafford Centre. Back in 2012, during the last retail crisis at the time of the Portas Review, the average vacancy rate of these four malls was just 5.3%, less than half that of traditional town centres. At the time, out-of-town centres were part of the problem, and there was a feeling that traditional town centres needed to be managed more like malls if they were going to compete.

The threat of out-of-town centres was greater even than the internet. Now they are suffering as much if not more than traditional centres; by 2021, the vacancy rate in our case studies had increased to 15.2%, the second highest of all our categories, indeed the Metrocentre and Westfield Stratford had vacancy rates over 20%. In-town malls are more difficult to separate out in the data. However, THE British Retail Consortium's Local Data Company Vacancy Monitor provides vacancy data for high streets, retail parks and shopping centres, the latter covering both in-town and out-of-town centres. In 2021, shopping centre vacancy rates peaked at 19.5%, compared to 14.1% on the high street and 11.1% in retail parks.[1]

As described in Chapter 3, the story of shopping centres in the UK originates in the 1960s and 1970s with the early attempts to import the American mall to the UK. The initial schemes, such as the huge mall proposed at Haydock between Liverpool and Manchester, were seen off by the UK planning system. As a result,

The Trafford Centre: With debts of more than £4.5 billion and a share price that had fallen 94%, Intu the owners of the Trafford Centre collapsed in 2020. But the vast out-of-town mall continues to trade.

most of the early shopping centres were built within existing town centres such as the original Bull Ring in Birmingham (1964) or the Arndale Centre in Manchester (1976). On the inside these malls were very like their American predecessors, but rather than being surrounded by parking, they were shoehorned into tight urban sites. Far from being resisted, many of these in-town malls were promoted by local authorities – there was no other way in which such complex sites could have been assembled. They were seen as essential if town and city centres were going to compete. The only other malls built in the UK at the time were the centres of new towns like Milton Keynes, Cwmbran, Winsford, Irvine and Cumbernauld, where the entire town centre was designed as an internalised shopping mall.

Then there was a loosening of planning policy under the Thatcher government of the 1980s leading to a raft of proposals for large out-of-town malls and retail parks. Only a handful of the regional shopping centres (as the out-of-town malls were called) made it off the drawing board, again normally with the support of local councils. These included Meadowhall, promoted by Sheffield Council and implemented with the help of a government development corporation, and Metrocentre near Newcastle, built without planning permission in an Enterprise Zone and accessed by a publicly funded road junction. Others included the Trafford Centre in Manchester, Cribbs Causeway in Bristol, Bluewater in Kent, Merry Hill in the Midlands, the White Rose Centre in Leeds and Lakeside Thurrock.

A further change in planning policy in the mid-1990s closed the door on further out-of-town developments. Since then, all new malls have been built within existing town and city centres. As we described in Chapter 4, there was a great rush of mall developments in the 2000s, including the redevelopment of the Bullring in Birmingham, Liverpool ONE, High Cross in Leicester and the two Westfield Centres in London. There were also scores of smaller schemes: indeed most of our case studies were actively seeking to build a new shopping centre following advice by retail agents. A slew of these centres were completed in 2008 on the eve of the financial crisis. Those that didn't make it limped on for a few years as councils and their development partners sought to make them work. Most were eventually abandoned and are now being developed as mixed-use schemes like Winchester, Coventry and Guildford. A few were eventually completed, like Bradford, Stafford and Wrexham, in a brief window of viability between 2014 and 2017.

This brief history gives us a legacy of 700 malls in the UK today: a very small number of large out-of-town malls, and a huge number of in-town malls ranging from mega malls in large cities to small shopping centres and precincts in all but the smallest places. Most medium-sized towns have more than one mall and some have three or four. These malls end up competing with each other, the newer malls cannibalising the trade of the older malls.

THE LAST MALLS

It is worth spending a moment looking at some of the newer malls that were built or almost built in the late 2000s because in many respects they had started to evolve into something different that urbanists didn't hate (quite so much). A good example is the Princesshay Shopping Centre in Exeter, a scheme by Land Securities together with the Crown Estate. This was the redevelopment of an earlier retail scheme built after the city centre had been damaged by wartime bombing. Long before it had been conceived, Exeter had been named by the New Economics Foundation as the least diverse shopping centre in their 'Clone Towns Britain' report.[2] There

was just one independent store, and most of the other units were clothes and fashion outlets. Retail rents were high, partly because of its popularity with the big retailers, but this was also the reason for the lack of diversity because independent retailers couldn't afford the rent. From the perspective of a retail agent this is what success looks like and it is what made the redevelopment an enticing commercial proposition.

The Exeter scheme was one of a series at the time that started to reimagine what a shopping centre could be. It is part arcade and part open street with 530,000ft^2 (50,000m^2) of retail space with 60 stores that now attracts 9.5 million people annually.[3] A second phase includes a John Lewis store, and the overall effect has been to reinforce Exeter's retail ranking (if not its clone town rating). It is one of a series of shopping centres built at the time, the main feature of which

Princesshay Exeter:
One of a new breed of shopping centres, the distinguishing feature being the lack of a roof.

was that they didn't have a roof. Prime amongst these was Liverpool ONE that we have describe in Chapter 11 and the redeveloped Bullring Centre in Birmingham that we visited in Chapter 4. On a smaller scale it includes Eagles Meadow in Wrexham and the Rock in Bury. This new generation of malls would have been joined by others had it not been for the 2008 financial crisis. The next step would have been the Retail Quarter in Sheffield, which was planned as a major shopping centre anchored by a huge new John Lewis but designed around a street network, without a roof and as a series of buildings each designed by a different architect rather than a single mega structure. Like Liverpool ONE, it would have been a mall hiding in plain sight without any clear indication of where the mall ends and the city starts.

Princesshay in Exeter was nominated for a 'Great Place' award by The Academy of Urbanism,[4] sparking a debate about whether a mall, however well designed, can be a real place, because these are still malls as in privatised spaces under a single management. There was controversy in Exeter soon after the centre opened, when it was revealed that the management was employing mobile device tracking technology to plot the movements of customers via their phones.[5] The 'streets' are private spaces, patrolled by security guards and CCTV and occupied exclusively by national retail chains. It is certainly a very good mall but whether it is a very good piece of urbanism is a moot point.

DEAD MALLS?

The vulnerability of malls can best be seen in the US where there are up to 1,800 malls and where in the 1990s an average of 140 malls opened every year. Since 2007, no new malls have opened in the US and today a quarter have been, or are at risk of being, abandoned.[6] Indeed, there is an entire genre of 'dead mall' photography with eerie pictures of abandoned concourses, dust-dry fountains and frozen escalators. Most US malls were built out of town, and while some have been the victim of demographic change in their catchment area, most have died because they have lost one or both of their anchor department stores. Department stores in the US have suffered like those in the UK. In 2011, US department stores had 1.2 million employees and 8,600 outlets whereas the research firm IBISWorld estimates that they now have fewer than 700,000 employees and 6,000 outlets.[7] An out-of-town mall might be full of successful small shops but without its department store it is doomed as footfall drains away and all the smaller traders are forced to close.

At present, around 300 US malls are derelict and their peripheral locations, scale and introspective nature mean they are not easy to adapt. Some have been redeveloped as residential districts, as documented by Ellen Dunham-Jones at the Georgia Institute of Technology.[8] Others have been imaginatively transformed into college campuses, offices, parks, cinemas, fishing lakes, gyms ... There is at least one example of a conversion to a 'mega-church' (Lexington Mall in Kentucky) and a meanwhile use as a homeless shelter (the former Macy's store in Landmark Mall, Virginia). In Tennessee, a private healthcare provider has bought up half of the dead malls, repurposing them as huge medical centres with a wide range of specialities and surgical centres all under one roof. Other ghost malls have been demolished and the land acquired by the likes of Amazon and FedEx to build fulfilment centres.

There are also dead malls in the UK. According to analysis by the Local Data Company, there are 70 malls in the UK that are unviable; five of them have a vacancy rate of more than 80%, another 25 are more than half empty and 34 have vacancy rates of 40–50%.[9] Knight Frank estimate that a further 200 malls are at risk without major refurbishment.[10] We have come across a number of these 'zombie malls' in our case studies. They are generally the second or third shopping centre in the town and have lost out to more modern developments like the Guildhall Centre in Stafford, the Alhambra in Bradford or the Paisley Centre in Paisley. The Alhambra has been acquired by Bradford Council to redevelop as housing while the Paisley Centre has been bought by the Beyond Retail Property Fund to create a residential quarter and hotel with ground floor retail and leisure. Other struggling malls include Stockton's Castlegate (which is being demolished to create a park), the Riverside in Shrewsbury, the Chilterns in High Wycombe and Nicholsons in Maidenhead.

THE FALL OF INTU

The biggest casualty of these trends is Intu, which was one of the largest shopping centre owners in the UK. They were the owners of the Trafford Centre in Manchester, Cribbs Causeway near Bristol, Lakeside in Thurrock, Merry Hill in the Midlands and the Metrocentre in Gateshead. They also owned the Arndale Centre in central Manchester, both of Nottingham's shopping centres and the Potteries Centre in Stoke. At the beginning of March 2020, Intu were forced to abandon their attempts to raise £1 billion in equity due to lack of interest from investors. The date is relevant – it would be another four weeks before the first COVID lockdown was imposed, but Intu's problems stemmed from what had happened in the past rather than the prospect of lockdown. Its share price had fallen from £2.8 billion in November 2018 to just £164 million in March 2020, a drop of 94%. The failure to secure investment meant that Intu, with debts of more than £4.5 billion, failed to meet the criteria set by their banks, making their collapse on 26 June all but inevitable.

Footfall at the Trafford Centre in the first three months of 2020 had actually been slightly up on the previous year and occupancy rates were steady. Rental income was down by 9.1% due to the closure of a number of its retailers, but the figures were far from disastrous. With the exception of the Broadmarsh Centre in Nottingham, which was about to be redeveloped, the same was true of the other Intu centres, these were not zombie malls. The problem was that investor confidence in big retail had collapsed and for companies with debts as big as Intu's this put them in an impossible position. All the former Intu shopping centres have continued trading despite its collapse. They are mostly owned by special purpose vehicles and Intu's administrators KPMG have been trying to find buyers. The best bid for the Trafford Centre was just £800 million, half its valuation a year earlier. Intu's biggest investor, the Canadian Pension Plan Investment Board, has therefore decided not to sell and has appointed Savills to run the centre on its behalf.

REINVENTING THE MALL

There was a time in the early 1960s, soon after the Merseyway Shopping Centre opened, when Manchester was so concerned about the growing threat of Stockport town centre that it used it to justify the development of the Arndale Centre. But Stockport and the Merseyway Shopping Centre in particular was badly hit by the opening of the Trafford Centre and by 2016 the centre's owners had collapsed into administration. It was at that point that the council stepped in to acquire the centre. This is not unusual – many of the councils in our case studies have taken a similar step, often buying centres for a fraction of the price they sold them for years ago. As

WINSFORD

You arrive in Winsford along a road that is called a high street but is in fact an impossibly broad dual carriageway with a 40-mile speed limit. Ahead of you the clock tower of the town centre rises above the trees but once you arrive, on a road that has now increased to six lanes, it becomes clear that the clock tower marks the edge not of a traditional town centre but a large and aging mall. Winsford may be an ancient town with a market charter dating back to 1280 but it is also a new town, and an old one at that.

It was one of a series of expanded towns around Liverpool and Manchester designated in the 1950s. Much of the town's terraced housing was demolished in a comprehensive plan that included a brand-new town centre including shops, market hall, library, sports centre and civic hall. Unfortunately, the projected population fell short of the target so that the new town centre was too large.

The entire town centre is contained within a single shopping mall – the Winsford Cross Centre. This was sold many years ago and passed through the hands of a number of owners, eventually being bought by an Irish property company. They produced several plans for the centre, none of which the council felt able to support. Meanwhile, the centre was showing increasing signs of decay, part of it collapsing in 2005.

The council stepped in and purchased the centre for just under £20 million and a budget was set aside for essential repairs including partial demolition, which made the vacancy rate look much better. By June 2019 the council had made a profit of £700,000 after the repayment of the loans.

This is only the start of a long-term plan to transform the centre, supported by £10 million from the government's Future High Streets Fund and £17 million of further borrowing. The retailing is to be reduced by 40% with new uses introduced, including a social hub, to make the centre more outward-facing with improved entrances and public realm. It is a good example of how a council can proactively intervene to transform a failing centre.

we have heard, Stockton acquired its centre so that it could be demolished to make way for a park. Other places are proposing to redevelop centres for housing or a mix of leisure uses. Stockport however did not buy the centre with a view to redevelopment but rather to evolve the Merseyway Centre into something very different.

Originally, Stockport town centre was anchored by three department stores – BHS, M&S and Debenhams – all of which have now closed. The council's acquisition of the Merseyway Centre was seen as necessary to stop the slide. Other councils have unwisely acquired retail property as an investment; in Stockport the hope was that the council would cover its costs but there was no expectation that they would make money. The strategy was based on an analysis that there was too much retail space in the town, so the aim was to manage the transition of the town centre away from an overreliance on retail.

The process is being managed by James Chapman, who used to advise the council as a consultant with CBRE and has now been taken on by the council. As he told us, the problem with shopping centres lies in the collapse of their capital value. Often the headline rent has not fallen greatly but, as historic leases come to an end, retailers are either leaving or renegotiating new shorter leases with an expectation of rent-free deals, a contribution to fit-out costs or even turnover rents linked to the shops takings. Whilst these deals don't necessarily harm income, they do destroy capital value. Thus, the capital value of many retail assets is now more likely to be based on the underlying value of the land rather than the income from the units.

The Strand Shopping Centre in Bootle: One of a number of shopping centres that have been bought by their local council.

This is a major problem for retail landlords with stock market valuations. It is less of a problem for Councils who are not so worried about capital value provided that they have enough income to cover their costs (including borrowing) and are achieving regeneration benefits.

Stockport is not alone. In Bootle the council paid £32.5 million to purchase the Strand Shopping Centre, a decision that came under public scrutiny since the centre was valued at just £27.2 million, however the council has since managed to generate a £1 million surplus from rental income. The same has happened in Winsford where Cheshire West and Chester Council paid £20 million for the Winsford Cross Centre (which encompasses the entire town centre), frustrated at the lack of investment by the previous owners. The centre generated £700,000 in its first year of trading after borrowing costs and the council have combined a £10 million grant from the Future High Streets Fund with further borrowing and reserves to invest £37 million in the centre, reducing the retail space by 40% and consolidating the remaining retail, making the centre more outward-looking and introducing other uses including a community hub.

Back in Stockport, James Chapman tells us that the fundamentals of the town centre are strong. Almost 5,000 apartments are being constructed and its changing

The Westfield shopping centre in Stratford London: Rethinking the role of a mall prompted by vacancy rates of over 20%.

demographics are already increasing demand for bars and food outlets. The council has secured a £14.5 million grant from the Future High Streets Fund, which it is using to transform the Merseyway Centre. The first project is the 'Stockroom', the repurposing of a former Mothercare unit and back office space to create a new library, community facility, council service point and a performance space. They are also experimenting with ways to get more independent shops and other activities into the centre. They agreed a deal with a plastics recycling company to take a vacant unit, upcycling the fittings left by previous tenants and paying part of their rent in kind by organising events. A pop-up unit has also been created featuring different retailers each week. The strategy is to focus on low-hanging fruit – vacant units that may not be in the most lettable position but are in good condition, recognising the need to be creative in accommodating independents who lack capital for fit-out.

The old Marks & Spencer has been rebranded as Stok and is being converted by local property firm Glenbrook into high quality offices around a central glazed atrium. It will further diversify the centre, which doesn't have a great deal of office space, and in turn help with lunchtime trade. That leaves the vacant Debenhams, which is currently being used for storage while the 'Stockroom' scheme takes place. In the longer term, the council is planning to redevelop the store along with the adjacent multistorey car park to build a new hospital. This will replace the existing Stepping Hill Hospital, so releasing an out-of-town site for housing development and focussing all the activity generated by the hospital in the town centre.

Stockport shows one possible future for in-town malls, publicly owned, and managed for the benefit of the town centre rather than distant investors and with a much greater mix of uses and activities – a bit like town centres used to be before they were hijacked by the big retailers and retail developers/landlords. There will still be plenty of shops, but they will form just part of a town centre mix of apartments, office space, health facilities and public services.

WESTFIELD STRATFORD CITY

Privately owned malls will also need to evolve both in town and out of town. One of the leaders in this respect is the Westfield Stratford City. Our case study data shows that it currently has a vacancy rate over 20%, but even before the retail crisis the centre was having to work hard to maintain footfall and occupancy because of its unique position. The mall sits next to the London Olympic Park and was developed as part of the huge Stratford City development and the opening of the shopping centre was timed to coincide with the Olympic Games. It is not however a particularly promising site for a shopping centre, being entirely surrounded by railway lines, with only three long pedestrian bridges connecting the centre to Stratford town centre, the Olympic Park and the surrounding new residential neighbourhoods. It was the only mall to be opened between 2009 and 2014 at a time when retailing was still recovering from the financial crisis, and it took a number of years for housing to be built on the Olympic Park, so the location wasn't ideal and Westfield has had to work hard to maintain its occupancy. This is why its management is arguably more innovative than other malls in maintaining its appeal.

In 2020, the centre's owners Unibail-Rodamco-Westfield commissioned a report; 'How We Shop: The Next Decade'. It concluded that by 2025 more than half of retail space would be dedicated to providing customer experiences, not products. Noting that traditional retailers on longer-term leases may not come back to shopping centres the report recommended that retail landlords will need to be more flexible in providing short-term leases and pop-up spaces.[11] As described in Chapter 11, Westfield piloted a scheme to give shop window spaces to small online start-up businesses. Each shop unit had a QR code on the store window that could be scanned as a gateway into the company's social media and digital online store.

Harita Shah, Westfield's Marketing Director UK, was quoted in an interview with Fashion United UK: 'With people craving physical experiences more so than ever before and with 49 percent of consumers wanting to buy more locally sourced products, we're bringing these online brands offline into a physical space for the first time.'[12] This is part of a growing interest in showrooming, by which products are displayed in physical spaces but still bought online. It is something that is happening in a number of retail sectors, creating a hybrid retail model that lies at the heart of the Westfield strategy and is probably the future of other malls.

LIFE AFTER MALLS, CHESTER

This leaves us with the question of what happens to all the malls that never were. The schemes that had been nurtured by councils for years and seen as essential to the success of the town centre but which they have now been forced to abandon. A good example is the Northgate scheme in Chester. As Rob Monaghan, the regeneration officer brought in by the city to manage the development told us,[13] the scheme was first proposed in the early 2000s on a site within the city walls, next to the Cathedral. It was the site of Chester's original market and in the 1970s had been redeveloped to build the Forum Shopping Centre, a new covered market, library and bus station. The plan in the 2000s had been to relocate the bus station and to build a new large mall anchored by a House of Fraser department store and incorporating a new market, library, hotel and car park. The initial scheme was promoted by Scottish Widows who were then replaced by ING. They worked up the scheme and secured planning permission but struggled with viability as the financial crisis took hold, eventually pulling out in 2010. At this point, the council decided to step in and act as developers themselves. New plans were draw up by Acme Architects for a £360 million retail-led mixed-use scheme that secured planning in 2016 and completed the compulsory purchase of the site.

However, before construction could start, House of Fraser went into receivership and its new owners Sports Direct pulled out. One by one, the other 'big seven' retailers that had provisionally been signed up also pulled out and it became clear by 2018 that a rethink was necessary. By this time, the bus station had been moved and the council decided to proceed with a first phase on the northern third of the site. It includes the conversion of an old Odeon cinema into the Storyhouse cultural centre with a new library and theatre. Behind this is a new public square leads to the new market hall, multiplex cinema and multistorey car park. The anchor for the site will be the market rather than a department store and the council has been putting a lot of thought into the market, which it sees not as an 'Altrincham-style' food operation but somewhere that you can buy groceries, get your phone fixed and have your hair cut, as well as something to eat. In preparation for the move the council has been working to modernise the existing market, successfully raising annual footfall from 300,000 to 1.2 million. The plan is that this will further increase to 2 million in the new market.

The question is, what happens to the remaining two-thirds of the site when the old market and Forum Shopping Centre is demolished? It is a question being asked by other towns and cities with abandoned retail schemes like the Tithebarn

Centre in Preston, the North Street Centre in Guildford, the Waterside North scheme in Aylesbury, the Silver Hill scheme in Winchester and the City Centre South scheme in Coventry. All of these schemes have become residential-led developments with a ground-floor fringe of small-scale retail and leisure. Some, like Preston, include significant leisure uses and others have a significant amount of offices and other uses but the viability is based on the sale of apartments. Whether this is a welcome diversification of town centres or the erosion of the town's retail offer depends on your viewpoint but this is where the history of malls in the UK has ended up – it is hard to see any more malls being built in the UK for the foreseeable future.

The current retail crisis has hit malls as much, if not more, than traditional town centres and there is a significant risk to smaller secondary malls. The larger, more modern malls are not going to fail but they too need to reinvent themselves so that they are less dependent on a narrow set of multiple retailers. They will need to find ways to introduce a broader range of retailers including independents and a broader range of uses including leisure as well as public services. The question is, what effect does this have on the financial model on which malls are based? For the malls that were never built, the future lies in an alternative mixed-use development model. For those that are struggling the future may lie with the public sector, harking back to the days of the original municipal market halls. Either way, urbanists can come to terms with a form of retailing that has in the past done so much damage to traditional town centres but may now be part of the solution to their revival.

The Rows in Chester: With retailing at street level and on an elevated walkway, this has provided a model for many shopping centres. However the city's attempts to build the new Northgate shopping centre have failed and the scheme is being rethought.

14 THE TOWN

I n the early 2000s, the institutional investor that owned the Metropolitan Centre in Barnsley put their stake up for sale together with a number of other shopping centres. Humiliatingly for Barnsley, prospective buyers were interested in the package but only if Barnsley were excluded. That was perhaps the town's low point and yet in less than 20 years the vacancy rate in the town has dropped to just 7.1%, a new indoor market is thriving together with the Lightbox, a new library/ community hub, and construction has started on a new shopping arcade called The Glass Works. None of this would have been possible had it not been for a process that started with Barnsley being compared to a Tuscan hill town.

BARNSLEY'S HALO OF CONFIDENCE

The Metropolitan Centre was a huge complex including a covered market, office building and multistorey car park. It was eventually offered for sale on its own and after a frantic scramble involving a number of government agencies, the council was able to buy it. As David Kennedy, who was then Barnsley's Director of Development recounts, in the early 2000s Barnsley was a mining town that had seen the closure of all 10 of its coal mines and had yet to find a new role.[1] Its population was falling and it was the 16th most deprived borough in the country. Together with Steve Houghton (who has been council leader throughout this story), David Kennedy contacted the Regional Development Agency, Yorkshire Forward. The agency had recently set up a *Renaissance Towns Programme* and appointed an international team of architects and urbanists to work with the towns of Yorkshire on strategies for their regeneration.[2] Alan Simpson, head of the programme, said he knew just the person Barnsley needed.

The person Alan had in mind was the most flamboyant member of the panel, the late Will Alsop. On being told at an initial meeting that the vision was to put Barnsley on the itinerary of every visitor to the UK alongside Durham and York, he responded, 'Fucking hell, we have our work cut out then!' The process started with a series of 'charrettes', with town centre businesses and users from which council officials were excluded. After a few months, Alsop's vision was ready and David Kennedy and Steve Houghton were invited to the town's best restaurant for a preview in advance of a presentation he was due to make to a town meeting a few days later. Over a couple of bottles of red wine, Alsop explained his thinking.

The vision was subsequently published as 'Remaking Barnsley 2003–2033', proclaiming that 'Barnsley can rewrite the rules about post-industrial economies'. The core of its vision was that Barnsley should become a '21st century market town', something that went down very well at the town meeting. The report is full of 'step changes' and 'fundamental rethinks' claiming that the town 'will have a track record of business incubation second to none in Yorkshire and amongst the best in the UK and Europe'. It will be home to 'lawyers, carpenters, doctors, plumbers, stockbrokers, train drivers, journalists, green grocers, poets, builders and artists'.[3]

Barnsley Market Place: No longer the centre for the town's retailing but still very much the focus for the town's pride and community.

This is a slightly more poetic version of the vacuous boosterism found in many regeneration strategies, but it was only the starting point for the Alsop team.

The Barnsley skyline, with its town hall tower standing on a hilltop, led him to suggest that Barnsley should be modelled on the Tuscan city of Lucca. It would have a small compact town centre ('where everything is close at hand') surrounded by beautiful, productive countryside. He proposed a 'living wall' of buildings to encircle the town centre, made up of abstract, amorphous buildings, many on stilts, and capped with a rooftop park. All new development would be located within this wall and beyond it the urban sprawl would 'slowly dissipate' (as in somehow disappear, to be replaced by fields). The circular wall became a halo, and it was suggested that, as a first step, a halo of light should be projected into the sky above the town to symbolise its rebirth.

There was a certain nervousness on the part of the council as the great and the good of the town filed into the public meeting. The presentation was made in inimitable Will Alsop style and, when it finished, there was quiet as the chairman of the market traders got to his feet and said, 'I think ...' (long pause while the room held its breath) ... 'Steve Houghton (the council leader) is to be congratulated'. As David Kennedy recalls, 'it was so off the wall that it bypassed knotty issues like parking and market stalls', which had dominated arguments about the town centre for years. It tapped instead straight into the town's pride and engendered a sense of optimism about the possibility of change. Yorkshire Forward even allocated money to realise the halo of light, although air traffic control issues could never quite be overcome. Nevertheless, the halo became a symbol of the regeneration of the town and, while nothing from the Alsop vision was ever built, it didn't matter, Barnsley would never be the same again, as we will return to later in this chapter.

THE FRONT LINE OF THE RETAIL CRISIS

Towns are the most numerous of the 100 case studies on which this book is based. We have looked at 12 large towns/small cities, 35 towns and 10 smaller towns/villages and the variety is such that drawing conclusions is difficult. There are industrial towns like Barnsley, Doncaster and Wolverhampton in the North and Midlands, in what we now call 'red wall' seats. These are places whose people have become disillusioned and where boarded-up shops in the town centre are often symbolic of their sense of being bypassed and taken for granted. By contrast, there are prosperous historic towns like Winchester, Guildford, Harrogate or Chester (not all of which are in the south), struggling to accommodate modern retailing in beautiful but constrained town centres. Here the issue that recurs through our case studies has been the drive to build new shopping centres to provide 'modern' units able to accommodate mainstream retailers, just at a time when many of these retailers were collapsing into administration. Then there are the new towns like Milton Keynes, Cwmbran and Corby, and other modernist centres like Coventry, Winsford and Bootle, conceived by the architects and planners of the 1960s and 1970s rather than retailers and presenting very different challenges.

There are issues of scale, from towns with populations in the hundreds of thousands like Reading, Preston and Lincoln (some of which have been granted city status), to tiny places like Totnes, Ludlow, Slaithwaite or Ashington. Location is also a factor, from the splendid isolation of Wisbech and Penzance to the towns crowded around big cities like Bury, Paisley, Skipton and Todmorden. Some of the latter have struggled to compete with their larger neighbours, while others have attracted affluent commuters, using their energy and spending power as a spur to regeneration.

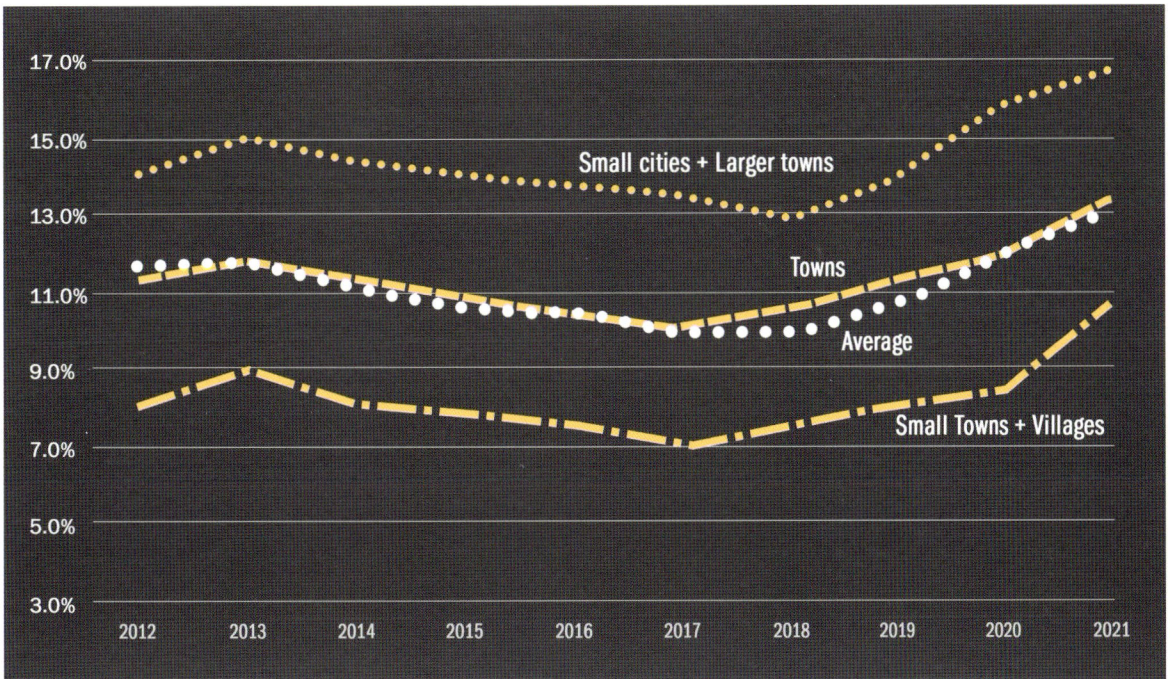

Retail vacancies in towns: This graph shows the percentage of vacant units in our 57 case study towns, based on data from Experian.

However, in a world where physical retailing is predicted to contract by between 25 and 40%, what unites all of these towns is that they are on the front line of the retail crisis.[4] As we suggested in Chapter 4, mainstream retailers once needed as many as 400 branches to cover the whole of the UK.[5] That would have meant a branch in all but the smallest of our case study towns. Now they can get away with as few as 80 branches, which would cover only the very largest towns. The number of branches varies by retailer, from John Lewis with stores in just 36 places, to Boots with a presence in more than 2,200. But the threshold for most retailers runs through the centre of towns, many of which will no longer be on the radar of the remaining national retailers.

You might therefore expect the smaller towns to be doing less well, but our data suggests that the opposite is true (as the graph above illustrates). This is not just a matter of size, because the average vacancy rate of the large cities would be below the average line on this graph. It may be that the smaller towns were never so reliant on the big retailers and therefore have not suffered the brunt of the 2008 and 2019 retail crises.

SEEKING SALVATION IN A SHOPPING CENTRE

In Chapter 4 we told the salutary tales of Bradford and Stafford. Both had been desperate to build a shopping centre, based on advice that their town centres were missing out on a long list of multiple retailers that would normally be expected in a centre like theirs. Having not managed to build their shopping centre prior to the 2008 financial crash, they struggled on and finally succeeded in a brief window of retail optimism between 2013 and 2015. In both cases, the shopping centre filled up largely with shops that had previously been trading elsewhere in the town centre, most significantly the Marks & Spencer. The resulting problems in the old town centre might have been temporary, except for the advent of a new retail crisis in 2018 so that now Bradford has the highest vacancy rate of all our case studies, with almost one in four of its shop units vacant; Stafford is 7th worst with just over one in five units vacant. It seems that the salvation for the town centres does not lie in new shopping centres, but if not that, then what?

There is a longer list of towns in our case studies that didn't manage to build their shopping centres, including Winchester, Chester, Preston, Guildford, Coventry, Norwich and Dundee. These places pursued their plans every bit as enthusiastically as Bradford and Stafford but they didn't manage to get the scheme over the line and are now having to think very differently.

Winchester

As Bláthnaid Duffy, Director of Planning at Lambert Smith Hanson told us, pre-pandemic there was 'a line of retailers queuing up to be in Winchester but they just couldn't find the units'.[6] The council's solution was Silver Hill, a covered shopping centre planned for a site one block back from the high street. The scheme looked set to start in 2010, with a development partner in place and planning consent granted. However, it had been subject to a vociferous campaign under the banner 'Winchester Deserved Better', spearheaded by local developer and Councillor Kim Gottlieb. He used his own money to secure a judicial review, arguing that the scheme had changed so much since the appointment of the development partner that the procurement process was no longer sound. The High Court agreed and the scheme collapsed. Soon after, Councillor Gottlieb bought the doctors surgery in the centre of the site, ostensibly protecting the surgery but also giving him a ransom over the scheme. The resulting chaos saw the resignation of the council leader and chief executive, an investigation by the council's Standard's Committee, accusations of a conflict of interest and even at one point a police investigation. Councillor Gottlieb was cleared but his actions were criticised as 'ill judged, undisciplined, and might be viewed as reckless'.[7]

Meanwhile Ian Charie, the newly appointed Head of Programme, sought to rethink the proposals.[8] JTP Architects were appointed to run a community planning event to develop a very different scheme with a mix of small-scale retail, commercial and community space on the ground floor and with up to 300 homes and office space on the upper floors.[9] It is a street-based scheme that is integrated into the city and is guided by the notion of 'Winchesterness' in terms of its form, height, roofscape and design. Crucially, one of the design principles is 'incremental delivery', allowing the blocks to be brought forward over time by a range of developers. The opposition groups were largely won over and the SPD was adopted in 2018.[10] The mixed-use scheme, with active ground floors targeted at independent retailers and made viable by the residential and office uses, is very much the future direction of town centre development. But whether it will be built, with the now former Councillor Gottlieb describing it as a 'sell out' and once more demanding the resignation of the Chief Executive, remains in doubt.[11]

Guildford

A similar story can be told in Guildford, a town hailed by Experian in 2013 as the 'luxury shopping capital of the UK'.[12] It was also the place that John Lewis had identified as their top target for a new store.[13] The difficulty, as the 2015 Town Centre Masterplan stated, was that 'whilst the town's historic core makes for a

Guildford: The 'luxury shopping capital of the UK', with huge demand for retailing but still with a diminishing number of shops.

pleasant shopping environment, many of the available units are small and poorly shaped, inconsistent with modern retail requirements'.[14] The masterplan included the North Street development, a 430,500ft² (40,000m²) shopping centre anchored by a John Lewis store that the council had been promoting for a number of years. It was, however, never built and in the years since the masterplan was published the amount of retailing in Guildford, far from expanding, has contracted markedly. The large Debenhams stands empty and is now being proposed as a residential scheme. The House of Fraser store on the high street received a temporary reprieve, but is now up for sale, with the Guildford Society reporting plans for it to become a hotel.[15] Meanwhile, the North Street scheme was shelved and new development partners, Berkeley Group and M&G Real Estate, are developing plans for 500 new homes and

20,000ft^2 (1,800m^2) of 'flexible commercial space, F&B and experiential ground floor uses'.[16]

So, Guildford, the town where the supply of shops was unable to meet demand, has seen a significant reduction in its retail floor area, such is the changing face of the high street. The pressure on units is having the effect of squeezing out smaller and independent shops. As local retailer Andrew Colborne-Baber told *Surrey Live*: 'People want to see small, independent traders who offer something a bit different ... but the sky-high rents in Guildford risk making that impossible.'[17]

Preston

This is not just a phenomenon of southern towns. For much of the 2000s, Preston sought to promote the huge Tithebarn scheme, which would have redeveloped 13ha of the city centre with a million square feet of space. A joint venture was signed with Grosvenor and Lend Lease in 2007 and the scheme was to have been similar in design and size to Liverpool ONE; a street-based redevelopment anchored by John Lewis and Marks & Spencer. Planning permission was secured in July 2009, but it was called in and subject to a public enquiry. There was controversy over the proposed demolition of the town's iconic modernist bus station as well as from neighbouring councils Blackburn and Blackpool, fearing the impact on their town centres.[18] The scheme was eventually granted permission only to collapse a year later when John Lewis pulled out. As the council leader Peter Rankin said at the time: 'We are in the middle of one of the worst economic and financial situations since the 1930s and it is now clear that the large scale comprehensive Tithebarn scheme is financially unviable. The world has simply changed and we have to move on and be realistic about what can be achieved.'[19] The council has instead progressed elements of the scheme on an incremental basis, including the refurbishment of the old market hall, an eight-screen cinema, and a bowling alley along with restaurants, bars and a street food hub. The bus station has also been saved, after being granted listed status.

These examples, along with Chester, represent a lost generation of town centre retail schemes that will not be missed. Given the problems experienced by Bradford and Stafford, these towns, along with others in our case studies that have seen schemes collapse, might consider themselves to have had a lucky escape. The shopping centres would have opened in the teeth of a new retail crisis without their anchor department store and, even if they had succeeded, they would probably have done so at the expense of the rest of the town centre.

The question is: what to do next? The problems that these retail schemes were meant to solve have not gone away. Many of the sites are now being brought forward as housing- or office-led schemes and, while town centre living is no bad thing, office jobs have been hit hard by the post-pandemic trend to continue homeworking for at least part of the week. There is also the question of what happens at ground level and how the schemes can add to the vitality of the town centre at a time when retail development is not viable.

BARNSLEY – THE COUNCIL TAKES THE LEAD

This brings us back to Barnsley in the mid-2000s, where the council now owns the Metropolitan Centre and has just seen its development partner Multiplex walk away, prompting *The Guardian* to proclaim 'controversial architect Will Alsop's plan to transform Barnsley into a Tuscan hill town has collapsed'.[20]

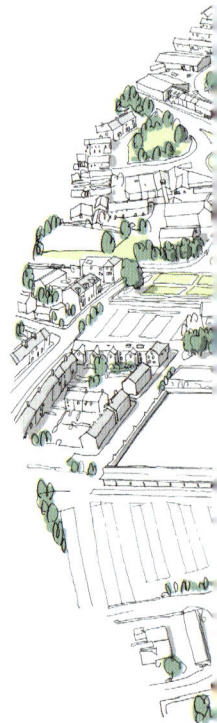

Barnsley Town Centre:
This is a drawing from a recent town centre masterplan undertaken by our company URBED showing the metropolitan Centre (1) and the Light Box (2) and the Alhambra Centre (3). The strategy is to build on the success of the market by diversifying the centre and promoting independent businesses.

Undeterred, the council established the 1249 Partnership (the date of the town's market charter), appointed new development partners and set about designing a new scheme. This was a relatively conventional covered shopping centre anchored by a Debenhams, alongside a slightly more architecturally expressive market hall which, to the disappointment of Will Alsop, was designed by Piers Gough of CZWG Architects. By 2007 the scheme was, in the words of David Kennedy, 'oven ready', with planning permission for 570,500ft² (53,000m²) of space, a price tag of £70 million and a start date of 2008.[21] The financial crisis put paid to those plans although they limped on through a series of redesigns and value engineering exercises for a full five years before the council eventually accepted that the scheme was unviable. In early 2014, the development agreement was terminated and the Partnership dissolved.

Thus far, the story is the same as the examples above. But then Barnsley took a different path. They found themselves owners of a run-down complex of buildings

looming over a town centre where expectations had been raised – something needed to happen. It is at this point that David Shepherd, who had taken over from David Kennedy, takes up the story.[22] He spent some time talking to other councils with stalled retail schemes. As dark skies gathered over the retail market, these councils were taking the brunt of criticism about lack of progress and yet had little influence over increasingly nervous developers and investors. They were being told they had no choice but to accept schemes that had been dumbed down and were being asked to invest more money and take on more risk. Many felt they had no choice given the political capital that had been invested. As David Shepherd told us, councils were finding themselves 'hoodwinked by a commercialised model that was using viability as an excuse to justify sub-standard schemes'.

Barnsley decided instead to develop the scheme themselves. They would employ development managers and a construction partner because they recognised that they lacked those skills, but the council would put up the funds, take the risk and call the shots. In March 2017, the council agreed to use a combination of reserves and borrowing from the Public Works Loan Board to fund the scheme that had been rebranded as The Glass Works with a price tag of £180 million. They also agreed to factor in an ongoing subsidy for running costs, accepting that this would no longer be a commercial scheme, at least not one that would interest private investors. As David Shepherd says, 'It was a scheme with a 300-year business plan, an investment in the future and the pride of the town.' The town centre was too important to the economy and psyche of Barnsley to be left to the private sector.

This philosophy fed through into the design of the new scheme, which was based around the public commons rather than a commercial mall. The market became the heart of the scheme and the team spent time visiting other markets for inspiration including Borough Market in London, Bolton Market, Altrincham Market and the Foodhallen in Amsterdam. The new market opened in November 2018, in a building that reuses the concrete structure of the original complex. The market stretches over two levels along with a Market Kitchen accommodating 10 independent food outlets. Despite some of the precedents that they visited, the aim was very definitely to avoid a 'hipster' market full of expensive 'craft' produce. The Market Kitchen, for example, included the original 'greasy spoon' cafés alongside a craft beer bar.

The result is a modern reworking of a traditional market and the scheme also includes a new public library and community/arts space called the Lightbox. There are also 25 retail units in a new arcade, which is anchored by a Next store that has relocated from a cramped unit elsewhere in the town. There is also a cinema and bowling alley and a new landscaped public square.

It is a big risk and it's too early to say whether it has worked. Having dropped as low as 6.4%, the town's vacancy rate has risen to 11.5% post-pandemic, although it is still two points below the average of our case studies. However, the owners of the town's other shopping centre, the Alhambra, where Next is currently located, have announced that it is going into administration. Barnsley is a mid-sized northern industrial town, within easy reach of Leeds, Sheffield and Meadowhall. It never had major department stores and so had less to lose than other towns in the current retail crisis. However, its strategy to reinvent itself based on its working class roots and the pride that people have in the town, together with public sector investment, shows one potential way forward for town centres. Analysis by the council after the 2008 recession showed that most of the new jobs in the borough were created

COVENTRY: MODERN HERITAGE

The city centre of Coventry, comprehensively rebuilt after the bombing raids of the Second World War, was for many years seen as a model of modern retailing that many other places would emulate. Concrete pedestrianised precincts and unloved modernist buildings became all too familiar and it's easy to forget that Coventry was the first and arguably the finest example of this 20th-century retail model. Elsewhere these modernist set pieces have been swept away, often to be replaced with malls, but what is to be done with Coventry?

There are currently plans to demolish the southern part of the city centre for the £320 million City Centre South scheme which includes almost £100 million of public money. The original shopping precinct and circular market hall are to be retained, but the plans show City Arcade, Bull Yard and Sheldon Square being replaced with a scheme that includes new retailing, leisure uses, a hotel, 1,300 apartments and a new Pavilion building, to which we will return in a moment.

Many people, including members of the Coventry Society, are horrified by the loss of this modernist townscape. The centre does however have many problems and many other people probably welcome the redevelopment, even if it does mean that Coventry would end up looking like every other city centre. However, the City Centre South scheme has been forced to evolve by the changing retail market. The early versions were much more retail-based whereas the current scheme is largely residential.

One of the most interesting elements of the scheme, which received planning permission in May 2021, is the Pavilion. This is described as featuring 'a dynamic variety of pop-up retail and leisure providers ... allowing the mix of offers to change and evolve to promote new local independent initiatives and artisans', as well as providing space for public events. This is an attempt to incorporate the pop-up retail into mainstream development as an alternative to a reliance on mainstream retailers. We are told, however, by sources close to the scheme that the developer is struggling with the viability of the Pavilion building and its inclusion in the scheme is in doubt.

in the town centre. It therefore makes sense to invest public money in the centre – although it may not make a commercial return it will generate sufficient income to cover borrowing and even potentially break even. It harks back to an age when retailing in the form of markets was seen as public infrastructure rather than the preserve of private developers.

THE DONCOPOLITAN

Another approach to town centre regeneration is illustrated by Doncaster, just 15 miles due west of Barnsley. In 2012 Doncaster was one of a number of towns bidding to be granted city status. One contribution to the discussion, posted by a self-proclaimed, old-school anarchist Warren Draper on a council-run arts forum, suggested that, if Doncaster wanted to be a city, it should start acting like one. He suggested that they set up a magazine that treated cultural life in Doncaster seriously, as if it were a city. The editorial in the first edition would proclaim, 'fake it until you make it'.[23]

Doncaster didn't achieve city status and only one person – the artist Rachel Horne – responded to the post. Together with Warren she formed the Doncopolitan, starting as a blog, then a radio show and magazine. Their strapline was 'building bohemia in the best little city in England', as Rachel wrote in the first edition, 'just because we are working class doesn't mean we are idiots'.[24] As well as publishing the magazine, the Doncopolitan organised pop-up events, exhibitions and poetry readings, drawing together and taking seriously all of the town's existing culture, culminating in a series of Culture Crawls linking 13 places hosting exhibitions, music and poetry. In 2015, the Chief Executive of Doncaster Council, Jo Miller, asked to meet Rachel and Warren. She said that the term 'Doncopolitanisation' had been used in cabinet meetings to describe the council's emerging strategy for the town. A strategy John Harris in *The Guardian* in October described as seeking to create a 'noisy, very human-focussed place for socialising and collective experience'.[25] Scott Cardwell, Assistant Director of Economic Development, told *The Guardian* that the strategy was 'perhaps not do an exact Hebden Bridge, but something along those lines' by latching onto the town's 'bohemian' potential.

The importance of grassroots culture has long been recognised in the big cities – that is why so many young people from towns end up heading for them – but there is no reason why this can't also happen in towns as we have seen in other places such as Sunderland and Wrexham. In Doncaster the council has been buying up vacant retail units and looking to let them for creative uses. The Cast Arts Centre, developed on a former car park on the edge of the town centre, is home to a programme of world-class theatre. The library and museum have been combined in a brand-new Cultural and Learning Centre and the old Wool Market has been opened as a food market selling artisan food and craft beer.

And yet the most recent retail strategy published in 2019 makes no mention of any of this. It states that Doncaster is a 'generally healthy town centre performing in accordance with its role' with a 'good range of retailer representation'.[26] Since then the town has lost its House of Fraser and Debenhams and its vacancy rate in 2021 was 20.6%, the fourth highest of all our case studies. As with many places, the link is not being made between retail policy and wider conversations about culture and creativity. Whether the council's Hebden Bridge-influenced bohemia vision is an appropriate strategy for an ex-mining town whose main industry is now Amazon fulfilment warehouses and call centres is still unclear. Certainly, the

Doncopolitan say that this is the exact opposite of what they were suggesting. It may be that this is the type of thing that needs to grow from the grassroots rather than via a council strategy.

SOUTH LANES, COLCHESTER

Just such an upswelling of grassroots retail can be found in Colchester, not that this was recognised by its two recent town centre assessments. The first of these studies, completed in 2016, states that: 'With major retailers looking to consolidate their space requirements into a smaller number of prime locations, Colchester Town Centre's declining status and performance makes it vulnerable and at risk in terms of its ability to attract and retain investment.' Of particular concern was the rise of its great rival Chelmsford, which had just opened a new shopping centre anchored by a John Lewis department store. The solution, according to the report, was to make the centre an 'attractive place to shop' (a statement of the blindingly obvious typical of these retail assessments), along with the provision of 'convenient and affordable parking' and the diversification into leisure uses and independent retailers.[27]

Despite that mention of independents, most of the report is concerned with Colchester's two shopping centres: Culver Square and Lion Walk (identified as needing major investment), the Fenwick department store and the fact that the town only has 24 of the 29 major retailers seen as essential to the retail health of a town. One of their recommendations was that there 'is a qualitative need for modern, larger units to provide "prime" space for retailers looking to locate to or re-locate within the town centre'. In other words, the town should respond to the contraction of retailing by building more retail space.

The South Lanes in Guildford: A thriving centre for independent traders hardly mentioned in the town's retail assessment.

Colchester's independent retailers are clustered around Sir Isaac's Walk, Eld Lane and Trinity Street near the old Roman Wall. It is an area where the traders have organised themselves, rebranding the area as the South Lanes and developing a package of measures to promote the area. As Neil Gibb, an independent retail consultant based in Colchester and one of the organisers of the initiative, told the local paper: 'Colchester's greatest asset is the network of small streets and lanes which contain a hive of small businesses, community projects and unique, one-off cafes and independent shops.'[28]

The South Lanes Project ran community days and clean-up campaigns. They organised a successful 'After Dark' project to persuade people to come out on winter's evenings. Themed nights included street entertainment, tasting sessions, free film screenings and late-night shopping. They have pioneered ideas like 'clustering', in which neighbouring shops coordinate special deals, and 'daisy-chaining', in which local shops recommend each other. All of this was gaining momentum through 2019 but there was increasing frustration at the lack of official support and recognition. In February 2020, soon after being shortlisted for the Rising Star Award in the Great British High Street Awards,[29] the South Lanes Project announced that they were putting the project on hold until they received support from the council and the town's Business Improvement District (BID).

In response to the announcement a council spokesman told the local paper, 'We have met with members of the project on several occasions, offering to fund street bunting and improvements to the visual appearance of premises',[30] while the BID said that they had invited the South Lanes Project to their 'independent business focus group which looks at different creative ideas that could be implemented across Colchester town centre'. The underline is our addition but reading between the lines there seems to be a certain tension here, leaving the impression that the South Lanes Project might have been seen as troublemakers?

The council instead commissioned a further retail study during the first COVID lockdown. It covered the same ground as the earlier report and remarkably came to the same conclusions, despite the number of comparison goods stores (items like household goods and clothing) having fallen from 241 to 190. The report makes no reference to the South Lanes Project and even though it does at one point state: 'During our site inspections, we identified a high number of [independent] shops and stores along Sir Isaac's Walk / Eld Lane' and at another point identifies Sir Isaac's Walk as having one of the highest pedestrian flows in the period after the first lockdown.[31] On publication of the report the South Lanes Project put out a statement on its Facebook page with three demands: that the council recognises the South Lanes as a place; that they allow the erection of signs and interpretation using the branding and that they provide some funding – the £25,000 spent on the second retail study would have been a good start.

Colchester was finally granted city status in late 2022, but both of the examples above show the tensions that exist in town centres. The future of town centres does not lie in more big retail – as we write there are *no* developers or investors willing to invest in building new retail-led development and the amount of mainstream retail is predicted to contract. The best alternative is to promote independent retail and other local businesses with the potential to generate town centre vitality. Yet many towns and their retail consultants remain enthralled by the retail rankings and continue to cling to the idea that attracting and retaining multiple retailers is the answer to their town centre. Of course most councils continue to support culture and enterprise but those activities are in different silos and are seen as subsidiary to the retail approach to the town centre. The irony is that, as the South Lanes traders pointed out, the money spent on consultants to undertake a retail assessment could have a huge impact if used to support the South Lanes, the Doncopolitan or grassroots initiatives in many other towns.

FROME INDEPENDENT

This sort of assessment is something that small towns find easier to embrace. As described in Chapter 5, we have used our data to calculate an Indi Index for all our case studies based on the ratio of multiple to independent retailers. The top 10 places with the highest proportion of multiples are dominated by high streets (that we will return to in the next chapter) and smaller towns like Todmorden, Totnes, Wisbech and Frome. We could look at all these places, each of which has an interesting story, but let's focus for a moment on the ancient market town of Frome, 25km south of Bath.

In 1994, the retail vacancy rate in Frome stood at 28% and up the picturesque Catherine Hill 60% of the 35 units lay empty.[32] Shoppers had deserted the town in favour of Bath and Trowbridge and trade had also been lost to a large edge-of-town Sainsbury's, approved on appeal. A study was commissioned by the Civic Trust Regeneration Unit, its recommendations enthusiastically taken up by Julie Grael, a town centre manager responsible for Frome, and her successor Katy Duke.[33]

The strategy started with small steps: children's exhibitions filled vacant shop windows, a Shop Watch Scheme was set up in liaison with the police and a community clean-up scheme was organised with the council. On Catherine Hill, a vacant property schedule was drawn up and the landlords were wooed, eventually agreeing to flexible leases and a 30% blanket reduction in rents. This allowed a successful case to be put to the District Valuer to reduce business rates (which had become higher than rents). A brand was created for the area and links with the local press generated positive press stories. The District Council also secured £1.7 million from English Heritage, together with £1 million in planning contributions from Sainsbury's, to support the refurbishment of buildings and the town centre management budget. This included grants to independent businesses taking on vacant shops, to cover fit-out and set-up costs. The results were remarkable – by 2007 the vacancy rate for the town had dropped to 5% and Catherine Hill was fully occupied. As Katy Duke writes in her blog, the street started with collectibles and antiques, then in the early 2000s moved to art and crafts and is now a place for retro goods, cafés, gifts and crafts. As she writes: 'This didn't happen because a few Londoners recently came to Frome, it has been a concerted effort by local people willing to put their money and time into its regeneration.'

Initially, the lead was taken by Mendip District Council and Somerset County Council but by 2010, as the initial budgets were spent and the councils were hit by austerity, the lead passed to the Town Council. This is the other great lesson of Frome, the way in which the community has taken control of the town centre's regeneration. Former Mayor of Frome, Peter Macfadyen, describes the process in his book *Flatpack Democracy*.[34] The starting point was to abolish politics so that candidates for the Town Council no longer represented political parties but their constituents and the town. This changed the whole ethos of the Town Council from fractious opposition and political point scoring to collaboration. The Town Council now employs more than 30 people, including five town rangers, and, as the Academy of Urbanism stated when it was awarded the Great Town Award in 2015,

'Frome has reinvented the role of the town council'. The Deputy Town Clerk Peter Wheelhouse told us that Frome is a very 'eventful' town that has countered national trends because of the large number of local entrepreneurs and 'the incredible community spirit'.

A good example is the former Cheese & Grain market hall, which the Town Council took on and has converted into an 800 capacity performance venue and recording studio run as a community business. The space still operates as a weekly flea and antique market and is also a venue for the Frome Independent, a huge market that takes place on the first Sunday of the month from March through to December. The Frome Independent started on Catherine Street but grew in 2012 when a series of pilot events called the 'Frome Super Market' expanded the market across the whole town centre. Two years later it was branded as the Frome Independent under the slogan 'Shop (independently), Eat (seasonally), Sleep (easily), Repeat (monthly)' and grew to hundreds of stalls attracting around 800,000 people a year.[35] The market has sections including designer/maker stalls, a suitcase sale for start-ups, home and garden including a plant market and a flea market, as well as a farmers market and other food and drink stalls. Each market also incorporates live music, street performance, workshops and activities for children.

Frome: The town that abolished politics and worked together to revive a moribund town centre through markets and independent retail.

TOWN CENTRES IN TOWNS

The diversity of towns that we have covered in our case studies makes it difficult to draw firm conclusions about the future of town centres in towns. The largest towns, like the cities, will probably benefit from the consolidation of mainstream retailers. But others risk missing out, and the old assumptions about attracting a key set of multiple retailers in order to maintain the town's retail ranking will no longer apply. Our case studies suggest that the towns that succeeded in building a shopping centre, particularly those that opened in 2012–15 are doing significantly worse than those that failed to do so. Rather than rely on big retail, town centres need to diversify, particularly in terms of independents, leisure, food and beverage, culture, housing and community. The question is how this is to be achieved.

Some of these uses remain commercial propositions, and a number of our case studies have seen retail-led schemes repurposed as housing- or office-led schemes with the values generated on the upper floors subsidising retail and service uses on the ground floor.

It is also tempting to see a diversity of uses bubbling up from community activity and local entrepreneurship. The criticism of this approach is that it only applies to places like Frome where an influx of engaged middle-class people has helped turn the town around. Nevertheless, there are lots of places, like Stroud, Totnes, Todmorden, Ludlow and even tiny Slaithwaite, where the energy of incomers has made a huge difference. The dynamic is different in these small towns, where the whole community pulls together to regenerate the town. However, the examples of Doncaster and Colchester show that community dynamism exists in many places if only it can be recognised and nurtured.

However, the other lesson from our town case studies goes back to Barnsley and the role of the public sector. Just as the original market halls were built by councils as a public service, so future retail may need to be seen as a public good. Town centres remain crucial to the economic and social life of towns; they are the focus for the community, a source of pride, an economic driver and job generator, a cultural hub and social centre. None of this requires the presence of multiple retailers and is too important to be left to commercial developers. By all means towns should encourage commercial development where it is viable, but they should also invest and engage as a public sector where it is not. These are activities that generate an income, cover borrowing costs and even make a small surplus, they just no longer make a commercial return. This is a textbook case for public sector intervention as we can see happening in many of our case studies.

15 THE HIGH STREET

Walking down the Belgrave Road in Leicester with Karan Modha, the dapper and energetic owner of Anokhi House Of Sarees, can take a long time.[1] He also runs the Belgrave Business Association and every few paces he stops to exchange pleasantries with people he knows, mostly from his parents' and grandparents' generation. He is one of the few third-generation children who have stayed to run the family business, as his contemporaries left for university and the professions. Karan's grandfather established the family business on Belgrave Road in the late 1960s and the shop caters to a customer base from across the Midlands and beyond, proud that it is one of the only shops to retain the wide cushioned shelves typical of saree shops in India.

Belgrave Road gives us an insight into another type of retail centre – the high streets that were once to be found across the UK. This book is called *High Street* because the term is used to describe all retail centres, but it also has a specific meaning, referring to the radial routes that run in and out of our towns and cities. Many of these streets were once lined with shops for large parts of their length. Indeed, they almost certainly contained more shops than town and city centres. For decades these high streets were a dying breed, their vitality only being glimpsed occasionally in places like Belgrave Road. But as our case studies show and as we describe in this chapter, many of those that survived are now thriving.

BELGRAVE ROAD, LEICESTER

In 1972, Leicester City Council took out an advert in the *Uganda Argus* telling the country's Asian community *not* to come to Leicester.[2] The Uganda government under Idi Amin had given the country's 55,000-strong Asian community 90 days to leave the country. The council in Leicester, citing pressure on housing, schools and social services, were keen that they didn't come there. The community naturally wondered what was so special about the East Midlands town. 'The message my family sent back to relatives in Uganda', Karen recalls, was that 'Leicester is not as big, and much more friendly than London and there is already a strong Hindu community'. Around half of those expelled from Uganda had UK passports and came to the UK, with almost 6,000 defying the advice and settling in Leicester. So successful was the community that they established along the Belgrave Road in the north of the city that other families who had initially settled elsewhere subsequently gravitated to Leicester. Within 10 years, half of the Ugandan Asian community lived in the city. The result is one of the liveliest high streets in the country and a place that gives a feel for what all high streets were once like.

Belgrave Road: The Diwali celebrations are the largest of their kind outside India.

The street is known as the Golden Mile and is lined with 186 shops running northwards from the fringe of the city centre. There are a few multiples on the street, including Tesco Express, bank branches and betting shops, but they are outnumbered by independents almost nine to one, the highest proportion of independent businesses in any of our case studies. These are mostly family-run affairs; the Ugandan Asians were, after all, a community of business people. There are six sari shops plus the largest concentration of Asian jewellers in the UK, together with other specialist shops (fireworks, cakes, decorations) serving the lucrative Asian wedding market, attracting customers from a wide area. There are also numerous food outlets, from takeaways to high-end restaurants. One of the people Karan introduced us to was Dharmesh Lakhani, owner of Bobby's restaurant, named after a 1973 Bollywood rom-com starring Dimple Kapadia (think Indian Brigitte Bardot). The café is all bright colours and melamine-topped tables with an extensive Gujarati vegetarian menu, described in *The Guardian* as 'an eatery where people go to eat, not to ponce and pose'.[3] In addition to this there are all the usual high street shops, including butchers, grocers, travel agents and hardware stores, invariably run as family businesses. The data collected for this study shows that the vacancy rate was just 4.8% prior to lockdown, much of which was at the southern periphery of the street. This has risen steeply to 8.2% post-lockdown but is still lower than the average of our case studies.

In appearance, were it not for the Diwali decorations, it would look like any other high street. At its centre once stood the British United Shoe Machinery factory that employed 4,000 people. The tightly packed terraced streets surrounding this and other factories in the area housed workers who shopped and socialised on the bustling high street. The factory closed in 2000 but, long before that, the high street would have been in decline like hundreds of similar streets across the country, were it not for the Ugandan Asian community.

The vibrancy and resilience of the streets come from its role as both a high street serving a community who still shop locally, and regional shopping centre for jewellery, saris and restaurants. Around 60% of the local population are of Indian, Hindu origin. They live in the terraced streets and have built a strong social infrastructure. Many of the local churches and public buildings, including the library that has been saved from closure, have been refurbished and converted to temples and community spaces.

And yet the street is also a major arterial route (the A607) carrying 26,500 cars a day, the poor air quality meaning that it is designated as an Air Quality Management Area. The flyover that until a few years ago disgorged fast-moving traffic into the heart of the area has been removed and, at the time of writing, work is underway to widen pavements and create a median strip to accommodate tree planting.[4]

In early November, Belgrave Road hosts the Diwali celebrations where the Hindu Festival of Lights goes on for two weeks, during which the street is bedecked with illuminations. In the November before COVID, 35,000 people flocked to the largest event of its kind outside India. It is this 'Indian-ness' that is key to Belgrave Road's success. The high street benefits from a very Indian way of shopping, using specialist local shops and networks of family business connections, tailoring clothes rather than buying off-the-peg and eschewing the supermarkets. All of this can be gleaned as you walk with Karan down the street where his family have done business for more than 50 years.

CURRY MILES: THE BALTI TRIANGLE

Belgrave Road is not alone. Across the country, there are high streets that have become associated with particular ethnic groups and have thrived as a result. Our case studies include St Marks Road in Bristol, which is also related to the Ugandan Asian community. We have also looked at Ladypool Road in Birmingham, associated with the city's Pakistani and Kashmiri community. Examples also include the Sikh community of Broadway in Southall, West London, and the Pakistani community on Wilmslow Road in Manchester. Elsewhere, streets have become the focus for the West African, Somali and Libyan communities, while others are associated with the Chinese community, although the latter tend to be characterised as 'Chinatowns' rather than streets.

Most of these high streets have followed a similar path. They started off as run-down places where ethnic minority businesses could gain a foothold. Forces of agglomeration attracted similar business and the community grew in both numbers and confidence. Local shops developed, serving the needs of the community, alongside restaurants that often served a wider community.

The process can be seen at work in Birmingham where, in 1977, Mohammed Arif, the chef at Adil's restaurant on Ladypool Road invented the balti. It was a dish inspired by the cuisines of Pakistan and Kashmir, its main feature being that it was served bubbling hot in the same wok-style dish in which it had been cooked. Within a decade the popularity of the balti had grown hugely and the area of south Birmingham where it had been created became known as the Balti Triangle. The Triangle consists of Ladypool Road, Stratford Road and Stoney Lane and, by the 1990s, there were 46 balti restaurants in the area, 26 of them on Ladypool Road. At the time, civil servant Andy Munro, author of *Going for a Balti*, used to run a balti club in the city.[5] Each month its members would visit a new restaurant dressed in their club ties sporting a wok motif, and debating how the restaurant should be scored on their star rating system. However, many of the Balti Triangle's clientele

Ladypool Road in Birmingham: One arm of the city's Balti Triangle.

were less discerning. This was where people came for a curry after a night on the town and Munro tells horror stories of the 'balti bovver boys' abusing waiters and scrawling offensive graffiti in the toilets. This was part of a wider phenomenon of 'curry miles', as satirised by the 'Going for an English' sketch in the BBC comedy series 'Goodness Gracious Me'.[6]

Today there are just eight balti restaurants left in the Balti Triangle, including the original Adil's and Shahi Nan Kebab, which also dates back to 1977. As Shahi's owner Azer told the *Birmingham Mail*, the 'white English' trade has largely gone and 'our main trade is from our own community'.[7] This has not heralded the decline of Ladypool Road, far from it. The restaurants have been replaced by a huge variety of independent shops, mostly serving the Asian market from a catchment area that stretches as far as Oxford, Bristol and Newcastle. In the same way that Belgrave Road has grown to serve the Indian Hindu community, so Ladypool Road serves the Pakistani Muslim community, who are becoming increasingly affluent. As Mohammed Ishtiaq, owner of Raj Brothers, which has also been trading since the 1970s, told the *Birmingham Mail*: 'Asian wedding dresses have become big business. In the 1980s and 1990s, first and second generation families would never have dreamt of spending up to £4,000 on wedding dresses.'

He explains that younger people 'come here to do some shopping – then eat something afterwards. They're not really specifically in the area to try a balti. So Balti Triangle for me represents shopping now'. Indeed the tastes of this group are far more cosmopolitan, and the area's most successful restaurant is now Turkish, with others serving cuisine from across the world. As Andy Munro says, the balti became so ubiquitous that people forgot how good the genuine dish was. 'What are left are mostly genuine decent ones (restaurants). I think it's about quality rather than quantity.' The Balti Triangle remains, but to serve the connoisseur rather than Birmingham's late-night hordes.

LOST HIGH STREETS

In his book *The Conditions of the Working Class in England*, Friedrich Engels suggests that 'by unconscious tacit agreement as well as with outspoken conscious determination' you could travel around Manchester on civilised streets, lined with shops and services, and be entirely unaware of the poverty to be found a few blocks away. The high street, in his view, was a conspiracy by the middle classes to avoid confronting the inequity of the city.[8] At the time all the major radial routes in Manchester were lined almost continuously by shops – Oldham Road, Rochdale Road and Cheetham Hill to the north, Bury New Road and Chapel Street through Salford, Ashton Old and New Roads to the east and Stockport, Wilmslow and Chester Roads to the south. There were also great high streets running off these radials, like Great Cheetham Street to the north and Stretford Road through Hulme, the latter once home to Paulden's department store, which we encountered in Chapter 1, the first in the city to have electric lighting, escalators and to sell Danish pastries.

John Cooper Clarke, in his book *I Wanna Be Yours*, describes growing up in 1950s Salford in a flat overlooking the junction of Bury New Road and Great Cheetham Street. The former, in that pre-motorway age, was still the road from London to Glasgow, while the latter was the main route from Liverpool to Sheffield. It may have been the 'busiest intersection in Northern England' but as he writes, it was also home to: 'three barber shops, Millicent's the ladies hairdressers, snooker halls, two cabaret joints, two dispensing pharmacies, three medical practices,

Stockport Road in South Manchester remains an important traffic route and a high street that has been through difficult times but is now thriving.

several movie theatres [including the Rialto super cinema], various car showrooms, two gentleman's outfitters, several patisseries, Freda Steff's bagel joint, Barclays Bank, a launderette, three pubs, three coffee bars, countless confectioners/tobacconists/newsagents, a wine shop, a valet service ... and UCP (United Cow Products) known throughout the industrial northwest as 'the Tripe Shop'. There was also Harry Davis's hotel, 'the hang out of Manchester's drag mafia' and the Assembly Rooms with its 'Louis XIV interior' that morphed into the Whisky A GoGo.[9] All of this (except the car showrooms) has gone, to such an extent that it's hard to imagine it ever existed. The junction today has one remaining parade of run-down shops, a McDonald's drive-thru and a council estate shielded from the road by railings and a hedge.

The radial routes through the affluent southern parts of Manchester have largely been spared this fate; Stockport Road is still lined with shops, Wilmslow Road is the Curry Mile and Chester Road through Sale and Altrincham is largely intact. But the others, together with hundreds of great high streets in cities across the country have gone, sometimes as a result of economic decline, but more often the victims of slum clearance and road widening schemes. Only in London do significant radial high streets remain as an example of what all UK towns and cities used to be like.

This is where the term 'high street' is confusing. It has become a term used to describe all in-town retailing (as opposed to retail parks) but, in the past, high streets and town centres were quite different. Town centres may have had the department stores and great markets but, in terms of sheer scale and diversity, the radial routes stretching out from the town centre through its inner and outer suburbs were at least as important. They were based on what Bill Hillier called the 'movement economy', the shops along the street finding it advantageous to locate where there was passing trade, good footfall and accessibility by public transport.[10] These high streets served their tightly packed surrounding communities as well as providing specialised activities that served much wider markets. The intensity of the movement economy determined the scale of economic activity. In small towns and low-density suburbs, the streets may only support occasional shopping parades but in the big cities the retail frontage spread to become continuous along the main radial routes, stretching its tentacles along secondary streets and down local streets until the whole city became one vast high street.

As Matthew Carmona describes, these high streets were about far more than retailing.[11] The economic activity spread upwards into the floors above the shops and stretched backwards into courtyards and alleyways to the rear, creating a strip of 'super diversity' that ran for miles through a city. The amount of office space, workshops, studios, community uses, small-scale industry and housing was far greater than the retail floor area – as the ONS has shown, retail jobs account for only a quarter of high street employment.[12] The diversity also encompassed the users of high streets, which were the places where people from all backgrounds came together, where immigrant communities were assimilated, were able to start businesses and find a sense of identity and belonging.

However, just as the few remaining patches of ancient woodland bear witness to the fact that Britain was once covered with forest, so the high streets that remain are remnants of this once great economic ecosystem. They have disappeared to a far greater extent than town centre retailing, such that it can be hard to envisage what these great streets were once like. Their decline has many causes, but, almost certainly the growth in the volume of traffic has made many streets unpleasant places to be. The activities of highway engineers, who have added more traffic lanes, narrowing pavements and removing on-street parking. In some cases, the shops have been demolished in anticipation of future road widening schemes, some of which happened, some of which remained as strips of grass. The economy of high streets was undermined as slum clearance demolished the surrounding communities, the new housing often turning its back on the street. The factories, with their workers who had flocked to the streets in their lunch break and after work, closed down. Then came the supermarkets, many of which, like Sainsbury's, had grown up on these great streets but outgrew them and moved away, taking with them many of the functions that had sustained the street.

Matthew Carmona compares these streets to the canal network, an infrastructure that is essentially obsolete, built for a world that no longer exists. Just as the canals have been repurposed as leisure destinations, because there was no point pretending that the railways had not been invented, so high streets need to find a new role. To do this we need to explore some of the remnants that survive and what they can tell us about the future of the high street.

HIGH STREETS IN LONDON: WELLING AND PECKHAM

Matthew Carmona starts his paper on 'The existential crisis of traditional shopping streets' with two pictures of Poplar High Street in London. In the first, taken around 1910, the street is thronged with people and lined with grand shopfronts. At the time, its 1km length included 'ten pubs, a bowling green, music hall, public library, vicarage (with church behind), two schools, a council office and a mortuary, all this embedded in a tight-knit urban grain that supported a diverse ecology of retail,

Welling High Street:
An ordinary high street,
full of traffic, which is
nevertheless doing
surprisingly well.

small-scale manufacturing, and service businesses.' The second photo shows a nondescript street with a few parked cars and high railings around a housing estate. Out of frame there are a couple of remaining takeaways, local shops and the bowling green, but 'little gives away its former role as the central social and civic artery of a community'. It is true that many London high streets have disappeared, but it is also the case that more high streets survive in London than in other places, and London is a good place to start in considering their future.

The case studies on which this book is based include a number of London high streets, one of the most ordinary being Welling in South East London. This was originally Watling Street, the Roman road from London to Dover that, for centuries, was the main route to the continent from the capital. The road is an intermittent high street running as straight as a die for 14km between Greenwich and Dartford. In Welling the high street stretches for 2.5km with just over 300 shops, almost 80% of which are independents. They include 48 beauty establishments (up from 35 in 2021), plus around 30 food shops including three butchers, a baker and a greengrocers (the fishmonger didn't survive lockdown). There are also 17 restaurants of various kinds and another 17 takeaways, both up on the figure 10 years ago. Its vacancy rate prior to lockdown in 2019 was just 4.5% and even now it is less than half the average vacancy rate of our case studies. It's not a particularly attractive high street – most of its buildings are post-war, it remains busy with traffic and buses and is lined with parking bays – and yet it is clearly doing well.

One reason for this became apparent in 2008 when the street's two supermarkets happened to close at the same time. The Tesco was being redeveloped, with housing on the upper floors, and the Co-op was being refitted as a Morrisons. The owner of the local record shop, Cruisin Records, told the local paper: 'I have never known things as bad as this, business has just died.'[13] Now that both stores have reopened, they anchor the street and provide parking. Welling is typical of many London high streets – it is busy with traffic and buses and surrounded by residential streets. It may have been through difficult years but it has avoided the fate of Poplar High Street and is far from being an anachronism like the canal system. The return of the supermarkets means that the role they perform as local shopping and service centres is similar to the role they have always played. Maybe the high street isn't dead after all?

One of our other London case studies is Rye Lane in Peckham, a very different type of street, in fact two types of street. By day it is dominated by the West African community (just under 37% of the population in the 2011 Census). The daytime street, in the words of Mark Davey, is all 'Chinese grocers pumping out Asian techno … markets offering an Africa and Asian focussed cultural cornucopia of fruit and veg, halal meat and fish, dispersed in climate denying blue plastic bags'.[14] Then after 6pm the street changes, as the hipsters emerge, the craft beer and specialist bars start to fill, the students emerge from the Music Theatre School and the Peckham Plex – Olivia Colman's favourite cinema – opens its box office.

As the street emerged from COVID lockdowns, like Welling it was in a healthy state, with a vacancy rate of 10.5% compared to the average of our case studies of 13.2%. The problem in Rye Lane according to Neil Kirby, Head of Regeneration at the London Borough of Southwark, is not dealing with decline, but imposing some sort of order on the chaos of unauthorised stalls, barber shops and bars that keep appearing overnight: 'Regeneration is the last thing Rye Lane needs!'[15] The council's job has been to try and maintain the precarious balance that makes the street so special: to protect local businesses like the African-Caribbean barbers who are being relocated to allow the creation of a new station square; to speak up for the tenants of railway arches who are seeing their rents triple; to stay close to the owners of the Bussey Buildings workspace who receive weekly offers to sell out; to fight a constant battle with developers buying up retail frontage (the cause of many of the vacancies) in the hope of building new apartment blocks. Peckham is a thriving high street and the main threat to its diversity and vitality is gentrification.

One of the ways this threat is being countered is the Peckham Levels, a former 300-space council car park, next to the station that was being used by only a handful of cars. Rather than sell to a developer, the council announced an open call for a 'positive alternative use' that would support arts and employment. Hundreds of ideas were proposed and, in November 2015, it was announced that a team led by the Make Shift Foundation (now Make Shift Create) would take the scheme forward.[16] In addition to a rooftop bar with views across London, the levels of the car park were divided up on the basis of the parking spaces into 50 studios for artists, makers and small businesses, space for retailers, markets and events as well as units for food businesses. The building opened its doors in December 2017 and now supports 300 jobs while saving the council £250,000 a year.[17]

Rye Lane may not be typical – not everywhere can be *Time Out* magazine's 11th coolest place on the planet (absolutely nothing to do with the number of *Time Out* journalists who live there).[18] But, along with the more prosaic example of Welling, it begs the question of whether it is premature to announce the death of the high street. The trend is actually one of improvement – in both cases the vacancy rate is lower than it was 10 years ago when Peckham was notorious for drugs and shootings. The question is whether these trends can also be found outside London.

Rye Lane in Peckham: where the difficulty is imposing some sense of order on the street's vitality rather than promoting regeneration.

RADIAL HIGH STREETS, GOSFORTH AND ECCLESHALL ROAD

To answer that question, let us start with a couple of radial roads in large cities. Gosforth straddles the Great North Road as it heads out of Newcastle, which no longer carries traffic heading for Scotland, but is still congested with cars and buses. Eccleshall Road is a former turnpike heading south out of Sheffield and likewise remains a busy traffic and public transport route. Both are also great high streets.

Gosforth is a classic high street, stretching for 1.5km with 166 shops including an Asda, Sainsbury's and M&S Food, the latter attesting to the affluence of the surrounding area, which boasts two of Newcastle's most expensive streets. Despite the supermarkets, convenience retail makes up only a small proportion (9.5%) of floor area and comparison shopping is also low (17.1%), meaning that 73.4% of shops are occupied by services. Our data allows us to explore these services, the most common of which are the 23 hairdressers and beauty salons (up from 13 in 2012). As the house prices might lead you to expect, there are also nine estate agents, although this is down from 12 in 2017. The centre has also held on to its six banks and its seven pubs but has not yet been colonised by the bars and restaurants seen in similar centres.

Eccleshall Road runs for 2.5km from the edge of Sheffield City Centre and includes 321 outlets. Approximately 18.6% of its floorspace is convenience, with 25 food shops, also including an M&S Food and a Tesco but no longer a grocers or greengrocers; 66.5% of the floor space is services, including 47 beauty outlets (up from 36 in 2012), 20 restaurants and 21 takeaways. However, the recent growth has been in bars, which have increased from nine in 2012 to 24 today (including the pubs). Eccleshall Road has an Indi ratio of 5.5 (52 independent businesses for every 10 multiples) whereas the figure in Gosforth is 2.1, which is surprisingly low. In both cases, the vacancy rate post-COVID (8.4% and 7.8%) is well below the average of our case studies and one is drawn to the inevitable conclusion that these streets are also doing well, certainly better than the death of the high street narrative would suggest.

MARYLEBONE HIGH STREET

Walking down Marylebone High Street you see what you might expect from one of the most affluent parts of London, an attractive street with beautiful shops, busy with people and with virtually no vacancies. It's true that it has been like this for nearly 20 years, but it was not always the case. In the 1990s it was run-down and shabby, many units were boarded up and many others were charity shops. The story of its transformation has lessons for other centres.

The street has just under 230 outlets and the most recent data suggests a pre-lockdown vacancy rate of just under 7%. The street boasts two international retailers, 23 national chains, 30 specialist independents and 72 independents, many of which are high-end luxury brands, alongside its role as a local convenience shopping centre.

None of this seemed possible in 1994 when the Howard de Walden Estate, which owns much of the street, employed Andrew Ashenden to turn the street around. In 2006 the street was shortlisted for The Academy of Urbanism's Great Street Award and Andrew Ashenden told the assessment panel his concept was to return Marylebone High Street to being a 'quintessential English high street'. He managed to persuade the estate to forego immediate profit but rather to curate the street over the long term. The first step was to attract two anchors – Conran's Orrery restaurant, which took over some derelict stables, and a Waitrose. The latter couldn't pay as much as the other supermarkets but helped set the tone for the street. Andrew Ashenden then 'touted' for the shops he wanted, identifying and attracting them with lower, or even peppercorn rents. One of the aims was to make it a 'foodie' street, an important component of which was the Sunday farmers market.

Marylebone High Street may seem like a unique situation, a few hundred metres from Oxford Street and surrounded by wealth, but there is a lesson in the way that high streets can be curated for long-term value rather than for immediate profit.

High Street Gosforth (above) and Eccleshall Road Sheffield (below): Two traditional high streets, full of traffic but still doing reasonably well.

DEALING WITH TRAFFIC: THE SALUTARY LESSON OF GARSTON

Before we get carried away with the success of high streets, we should remember the salutary case study of Garston in South Liverpool that we visited in Chapter 8, where we described the online business of The Liverpool Cake Fairy. In 2013 we were engaged to prepare a regeneration strategy for St Mary's Road and the surrounding area and The Liverpool Cake Fairy, with its bright pink shopfront, seemed to be one of the few sparks of hope on an otherwise desolate high street. Our client for that study was Rob Monaghan, who still lives in the area and updated us on progress.[19]

St Mary's Road used to be part of a high street, similar to the others we have been discussing in this chapter, a radial route running through South Liverpool to the airport and the industrial areas of Speke. The volume of traffic and the heavy lorries from the docks led to the road being widened and, in the 1970s, a bypass was built around the back of the shops in Garston. The bypass removed the through traffic, but St Mary's Road remained open to local traffic and buses, its wide carriageway suddenly feeling very empty. The street had a small supermarket at either end, a Netto (that became an Asda) with a frontage onto the new ring road and a Co-op that was more embedded in the street and perhaps because of this, struggled and eventually closed. The banks followed, along with a couple of pubs, and the street found itself in deep trouble. The bypass had robbed the street of passing trade and formed a barrier, cutting it off from part of its catchment area. But, more importantly, it hid the street from view so that soon everyone other than locals had forgotten it was there.

And yet, as Rob Monaghan tells us, even here there are signs of recovery. The Co-op store has been taken on by Aldi and the surrounding area is often cited as one of the city's upcoming districts, a place for young professionals to buy one of its affordable Victorian terraced houses and commute back into the city. The Liverpool Cake Fairy has moved on but other independent businesses have followed, one run by Rob Monaghan's niece, who has a children's party company in one of the old banks. All of this probably dates back to 2008 and Liverpool's year as Capital of Culture, when local artists declared the Independent Republic of Garston (with its own flag and passport).[20] The strategy we developed included the appointment of a local artist, Tina Ford, to paint the carriageway with brightly coloured paint along with planters and seating, and the Garston Space Agency, designed to allow independent businesses to take on empty shops.

As Garston demonstrates, the issue of traffic is not clear-cut. Shopping streets in town centres have been pedestrianised for years but high streets are a very different type of retail environment and taking away the traffic can risk undermining their 'movement economy'. And yet removing traffic is one of the measures most often proposed to revive high streets, particularly after the temporary measures that were introduced during COVID. Just north of Garston, the high street of Lark Lane, another one of our case studies, is debating whether the street should be closed to traffic. Elsewhere in London the debate about Low Traffic Neighbourhoods (LTNs) is also affecting high streets. In some cases, LTNs include local high streets and in affluent areas the exclusion of traffic can be a benefit, as would probably be the case in Lark Lane. The worry is where traffic is excluded from streets that rely on more than just their local catchment area, that are dependent on passing trade and the movement economy. As we saw in Chapter 4, the town of Ashington in the North East has reintroduced one-way traffic and chevron parking onto its high street as part of a successful strategy of regeneration. Another worry with LTNs is that they channel more traffic onto a small number of main roads, which in London are also probably high streets and become even more clogged with traffic and pollution as a result.

Of course, we all believe in the walkable city and the reduction in car use, but high streets existed long before mass car ownership and the exclusion of traffic needs to be handled with care. This doesn't rule out measures to reduce the impact of the car. As with Belgrave Road where we started this chapter, many streets are looking to make COVID measures permanent – widening pavements, reducing the number of carriageways, reducing speed and creating cycle lanes. On-street parking is perhaps less clear-cut. Ideally it should be removed, but in some places, passing trade will be car-borne and some provision for parking will be required.

In this chapter, we have gone in search of the 'crisis on the high street' and failed to find it. It's true that many of the great high streets that existed in the past, like Poplar High Street in London or Great Cheetham Street in Manchester, have disappeared, victim of the supermarkets, traffic engineering and bad planning. We may have lost a significant proportion of the high streets that existed in the 1950s, but that does not mean that the high street is dead, or that the ones that remain are an anachronism like the canal system. In the case studies on which this book is based the high streets have the lowest vacancy rates and the highest number of independent businesses. We might attribute this to lockdown and people shopping locally while working from home and shopping locally, but the trend was clear before the pandemic. High streets are not dead – the ones that remain (at least those in our case studies) are thriving. There is of course a tendency with case studies to only pick successful places and there are undoubtedly high streets in declining towns, with less affluent catchment populations, which are suffering. However, even where high streets have collapsed, like Garston, they contain within them the seeds of their revival too. The 'crisis on the high street' is a misleading term – there is a crisis of big retail and the town and city centres dependent on multiple retailers have suffered. But high streets, which have always been far more reliant on independent retailers and which are benefitting from retail trends like the growth of convenience shopping, are doing well. Because of this they hold lessons that are applicable to all town and city centres.

St Mary's Road in Garston: Until recently a street in deep trouble because of the removal of through traffic, but now showing signs of revival.

16 CONCLUSIONS: NEW LIFE FOR TOWN CENTRES

We started this book in the Castlegate district of Sheffield, once the beating heart of its shopping centre with six major department stores, but now largely devoid of shops. We told the story of the city's unsuccessful attempts to build a new city centre shopping scheme and the humiliating announcement that its John Lewis store was to close despite the council offering a £4 million rescue package. The roots of Sheffield's problems do not lie in the current retail crisis, or even the previous retail crisis of 2008–12. Sheffield's problems stem from the retail crisis in the 1990s and followed the completion of the Meadowhall shopping centre a few miles away. The city's story is a warning that town centre retailing is not a given – get things wrong and it can collapse.

This type of collapse has been the great fear of the current retail crisis, the start of which dates back to late 2017. In the two years that followed, there were 260,000 retail job losses and more than 30,000 store closures. Local papers were full of local traders saying that their high street had become a 'ghost town' while the national papers ran headlines about the impact of online retail and the scandal of how little tax they paid. Then, just as things seemingly could get no worse, we were hit by COVID and all non-essential retail was forced to close. Despite government support and the furlough scheme, 2020 saw a further 182,564 retail job losses, culminating in the collapse of Debenhams and Arcadia. And then, as the high street started to recover from COVID, retailers were hit by a cost of living crisis, reducing customer spending power. There were signs in 2022 that the situation was improving, with *Retail Week* reporting the lowest number of store closures for five years and the number of independent stores increasing by 1,335 units.[1] However by the end of 2022 the Centre for Retail Research was reporting just over 150,000 job losses, worse than 2021, suggesting we are not out of the woods yet.

Kingston-upon-Thames: One of 14 metropolitan shopping centres in London, Kingston is a county town that has been absorbed into the capital. Serving affluent South London its centre is ranked above many small cities elsewhere in the country.

WHERE DID THE CRISIS COME FROM?

One thing we have sought to understand is the cause of the current crisis and how it relates to previous crises that have hit the high street. The threats to town centres from COVID and the cost of living crisis are clear enough. What is less clear are the causes of the retail crisis that started two years earlier. At the time it had seemed that town centres were recovering after the 2008–12 crisis, the economy was not in recession, confidence was returning, and investment was once more flowing into retail development. Then, as if from a blue sky, we were plunged into a new retail crisis. Some say this was a result of the growth of online retail, others the pernicious impact of the 2017 business rate revaluation. The finger of blame has been pointed at the uneven tax burden between physical and online retail, at the rising cost of labour and the minimum wage, changing consumer trends, the fall in home ownership impacting on DIY and furniture sales, the trend towards buying experiences rather than stuff, the declining number of young people who drive and therefore can't reach out-of-town centres and the move away from the weekly shop and towards convenience purchases. Undoubtedly, all of these trends are likely contributory factors but none of them is a smoking gun – neither individually nor collectively do they explain the current retail crisis.

We do however know that gradual trends can precipitate dramatic change – the gradual impact of the issues listed above will eventually become the straw that breaks the camel's back. The book *Climax City* describes how complex systems do not change in a linear fashion.[2] Patterns remain stable as the inputs to the system gradually change, but then there is a 'phase transition' as the pattern dissolves and a new pattern emerges. The current retail crisis is just such a transition – a series of factors that have been building for years caused the pattern of retailing on high streets and town centres to collapse. However, complexity theory tells us that a phase transition is just that: a transition from one stable pattern to another. The hope must be that what we are looking at is not the death of the high street but its transition into something different. It is a transition that has involved much pain but the hope is that we could transition into a better pattern, one which replaces the 'clone towns' of recent years with more diverse town centres with a greater variety of businesses and other uses.

THE LONG VIEW OF THE CURRENT CRISIS

In Part 1, we traced the roots of the current retail crisis from the arrival of supermarkets in the 1950s, via the explosion of out-of-town retailing in the 1980s and 1990s, the rise of the clone town in the 2000s, through the financial crisis after 2008 to the brief recovery of the mid-2010s. This is the story that contains the real explanation for the collapse of retailing at the beginning of 2018.

The story starts with the growth of retail chains, many dating back to the 19th century. For the first half of the 20th century these chains traded alongside independent businesses in town centres and along high streets. Self-service retail arrived from the US after the Second World War, allowing a handful of these chains to grow into supermarkets. Initially the supermarkets traded on high streets, knocking together neighbouring shops to create bigger units. However, they outgrew the high street, moving to large sites with parking as car ownership increased. They grew and grew, until there were 8,000 supermarkets in the UK accounting for 97% of grocery sales (which in turn makes up half of all retail spending). The supermarkets ate the high street. In many cases they caused terminal decline – hastened by road widening and slum clearance schemes, to such an extent that it is hard to grasp (at least outside London) how extensive these high streets once were. Those that remain are like isolated woodlands, remnants of a once vast ancient forest.

The supermarkets had less effect on larger town and city centres with their clothes shops and department stores. These places were, however, threatened by another American import – the mall. UK planning policy initially resisted out-of-town retail development and new retail investment tended to happen within existing town centres. A huge number of in-town malls – such as the Arndale Centre chain – were built with the connivance of local councils. They took a wrecking ball to large sections of town centres, destroying entire ecosystems of independent businesses. The 'Rape of Britain' as Colin Amery & Dan Cruickshank called it in the title of their 1975 book[3] could be seen as the start of the corporatisation of town centre retail, in which the diversity of independent businesses and the flexibility of traditional street patterns was sacrificed to big retail. To return once more to our forest analogy, ancient woodlands were cut down and replaced with a monoculture.

Then came the free market policies of the 1980s and the belief that the market knew best. The floodgates were opened to a wave of out-of-town retailing. Headlines focussed on proposals for up to 50 huge out-of-town malls, most of which were never built. Meanwhile, retail parks (strip malls as they are called in the US) were being consented to on the edge of every town. They initially catered to bulky goods like furniture, carpets and DIY, but soon all types of retail were heading out of town – a symbolic moment being the first out-of-town M&S in 1984.

By the early 1990s, there was growing concern about the impact on town centres. URBED were commissioned at the time to undertake a major government study published as *Vital and Viable Town Centres*, as part of a major change in planning policy.[4] And it worked! Only a handful of regional shopping centres were built, and a new planning 'sequential test' required developers to demonstrate that there were no in-town sites before they were allowed build out of town. In the US, traditional town centres had been wiped out by the uncontrolled growth of out-of-town malls but, by 2001 in the UK, 86% of retail development was being built in existing town centres.[5] This triggered a boom time for UK town centres, to an extent that would have been inconceivable 10 years earlier. However, two trends emerged during this period that help explain the current crisis.

The first of these was the asset-stripping of many of the major retailers. Profitable retail chains were acquired, their stores were sold and leased back, or mortgaged, huge dividends were paid to investors and the companies were left loaded with debt. In 2003 a debt-free Debenhams was sold to a private equity consortium for £600 million. Having taken out £1.2 billion in dividends they 'flipped' the company after a few years, floating it on the Stock Exchange with £1 billion of debt. These retailers, many with Victorian roots, were left in a precarious state, unable to invest in their stores and vulnerable to any downturn in the market.

The second trend relates to town centre development. As we have described, retail consultants would advise councils that their town centres were falling behind in the retail rankings and that they needed to build a new shopping centre to attract multiple retailers. Almost every large town and city in our case studies was promoting a retail scheme in the 2000s, many of which were finished in a great rush before the financial crisis of 2008. Other places were disappointed and spent years trying to revive their scheme. The lucky ones failed, and are now looking at alternative options with a greater mix of uses. The unlucky ones – Stafford and Bradford – managed to complete their schemes in the brief window of retail optimism after 2014. They now have some of the highest vacancy rates of all our case studies. They are left with an old town suffering high levels of vacancy, and a new mall having to survive without its Debenhams or Topshop.

A RETAIL CRISIS NOT A HIGH STREET CRISIS

This brings us to one of our most important conclusions: we don't have a crisis on the high street, we have a crisis in big retail. Over recent decades we allowed our town centres to be taken over by 100 or so retail chains, we even gauged the success of these town centres by counting how many of these retail chains were present. Many of these retail chains have collapsed in the last 10 years and most of those that survived have contracted, laid off staff and closed poorly performing stores. The blame for this lies with the retailers themselves and their corporate owners, not with town centres. Our town centres can be criticised for becoming over-reliant on these retailers, but cannot be blamed for their collapse.

The question is, what does life after big retail look like? We have quoted retail agents like Savills predicting that the UK may have 40% more retail space than it can support.[6] If true, this is a worrying figure for many town centres because it will not be evenly distributed – strong centres may lose only a small amount of retail, while weaker ones could be virtually wiped out. However, while the UK has around twice the retail floorspace per capita as Germany, the 4.6ft^2 of retail floor space per person in the UK is nothing compared to the 23ft^2 for every person in the US.[7]

It is also not clear how much of this projected surplus is based on assumptions about the space being occupied by mainstream retailers. Demand for space from the big retail brands will be down, but this doesn't stop space being let to other retailers. We have come across retail space being used as trampoline centres, crazy golf installations, escape rooms and ping-pong halls. We have heard also about beauty salons and nail bars moving from suburban parades into town centres because the rents allow them to do so, not to mention charity shops that have long kept the lights on in units that might otherwise be vacant. There are also examples of community uses, crèches, architects' offices and many other activities taking place in old retail space. In all but the most run-down centres, space can normally be let one way or another – that is not the issue.

The issue is that the space cannot be let on terms that make it a viable proposition for retail landlords and developers. We have been told by retail agents that trampolines and similar uses are all well and good, and can serve a useful function in maintaining activity and footfall, but the rent doesn't allow landlords to make a profit, doesn't provide a return on capital investment, doesn't even cover the cost of building upkeep and cyclical maintenance. Even when there is a prospect of letting space to a mainstream retailer, the demand for rent-free periods, short leases with regular break clauses and turnover rents makes it unviable. So, in addition to a crisis in big retail, we have a crisis in retail property that has seen the collapse of the retail landlord Intu and the suspension for a period of the M&G Real Estate portfolio that was heavily invested in shopping centres.

This collapse of retail property investment means the end of long cherished plans to build new retail space in many towns and cities. Painful as it might be to abandon schemes that have been in the pipeline for years, many places are realising that this may be a blessing in disguise, allowing them to rethink the role of their town centre. Within our case studies Guildford, Paisley, Chester, Preston, Aylesbury, Coventry, Nottingham, Sheffield, Norwich and Winchester are all developing mixed-use schemes on sites that were once earmarked for a new shopping centre. The viability of these new schemes is anchored by housing or offices on the upper floors with ground floor retail space being almost incidental. More worrying is the future of the shopping centres built in the last 10 years that are focussed almost entirely on serving the needs of the big retailers – what happens to them when they need to be refurbished and refreshed?

SIX TRENDS THAT WILL AFFECT FUTURE RETAIL

In Part 2 we reviewed future retail trends and came to a series of conclusions about how these trends may impact on town centres. These chapters were based on retail sectors but many faced similar issues and we can identify six trends that are likely to be important in the coming years:

1. The march of the independents

In many places independent businesses are rapidly filling the gaps left by the multiples. Independent and creative businesses, artisan food outlets, vinyl record shops, vintage clothing emporiums and independent bookshops are all growing. This is not only true of great independent shopping districts like Camden Lock, Brighton's North Laine or Manchester's Northern Quarter, it can also be found in smaller towns and villages (Frome, Todmorden, Slaithwaite) and suburban centres (Chorlton, Gosforth and Eccleshall Road) where there are lots of commuters. Independent businesses also dominate areas with large ethnic minority populations, like Belgrave Road in Leicester or Ladywood Road in Birmingham. These businesses are far from all being artisan hipsters; they include beauty salons, barbers, nail bars and vaping shops all of which are growing even more rapidly and moving into town centres.

Before we get too carried away, we should recall that at the height of the retail crisis in 2019 there were more job losses and business closures amongst independent businesses than the multiples. The independent sector is fragile, with limited reserves and high levels of debt. It is just that, for every independent business that folds, there is another one willing to give it a go. The vitality of the sector makes it a huge opportunity for authorities looking to regenerate their town centres. A relatively modest package of measures to support independents can have a huge impact. In our case studies, we have come across schemes making available small fit-out grants and rates relief, encouraging independents to take on vacant units. We have seen councils acting as intermediaries, taking on vacant units and letting them to independents. We have seen market stalls, pop-up units and even an independent department store in Bournemouth creating accessible, low commitment space that independents can take on. We also heard about 'daisy-chaining', 'clustering' and after-dark festivals linked to late-night opening in Colchester, as well as the usual business support and advice and promotion.

2. The return to the high street

The second trend has seen the return of activities to high streets that had been thought lost. This is happening in a number of sectors; IKEA, for example, are moving away from huge new out-of-town stores and instead looking to create high street stores where their products are on display but where most purchases are subsequently delivered from a distant warehouse. They have even taken on the flagship Topshop store in London's Oxford Street. The trend is known as 'showrooming', where physical stores are used to display goods and give advice but not to transact, with purchases being made online. It is driven by the 'halo effect' – online retailers receive significantly more web traffic from places where they have a physical store. As a result, many previously online-only retailers are opening physical stores – even Boohoo has opened a physical shop in Manchester.

However, the big return to the high street has been the supermarkets. For the last two decades the major supermarkets have been opening smaller convenience stores, normally on high streets. Since 2014, investment in large out-of-town stores has largely ceased and the convenience stores have been the main area of expansion, responding to people shopping little and often rather than doing a big weekly shop. Some feared that the supermarkets were targeting the last remaining independent convenience stores that had survived by being local and opening long hours. While we have not come across detailed research documenting the impact of smaller supermarkets on high streets, our data shows that the number of independent food shops has increased over the last 10 years. This is reinforced by a number of our case studies, such as Welling, which have shown that the presence of a supermarket is crucial to the success of the street, acting as an anchor that other shops rely upon.

Perhaps the most surprising new arrival on the high street is Amazon, and the contactless high street grocery stores that they have started to open. This is on a small scale at the moment but, given their ambition and resources, who knows where it will lead – their Chinese rivals Alibaba already have a chain of 250 contactless grocery stores using facial recognition software.

Epsom: The town had been seeking to use planning policy to prevent retail units from being converted to other uses, something that is no longer possible after the introduction of Class E.

3. Omni-channel retail

This brings us to the third trend – a convergence of online and physical retailing. The proportion of UK sales that take place online rose from 10% to 19.2% between 2012 and the first COVID lockdown in 2020. The rate spiked hugely during lockdown as non-essential physical retailing was forced to close, the big question being where will it settle? As we write, the rate is 26.1% and falling and as a result of this some online retailers are suffering. The furniture retailer Made.com has collapsed, as has Missguided, one of the biggest online fashion retailers. The latter has been bought out of administration by the physical retailer Fraser Group. Meanwhile, Boohoo have warned of lower sales and ASOS have issued profit warnings. We should not assume that the march of online retailing is inexorable and while no one knows, it may be that the online market share will stabilise at around a quarter of retail sales.

What will happen instead is a merging of physical and online retailing, what retailers call 'omni-channel' retailing. Companies will have physical shops, and their own website, plus virtual shops on Amazon, eBay, Facebook and Alibaba. The mainstream retailers that have thrived, like Next, have embraced this multi-channel world (in Next's case probably due to its origins as a catalogue retailer). There are also opportunities for smaller independent retailers who no longer need to rely on trade coming in through the front door of their shop. They can easily establish their own website using sites like Shopify or IONOS and sell via social media and on sites like Etsy, Discogs (for record stores), Bookshop.org (for independent bookshops) and a rash of vintage clothing sites like Depop and Thrifted. Online retail has disrupted the high street by levelling the playing field between the big legacy retailers and the small insurgents. Far from killing the high street it could be its saviour.

4. Touching, feeling and looking

One of the reasons for the enduring appeal of physical retail is the ability to experience products, to touch and feel, to sit on furniture and try on clothes. The trials and tribulations of online fashion brands have been blamed in part on the high volume of returns. People bracket their purchases, buying their size plus a size or two larger and smaller, returning everything but the one that fits. People are also becoming disillusioned with the manipulation of online images and the way that reality never quite lives up to the promise. Physical retailing overcomes this – it may be uncomfortable for your friend to tell you look awful when you come out of the changing room, but it saves a lot of hassle.

Physical retailing is also a collective experience as we learnt from our visit to Liverpool ONE, where the young people like to see and be seen, to strut and pose, check out what everyone else is wearing and build up to a big night out later in the day. The same may be true for very different demographics in bookshops, antique emporia and garden centres. They may not be building up to a big night out but there is theatre in seeing what is on display, nosing into other people's purchases, finding that treasure that you never realised you wanted until you saw it. These are all qualities you can't get in an online store.

5. Authenticity and uniqueness

It may be a relatively minor retail sector, but the story of record shops holds many lessons for town centres. The sector became dominated by a few major players as CD sales in the 1990s generated huge profits. With the advent of music streaming this market disappeared very rapidly – who's going to buy a CD when any track you could ever want is available for free online? The response was to return to vinyl and to discover that, when people loved an artist, they wanted to own a physical artefact and an LP is better than a CD in this respect. Our data shows record shops were still declining in 2012 but since then their numbers have seen a modest recovery. The same is true of bookshops for similar reasons.

The quest for authenticity has also seen the growth of the online store Etsy that, despite a recent relaxation in the rules, is a marketplace for either handmade crafts or vintage items. It caters for people craving something other than the mass-produced anonymous products of the mainstream retailers, be they physical or online. The trend can also be seen in food retail where there has been a growth of craft and artisan makers/retailers. Markets are up 31.7%, delicatessens by 12.5% and grocers by 67.6% (although this will include the small supermarkets) and even bakers are up 8%. There has been a growth in shops selling real food where you are served by someone who has probably been personally involved in the making of the product.

Bury: This industrial town on the northern edge of Greater Manchester thrives despite intense competition from other centres and a not particularly attractive town centre, because of the authenticity and vitality of its 'world-famous' market.

6. Experience rather than stuff

The final trend is one that has been widely cited by others – people's desire to spend their money on doing things, going on holiday, having a meal or a drink with friends, rather than buying ever more stuff. Of course, this took a knock with COVID lockdowns when people were not able to go out. However, the trend from our data is clear: the number of shops in town centres is on a downward trend while services are on the rise. Since 2012, the proportion of outlets in use as shops has fallen from 41.9% to 35%, so that 65% of all units are now services. In our case studies the number of hair and beauty outlets has risen by a third and food and beverage outlets are up by almost 20%, while clothing shops are down by 28.5%. Indeed, if you take out services that are declining, like banks and other offices (down by 16.4%), then the growth of experiential services is even greater. What this means is that town centres are places where shopping might be regarded as a secondary pursuit. Their primary role is as providers of services, or pampering, or drinks with friends (bars up 41%), or frappuccinos (cafés up 12.7%) or a good meal (restaurants up 20%).

But the diversification of town centres goes further than beauty parlours and coffee shops. We started this book with the story of Sheffield and how the city lost much of its retail role. But other than a few transitional places Sheffield City Centre is thriving. It is full of students from two universities, both of which are in the city centre. Its old cutlery factories have been colonised by creative businesses, new offices have been built and it is increasingly seen as a good place to live, has excellent theatres, art galleries and cinemas and its hotels are full of visitors and conferences. The notion that town centres are just about retailing is a historical aberration – town centres are about more than shops. It is something that we came to accept in the second half of the 20th century but it isn't inevitable.

These six trends may help explain the crisis in the big retail chains, but they also hold out hope for the future of high streets and town centres.

FUTURE TOWN CENTRES

In exploring how these trends will affect town centres we need to remember that the terms 'high street' and 'town centres' cover a huge diversity of places and their impact on big city centres will be very different to suburban parades, northern industrial towns or prosperous market towns. In Part 3, we therefore explored the issues facing city centres, malls, towns and high streets.

A few years ago, we would have told a fairly simple story of retail consolidation. The retail chains were looking to consolidate their operations into the largest town centres, using their online operations to reach the rest of the country. This was good news for the largest centres, which would continue to thrive, but was potentially very bad news for smaller towns. The retail crisis has changed this, partly because what the big retailers do is less consequential, but also because the whole retail hierarchy has been turned on its head. The big cities, reliant on office workers and tourists, found themselves hardest hit during the pandemic, especially London's West End. Meanwhile, suburban centres and smaller towns thrived on the back of home workers who were no longer in their city centre offices at lunchtime but popping out from home to shop locally. However, while the Centre for Cities High Streets Recovery Tracker showed the impact of COVID on cities in terms of footfall and other indicators, this is not particularly reflected in vacancy figures. The vacancy rate in our city case studies has risen slightly more rapidly than other categories but is still below

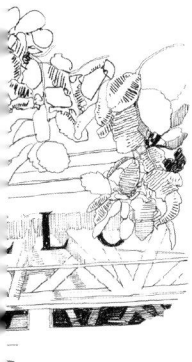

the overall average. The size and diversity of cities, and their large catchment areas, means that they will recover from COVID, even with the persistence of homeworking.

COVID has also affected out-of-town retail. Malls like the Metrocentre in Gateshead and the Westfield Centre in London (both with vacancy rates of more than 20%) found themselves over-reliant on retail chains while also being shunned by shoppers worried about social distancing even after the lockdowns were lifted. Meanwhile retail parks, with lots of parking and space for social distancing did well, and had the lowest vacancy rates in the year after COVID. The vacancy rate in our out-of-town case studies has risen from 5.3% in 2012, the lowest of all our categories, to 15.2% in 2022, the second highest. These out-of-town centres also have the lowest percentage of independent outlets, with an Indi Ratio of 0.5 (five independent businesses for every 10 multiples) compared to the average across our case studies of 2.7. They also have the highest level of comparison retailing (37.4% compared to an average across all case studies of 27%) and the lowest level of services (58.6% compared to an average of 65%). For these reasons, the retail trends described above make malls vulnerable, at least for the moment. Our case study figures relate to out-of-town malls but the trends equally affect in-town malls, it often being the case that the towns with the highest vacancy rates are being dragged down by a struggling mall.

None of this means that we can write off malls in the future. It is tempting to develop a narrative that out-of-town malls have had their day and that the future lies with traditional town centres; after all a third of the US's 1,200 malls have been abandoned or are in terminal decline. The UK has plenty of failed in-town malls, many of which have been acquired for redevelopment by the local council, like Bradford's Alhambra Centre. But there is no sign of the UK's clutch of large out-of-town malls failing and their owners will no doubt find ways to bounce back in the future.

The places that are doing best in our case studies are high streets, which is not what we were expecting when we started the work. We have looked at 13 high streets and suburban centres, of which only nine are covered by our data, so it is a small sample. But nevertheless the average vacancy rate is just 9.2% and the Indi Ratio is 3.8 (38 independents for every 10 multiples), much higher in some places. But it is striking that these high streets were doing well long before COVID. The vacancy rate in our sample had fallen to just 6.5% in 2018, and high streets have outperformed most other categories in our sample since 2012. And yet, as we describe in Chapter 14, the high streets that we have today are only a fragment of the great network of high streets that existed in the 1950s. If we take the long view, the UK's high streets have been decimated, but the world has turned, and they are thriving once more.

The category in our case studies that is doing least well is 'small cities and larger towns', in which we looked at 12 places. The data needs to be treated with a degree of care because the sample is also small. However, there does seem to be a pattern, with places like Bradford, Sunderland, Wrexham and Coventry being in the shadow of a larger centre. Smaller towns in similar geographical locations have managed to carve out a complementary niche, but the larger centres are competing head on with the big cities for a diminishing pool of mainstream retailers – and they are losing out.

These general trends are important but the other lesson from our case studies is that everywhere is different and local factors matter just as much. Why is the vacancy rate in the Metrocentre 22.1%, the third highest in our case studies, while the Trafford Centre has 11.1% vacancies and Meadowhall just 9.9%? The same is true of other categories – why is the vacancy rate in the historic market town of Skipton a minimal 7.7% while in the historic market town of Stafford it is up at 20.2%? Why is the rate 11.5% in Barnsley yet 20.6% in Doncaster, 12.2% in the Manchester satellite town of Bury but 20.2% in more affluent Stockport? Local factors matter and the actions of the local authority can make a huge difference, both positively and negatively. The places with the highest vacancy rates tend to be those that invested in new retail space at the wrong time, whereas other places have taken more successful action to turn around their centre.

TOWN CENTRE STRATEGIES

We have painted a picture of town centres that have suffered through the retail crisis, COVID and the rising cost of living, but have proven to be resilient. We have looked at 100 case studies, 87 of which are physical places and none of them has collapsed – even those that have experienced severe problems show signs of recovery. For all the dire predictions of the crisis on the high street, to paraphrase Jane Jacobs, it seems that town centres contain within them the seeds of their recovery. Many of the retail trends described in this chapter potentially aid this process and hold out the hope that the future high street could be more interesting, diverse and independent than the clone towns we've become used to. They will be places with a greater mix of uses, with people living there, with more services and hospitality, with a thriving evening economy and with a focus on public services – all of this sitting alongside a strong ongoing retail role with the most resilient of the multiple retailers and a strong independent retail sector. As we said in the Introduction, this book is meant as a diagnosis of what ails the high street, not a handbook for town centre regeneration. However, it is worth ending with some suggestions for what those concerned with town centres might do to nurture the seeds of recovery.

1. Town centre first

The huge wave of retail investment that took place in the early 2000s would not have happened in town centres had it not been for a town centre first planning policy that effectively put a stop to out-of-town development. The current retail crisis is affecting both in-town and out-of-town retail and while there is no great demand to build new out-of-town retail it is important to maintain a planning policy focus on town centres. This applies not just to retail but to a whole range of uses that should be located in town centres, where they can be served by public transport and where the activity they generate can support town centre uses. Stockport is proposing that the peripheral Stepping Hill Hospital be relocated to a new facility on the site of its vacant Debenhams department store, funded by the sale of the old site for housing. The same is true of council services, secondary schools, universities, libraries, venues and leisure facilities, as well as new offices and housing. Both through planning policy and other public policy levers, these activities should be located in and around town centres.

2. Positive planning

The UK's planning response to the current crisis has been to relax planning policy. In September 2020, a new Use Class E was introduced, including most town centre uses: shops, financial and professional services, cafés, restaurants, medical health facilities, crèche and nurseries, indoor sports and fitness, and office, business, light industrial uses (the exceptions being bars and takeaways). In our Epsom case study this change undermined a town centre planning policy protecting retail frontages that had been credited with helping regenerate the town centre. Then in March 2021, permitted development rights were extended to enable any Class E use to be converted to housing with 'prior approval' if the unit has been vacant for more than three months.

While it is clearly sensible to ensure that vacant units do not stay vacant because planners are unwilling to countenance a change of use, there is no evidence in our case studies that this has been happening. As one estate agent said, the conversion of shops to housing could mean 'town centres interspersed with "dead" retail frontages of converted former shops [that] may actually reduce the attractiveness and retail footfall rather than enliven it'.[8] There is a need for a mechanism to enable the conversion of surplus retail space to other uses, but enabling it to be replaced with a more profitable use without any controls is not the mechanism we need. Town centres need better planning, not less planning.

3. Plan for uncertainty

This planning needs to be done with a greater understanding and acceptance of the uncertainties facing town centres. Gone are the days of large single-use shopping malls, often built on the rubble of demolished small shops and businesses. Even if these large schemes were viable, which for the foreseeable future they are not, they are the town centre equivalent of putting all your eggs in one basket. There have been huge shifts in the retail landscape and there will likely be more to come, so the high streets of the future need to be ready for anything. When planning for the future we should be planning for uncertainty.

This has spatial implications – the urban environments that adapt best to change tend to be made up of small and medium-sized flexible units fronting onto streets and public spaces that are naturally busy because of their connected nature. By contrast, the shopping centre model is based on footfall being generated by an anchor department store, allowing it to be built off-pitch and leaving it vulnerable if that store closes. So, rather that redesigning town centres for one particular vision of their future, we should be creating town centres that can adapt to a range of different futures.

Shopping centres can be divided up into smaller units, the roof removed to let in light and air, and underused space can be repurposed for other uses including public facilities, leisure and offices. Where new development is taking place, as in our Nottingham case study where the monolithic Broadmarsh shopping centre is being redeveloped, it is sensible to reinstate historical street patterns or use techniques like Space Syntax and footfall modelling to understand what spatial configuration would have most likely evolved over time in that location. New space should be designed with floor-to-ceiling heights, fenestration, entrances, floor plates and servicing that could suit a range of uses. This will allow the development to weather inevitable change and to remain active and usable into the future.

4. Increasing the diversity of retail

Town centres rely on a variety of retailers and we shouldn't forget that despite all the retail failures that have happened during the retail crisis, a huge number of mainstream retailers are still with us. Some, like Frasers, are busy reinventing the department store format, others like Next have come through the crisis stronger, while high street giants like Marks & Spencer, John Lewis, JD Sports and Currys are battered but intact. We shouldn't write off these retailers; they retain huge pulling power and are vitally important in generating footfall. But we should stop measuring success based on the presence of a small number of national retailers.

These retailers will require fewer units and less space than they once did, leaving town centres with a choice – either to shrink the amount of retail space or to fill it with smaller independent businesses. Town centres will always bounce back provided that there are independent businesses willing to take a risk, invest their money and find a market. They include everything from creative outlets and artisan foods through to beauty salons, vape shops and convenience stores – we are not talking about turning every town centre into a hipster enclave. The churn of independent business is huge and the strategy needs to both encourage start-ups and support existing businesses. The techniques to do this are tried and tested and include business support and mentoring, access to finance and small grants, promotion and business networking. In most places the town centre has the greatest potential for business start-up and job creation and, if it is not already, it should be the main focus for economic development.

5. Tackling vacancy

Some of the biggest barriers to promoting smaller independent business relate to property. In an ideal market, when retail space falls vacant, its owners will seek to re-let it. If that proves difficult the rent will be dropped, incentives given and restrictions eased until the space is let. Retailing is not, however, an ideal market and often when space falls vacant it remains vacant. In many shopping centres the headline rent has not fallen in recent years because it is the basis for the capital valuation of the asset and therefore the share price of the centre's owners. However, landlords have found other ways of tempting new tenants, with shorter leases, rent-free periods or more frequent break clauses etc. In the past, retail leases could be as long as 20 years, with upward-only rent clauses, and when a retailer closed a branch they remained liable for the rent. This is why there have been so many Company Voluntary Liquidations (CVAs), in the retail sector, because they allow companies to get out of these leases.

A further problem is fit-out costs. Newly built retail space does not even come with a shopfront, the assumption being that most retailers would have stripped it out and put in their own. Even when space is re-let there is a requirement for considerable investment before it can be reoccupied. Retail landlords offer rent-free periods to cover fit-out but this is not enough for many independent businesses who can't finance such high upfront costs. We have talked to shopping centre owners who have tried to let vacant units to independent businesses and been told it just doesn't stack up.

Therefore the first strategy for town centres is to address the imperfections in the property re-letting process. We have seen examples of places creating low commitment pop-up leases to make the process easier for both landlords and business tenants. We have also seen places make available small fit-out grants, which only need to be a few thousand pounds to allow basic work to be done to bring space back into use. Property owners can also create opportunities for independents, by providing shop windows with QR codes, subdividing units and recycling fittings. We have seen artists and community groups taking on shop windows and whole units as galleries and other uses. The problem is that in shopping centres where there is one ownership, the economics are difficult, and on the high street where occupation costs are lower, ownership is fragmented. Vacancy is therefore a symptom of the economic model on which our town centres have been based for many years.

6. Reforming business rates

It is important to address the risk that any initiative is cancelled out by business rates. For many retailers, these are significantly higher than their rent. As we described in Chapter 4, the delayed 2017 business rate revaluation hit big retailers particularly hard and contributed amongst other things to the retail crisis. As Tony Brown, former chief executive of the collapsed Beales department store chain told *The Guardian*, its £2.8 million rates bill was the reason the company couldn't be saved. On some of its 23 stores, the rates were 10 times the rent: 'The system we have got at the moment is absolute lunacy.'[9] There is widespread consensus that the system is broken, as documented by the Treasury Select Committee. When chancellor, Rishi Sunak did instigate a review of business rates and some relief was offered in the Autumn Statement 2022, largely because retail rateable values had fallen, but the Labour Party have said they will abolish the system altogether. Until major reform takes place business rates will be a significant impediment to the regeneration of the high street.

7. Reforming the development model

Falling rents and shorter, less certain leases mean that retail development as we have known it over the last 20 years is no longer viable. The notion of building new shopping centres anchored by a department store and catering to a select group of blue-chip retailers is no longer an investable proposition – as many places have found to their cost. More worryingly, the cyclical maintenance and refurbishment of existing retail space is looking less and less viable in all but the strongest town centres. The situation may change in the future, but at present this is a major threat hanging over many town centres, particularly those with tired shopping centres in need of investment. We need a new development model and in our case studies three possibilities have emerged.

The first is for town centre development to base its viability on residential and office development. Many abandoned retail schemes are now being pursued as housing or office schemes, with the retailing on the ground floor being largely incidental. Sometimes the retailing is only there because it is a planning requirement and is likely to be targeted at food and drink uses rather than traditional retailers. Some schemes, like the City Centre South in Coventry, have been criticised because it is demolishing part of the retail centre for what is essentially a residential development. The scheme's attempt to develop the 'Pavilion' to promote new local independent businesses and artisans has unfortunately proved to be unviable.

The second approach is to find a different business model as we saw with Bobby's independent department store in Bournemouth, Kommune in the old Co-op department store in Sheffield and the market in Altrincham. All have been promoted by developers who know how to make a profit while nurturing small independent businesses. As the developer of Bobby's says, it is now possible for a small developer to buy good-quality retail space for less than it would cost to build. By keeping capital costs low, developing space incrementally, and being flexible and responsive to the needs of tenants, it's possible to develop a viable business model. It is something that market developers like those behind Camden Lock in London have known for years and is something that all towns are going to have to do as an alternative to being reliant on big retail developers and landlords.

The third approach is public intervention. As the leadership in Barnsley told us, investing public money in town centres is an important regeneration tool. We are not talking here about local authorities investing in retail to generate income – that is a very bad idea at the moment. We are talking about using public borrowing to buy vacant retail space or even whole shopping centres as a way of bringing them back into use. This may involve a fund to buy up or take on the lease of empty units. Councils can then use them as a tool for regeneration, letting them to local businesses and other activities, maybe moving the library into a vacant unit as Stockport have done. Many councils have taken the opportunity to buy old shopping centres and malls as they come on the market, often at knockdown prices. Councillors in Wigan were delighted to buy the Galleries shopping centre in 2018 for less than half what they sold it for 10 years earlier, and Bradford have recently bought the Alhambra Centre. Some councils have gone further, undertaking development directly, as we described in Barnsley in Chapter 14. The investment will generate an income sufficient to cover borrowing costs and may even generate a small surplus, if not one that a developer would regard as a commercial return. However, even if the development makes a small loss, the benefit in terms of jobs created, economic activity and investment in property make it very good value for money.

8. Unified ownership?

There are commentators like John Parmiter who see the main problem with town centres as fragmented ownership.[10] Like KPMG, who have put forward a similar model,[11] he suggests a model for town centre renewal that would see all property acquired either through a pooling arrangement or via a compulsory purchase order and then managed by an agency of some kind. The whole process would be self-funding following start-up costs and would allow institutional investment in town centres and for them to be managed like shopping centres.

The collapse in retail investment has rendered this idea moot because it wouldn't be fundable in the current market. However, the notion that coordinated management is preferable to the muddle of traditional town centres can also be called into question by the collapse of Intu. If it is true that town centres contain within them the seeds of their recovery then stifling that complexity under a single ownership may not be a good idea.

9. Improving the environment

We leave until last the town centre initiatives most commonly being deployed to address the retail crisis. Faced with empty shops and declining footfall, the easiest thing to do is change the paving and plant trees. The biggest example of this is probably Stockton-on-Tees, where the council acquired the Castlegate Shopping Centre so that it could be demolished to create a park. An intervention on this scale has the potential to be transformational. However, with smaller scale environmental works it is important to understand how they help, otherwise we are just fiddling while Rome burns.

It is true that the quality of the environment in a town centre is important. Back in the 1990s, URBED's town centre health check was based on four 'A's: Attractions, Access, Amenity and Action, with the 'amenity' relating to the quality of the environment. People are put off by an environment that is scruffy, litter-strewn and badly maintained. Environmental works can therefore instil confidence, change perceptions and also help with practical matters such as the width of pavements, the provision of seating and space for markets. In our Ashington case study, an environmental scheme that reintroduced cars and parking to a previously pedestrianised high street has been credited with its revival. Elsewhere, like Lark Lane in Liverpool, the debate has been about making temporary COVID measures permanent by restricting or excluding traffic. Environmental works therefore have a role to play as part of a wider strategy. The risk is that they are the first and sometimes the only measures implemented because they are the easiest to implement.

The message of this book is, perhaps surprisingly, optimistic. We went in search of the (latest) crisis on the high street through our 100 case studies and we found instead town centres and high streets in a state of transition. It is a painful transition involving the loss of many anchor retailers, COVID lockdowns and a cost of living crisis. But throughout, most of our town centres have proven resilient and most are showing signs of recovery. Indeed some are doing very well, confirming our initial hypothesis that every town centre is different. Sometimes local factors can be more important than national trends and the actions of entrepreneurial individuals, councils and companies can make a huge difference. There is no one-size-fits-all solution.

To call it a crisis on the high street is also a misnomer – the roots of the crisis lie not on the high street but in the boardrooms of some of the large retailers. They lie also with a retail development model that extinguished diversity and in any case is no longer viable. If we can transition to a town centre economy that is more diverse in terms of the type of retailers, mix of uses and range of activities, then the transition, painful as it might have been, may end up being positive. It might deliver us from the clone towns of the 2000s and create town centres nearer to those that exist in the popular imagination – community hubs with a range of distinctive retailers and leisure uses with a strong identity and a sense of place. These are all public goods and are too important to be left to the vagaries of the market. Just as public corporations set up and ran the markets and fairs where we started this story, town centres need to again be a focus for public policy at the national and local level to allow their diversity to flourish.

NOTES

Preface

1 Centre for Retail Research, 'The Crisis in Retailing: Closures and Job Losses', *Centre for Retail Research*, <https://www.retailresearch.org/retail-crisis.html>, (accessed 9 January 2023).
2 The full write-up of the case studies can be found on <https://www.talesofthehighstreet.com>.
3 Georgia Wright, 'The number of high street shops rise despite Covid lockdowns last year', *Retail Gazette*, 5 Jan. 2022, <https://www.retailgazette.co.uk/blog/2022/01/the-number-of-high-street-shops-rise-despite-covid-lockdowns-last-year/>, (accessed 31 January 2023).

Introduction

1 Kurious, 'Kommune', <https://www.kuriousworlds.com/kommune.html>, *Kurious* (accessed 31 January 2023).
2 Jarvis Cocker, 'Three Things Which Have Inspired Me', *Interior World*, a supplement to *The World of Interiors* magazine, January 2000.
3 This book is based in part on a series of interviews. The interview with Tony Coleman, a former director at Burtons and later a Labour MP and Minister, took place on 5 January 2021.
4 Simon Ogden, former Director of Development at Sheffield City Council [interviewed by author], February 2021.
5 BBC News, 'Sheffield's Moor to get a new market building', 29 July 2010, <http://news.bbc.co.uk/local/sheffield/hi/people_and_places/newsid_8868000/8868795.stm>, (accessed 6 January 2023).
6 David Walsh, 'Premium Sheffield shopping street Fargate is 'the worst it's been' – but don't write it off just yet', *Sheffield Star*, 25 August 2020, <https://www.thestar.co.uk/business/premium-sheffield-shopping-street-fargate-worst-its-been-dont-write-it-just-yet-2952006>, (accessed 6 January 2023).
7 The Academy of Urbanism, *Sheffield City Centre and New Retails Quarter*, <https://issuu.com/theaou/docs/aou-diagnostic-sheffield-nrq-final-?utm_medium=referral&utm_source=www.academyofurbanism.org.uk>, 5–6 Dec. 2013, (accessed 9 January 2023).
8 Hillier Parker & Oxford Institute of Retail Management, *Shopping Study*, Sheffield Development Corporation & Sheffield City Council, 1994.
9 BBC News, 'Meadowhall marks 20th anniversary', 3 September 2010, <http://news.bbc.co.uk/local/sheffield/hi/people_and_places/newsid_8961000/8961600.stm>, (accessed 6 January 2023).
10 URBED, *Vital and Viable Town Centres: Meeting the Challenge*, HMSO, London, 1994.
11 Elizabeth Howard, 'Assessing the impact of shopping-centre development: The Meadowhall case', *Journal of Property Research*, Vol. 10, issue 2, 1993 pp. 97–119.
12 Retail Economics, 'UK Retail Stats and Facts', *Retail Economics*, <https://www.retaileconomics.co.uk/library-retail-stats-and-facts>, (accessed 6 January 2023).
13 UK Hospitality, 'UK Hospitality Workforce Commission 2030 report: The changing face of hospitality', *UK Hospitality*, <https://www.ukhospitality.org.uk/page/WorkforceCommission>, September 2018, (accessed 6 January 2023).
14 Venuescore is an annual survey compiled by Javelin Group, which ranks the UK's top 3,500+ retail venues (including town centres, stand-alone shopping centres, retail warehouse parks and factory outlet centres).
15 See Peter Brett Associates, *Wrexham Retail Assessment*, Wrexham County Borough Council, July 2014.
16 Centre for Retail Research, 'The Crisis in Retailing: Closures and Job Losses', *Centre for Retail Research*, <https://www.retailresearch.org/retail-crisis.html>, (accessed 9 January 2023).
17 Caoimhe Gordon, 'Data: Shop vacancies 'at highest rate ever recorded' as uncertainty lingers', *Retail Week*, 30 July 2021, <https://www.retail-week.com/stores/data-shop-vacancies-at-highest-rate-ever-recorded-as-uncertainty-lingers/7040364.article>, (accessed 6 January 2023).
18 David Rudlin, Lucy Montague & Vicky Payne, 'Tales of the High Street', Built Environment Fellowship 2019, *Royal Commission for the Exhibition of 1851*, <https://royalcommission1851.org/tales-of-the-high-street>, (accessed 9 January 2023).
19 See David Rudlin, Lucy Montague & Vicky Payne, 'Tales of the High Street', *Tales of the High Street*, <http://talesofthehighstreet.com/>, (accessed 10 January 2023).
20 Mary Portas, 'The Portas Review: An independent review into the future of our high streets', *UK Government, Department for Business, Innovation and Skills*, <https://www.gov.uk/government/publications/the-portas-review-the-future-of-our-high-streets>, December 2011, (accessed 9 January 2023).
21 Office for National Statistics, 'Internet sales as a percentage of total retail sales (ratio) (%)', *Office for National Statistics*, <https://www.ons.gov.uk/businessindustryandtrade/retailindustry/timeseries/j4mc/drsi>, (accessed 18 November 2022).
22 Tom Whittington, 'How to repurpose retail space', *Savills Impacts*, May 2020, <https://www.savills.com/impacts/social-change/how-to-repurpose-retail-space.html>, (accessed 9 January 2023).
23 Office for National Statistics, 'Retail sales, Great Britain: January 2021', *Office for National Statistics*, <https://www.ons.gov.uk/releases/retailsalesgreatbritainjanuary2021>, (accessed 19 February 2021).
24 Ibid., Ref. 21.
25 Jonathan Eley & George Hammond, 'Crisis in retail: the UK town centres struggling to survive', *Financial Times*, 4 Feb. 2020, <https://www.ft.com/content/77b797fc-2fcf-420b-947c-a1a72109c231>, (accessed 9 January 2023).

Chapter 1: Places of Exchange

1 Andrew Simms, Petra Kjell & Ruth Potts, 'Clone Town Britain', *New Economics Foundation*, 5 June 2007, <https://neweconomics.org/2007/06/clone-town-britain>, (accessed 6 January 2023).
2 Harry Wallop, 'Skipton high street beats Portobello Road to win best street title', *Daily Telegraph*, 28 Nov. 2008, <https://www.telegraph.co.uk/news/uknews/3534209/Skipton-high-street-beats-Portobello-Road-to-win-best-street-title.html>, (accessed 9 January 2023).
3 Yuval Noah Harari, *Sapiens: A Brief History of Humankind*, Vintage Books, London, 2015.
4 David Harrison, 'Learning from the Past', *Urban Design Group Journal*, Issue 154, 2020.
5 Lucy Toulmin Smith, ed., *The Itinerary of John Leland in or about the years 1535–1543*, George Bell & Sons, London, 1907.
6 Ibid., Ref. 4.
7 H. G. Wells, *The History of Mr Polly*, Thomas Nelson and Sons, London, 2010.
8 Quoted by Simon Jenkins, 'Top of the shops: how has Oxford Street survived the slow death of the high street?', *The Guardian*, 5 March 2020, <https://www.theguardian.com/lifeandstyle/2020/mar/05/top-pf-the-shops-oxford-street-survived-death-high-street>, (accessed 11 January 2023).
9 Ike Ijeh, 'Could the pedestrianisation of London's busiest street work?', *Building Design*, 7 June 2016, <https://www.bdonline.co.uk/could-the-pedestrianisation-of-londons-busiest-street-work/5082030.article>, (accessed 31 January 2023).
10 Jon Stobart, 'Cathedrals of Consumption? Provincial Department Stores in England c. 1880–1930', *Enterprise & Society*, Vol. 18, Issue 4, 2017.
11 Abigail Jubb, 'What Debenhams' demise reveals about the future of fashion', *Prospect Magazine*, 31 Jan. 2021, <https://www.prospectmagazine.co.uk/society-and-culture/debenhams-closing-down-boohoo-fast-fashion-ethical-sustainable>, (accessed 9 January 2023).
12 Ibid., Ref. 7.
13 Ghostly Tom's Travel Blog, 'Oldham Street 2 ~ Affleck & Brown's', *Ghostly Tom's Travel Blog*, <www.toms-travels.net/?p=20462>, 21 May 2013, (accessed 6 January 2023).
14 David Boardman, 'Paulden's Department Store', *Manchester History*, <https://manchesterhistory.net/manchester/gone/pauldens.html>, (accessed 6 January 2023).
15 Deborah Linton, 'Tycoons support Afflecks', *Manchester Evening News*, <https://www.manchestereveningnews.co.uk/news/greater-manchester-news/tycoons-support-afflecks-939805>, 16 April 2010, (accessed 6 January 2023).
16 George MacDonald, Rosie Shepard & Hugh Radojev, 'Electric go-karts, arts fairs and whisky tours: Six innovative uses for empty department

stores', *Retail Week*, <https://www.retail-week.com/stores/electric-go-karts-arts-fairs-and-whisky-tours-six-innovative-uses-for-empty-department-stores/7040501.article?authent=1>, 31 Aug. 2021, (accessed 6 January 2023).

17 David Rudlin & Shruti Hemani, *Climax City: Masterplanning and the Complexity of Urban Growth*, RIBA Publishing, London, 2019.

18 See 'Space Syntax', <https://spacesyntax.com/>, *Space Syntax*, (accessed 9 January 2023).

19 Office for National Statistics & Ordnance Survey High Street, 'High streets in Great Britain', *Office for National Statistics*, <https://www.ons.gov.uk/peoplepopulationandcommunity/populationandmigration/populationestimates/articles/highstreetsingreatbritain/2019-06-06>, 2019, (accessed 9 January 2023).

20 Juliet Gardiner, 'A history of the high street', *BBC History Magazine*, <https://www.historyextra.com/period/modern/a-history-of-the-high-street/>, 6 Nov. 2010, (accessed 31 January 2023).

Chapter 2: Death by Supermarket

1 Bill Grimsey, *Sold Out*, Filament Publishing, London, 2012.

2 The Grocer in Jane Hamlett, Andrew Alexander, Adrian Bailey & Gareth Shaw, 'Regulating UK supermarkets: an oral-history perspective', *History & Policy*, <https://www.historyandpolicy.org/policy-papers/papers/regulating-uk-supermarkets-an-oral-history-perspective>, 17 Apr. 2008, (accessed 9 January 2023).

3 Helen Gregory, 'It's a super anniversary: it's 50 years since the first full size self-service supermarket was unveiled in the UK', *The Grocer*, <https://archive.ph/20120708193934/http://findarticles.com/p/articles/mi_hb5245/is_7528_224/ai_n28873842/>, 2001, (accessed 28 January 2023).

4 Ibid., Ref. 2.

5 Adam Schoenborn, 'The Right to Retail: Can localism save Britain's small retailers?', *ResPublica*, <https://www.respublica.org.uk/our-work/publications/right-retail-can-localism-save-britains-small-retailers/>, 2011, (accessed 9 January 2023).

6 Competition Commission, *The supply of groceries in the UK market investigation*, UK Government, Department for Business, Innovation and Skills, 2008.

7 Paul Whysall, 'GEM, 1964–1966: Britain's First Out-of-Town Retailer', *The International Review of Retail, Distribution and Consumer Research*, Vol. 15, Issue 2, 2015.

8 Jon Kelly, 'How first out-of-town superstore changed the UK', *BBC News*, 2 Sept. 2013, <https://www.bbc.co.uk/news/magazine-23900465>, (accessed 9 January 2023).

9 Asda, 'Our History', *Asda*, <https://corporate.asda.com/our-story/our-history>, (accessed 9 January 2023).

10 Dieter Brandes & Nils Brandes, *Bare Essentials: The Aldi Way to Retail Success*, Books On Demand, 2012.

11 Xan Rice, 'The Aldi effect: how one discount supermarket transformed the way Britain shops', *The Guardian*, 5 March 2019, <https://www.theguardian.com/business/2019/mar/05/long-read-aldi-discount-supermarket-changed-britain-shopping>, (accessed 9 January 2023).

12 The Grocer, 'Tesco's Defining Moments', *The Grocer*, 9 Aug. 2019, <https://www.thegrocer.co.uk/promotional-features/tescos-defining-moments/596508.article>, (accessed 9 January 2023).

13 Ibid., Ref. 12.

14 Peter Jackson, *Shopping, Place and Identity*, Routledge, London, 1998.

15 Ibid., Ref. 12.

16 Dan Hyde, 'One in three Aldi and Lidl shoppers is 'upper or middle class', *The Telegraph*, 15 March 2015, <https://www.telegraph.co.uk/news/shopping-and-consumer-news/11473701/One-in-three-Aldi-and-Lidl-shoppers-is-upper-or-middle-class.html>, (accessed 9 January 2023).

17 Ibid., Ref. 12.

18 Joanne Douglas, 'Why more wealthy people are shopping at discount stores Lidl and Aldi', *Yorkshire Live*, 25 Oct. 2017, <https://www.examinerlive.co.uk/news/west-yorkshire-news/more-wealthy-people-shopping-discount-13809413>, (accessed 9 January 2023).

19 Sarah Butler, 'Aldi and Lidl lose out as UK online grocery sales hit new heights', *The Guardian*, 2 March 2021, <https://www.theguardian.com/business/2021/mar/02/aldi-and-lidl-lose-out-as-uk-online-grocery-sales-hit-new-heights>, (accessed 9 January 2023).

20 Jacqui Parr, 'Big 4 line-up changes as Aldi confirmed to be UK's fourth largest supermarket', *Grocery Gazette*, 13 Sept. 2022, <https://www.grocerygazette.co.uk/2022/09/13/big-4-aldi-kantar/>, (accessed 9 January 2023).

21 Daniel Woolfson & Ian Quinn, 'The Tesco crisis: Timeline', The Grocer, 23 Oct. 2014, <https://www.thegrocer.co.uk/tesco/the-tesco-crisis-timeline/372259.article>, (accessed 9 January 2023).

22 Ibid., Ref. 12.

Chapter 3: Heading out of Town

1 The Newsroom, 'How Sir John Hall went from selling houses into Sunderland to building the Metrocentre', Sunderland Echo, 5 Nov. 2017, <https://www.sunderlandecho.com/news/how-sir-john-hall-went-selling-houses-sunderland-building-metrocentre-355662>, (accessed 9 January 2023).

2 Sam Wetherell, 'Duncan Tanner Essay Prize 2015: Freedom Planned: Enterprise Zones and Urban Non-Planning in Post-War Britain', *Twentieth Century British History*, Vol. 27, Issue 2, 2016.

3 Paul Barker, Cedric Price, Peter Hall & Reyner Banham, 'Non-Plan: An Experiment in Freedom', *New Society*, No. 338, 1969.

4 Barbara Hodgson, 'How Gateshead's Metrocentre was made – and why it was built on a great big clarty field', *Chronicle Live*, 29 Oct. 2016, <https://www.chroniclelive.co.uk/news/north-east-news/how-gatesheads-metrocentre-made-built-12096359>, (accessed 9 January 2023).

5 Ibid., Ref. 2.

6 Kieran Larkin, 'What would Maggie do?', *Centre for Cities*, <https://www.centreforcities.org/publication/what-would-maggie-do/>, 2011, (accessed 9 January 2023).

7 Ibid., Ref. 4.

8 Malcolm Gladwell, 'The Terrazzo Jungle', *The New Yorker*, 7 March 2004, <https://www.newyorker.com/magazine/2004/03/15/the-terrazzo-jungle>, (accessed 9 January 2023).

9 Jane Jacobs, 'Downtown is for People', *Fortune Magazine*, April 1958.

10 Timothy Mennel, 'Victor Gruen and the Construction of Cold War Utopias', *Journal of Planning History*, Vol. 3, Issue 2, 2004.

11 Ibid., Ref. 8.

12 Clifford Guy, 'Whatever happened to regional shopping centres?', *Journal of the Geographical Association*, Vol. 79, No. 4, 1994 pp. 293–312.

13 Statista Research Department, 'Retail space per capita in selected countries worldwide in 2018', *Statista*, <https://www.statista.com/statistics/1058852/retail-space-per-capita-selected-countries-worldwide/>, 2022, (accessed 9 January 2023).

14 J.A. Dawson, *Shopping Centre Development*, Longman, London, 1983.

15 Ibid., Ref. 12.

16 University of Manchester: Department of Town and Country Planning, *Regional Shopping Centres in North West England*, University of Manchester, 1964.

17 Distributive Trades E.D.C., *The Future Pattern of Shopping*, HMSO, London, 1971.

18 Colin Amery & Dan Cruickshank, *The Rape of Britain*, Harper Collins, UK, 1975.

19 Tony Travers, *London's Boroughs at 50*, Biteback Publishing, London, 2015.

20 Clifford Guy, 'Official Publications on Retail Development: A Review Article', *Planning Practice and Research*, Vol. 11, No. 2, 1994.

21 Nicholas Ridley in *The Times*, 17 Jan. 1987.

22 BDP Planning & Oxford Institute for Retail Management, *The effects of major out of town retail development: A literature review for the Department of the Environment*, HMSO, London, 1992.

23 Russell Shiller, 'Vitality and Viability: Challenge to the Town Centre', *International Journal of Retail Distribution and Management*, Vol. 22, No. 6, 1994.

24 Ibid., Ref. 23.

25 Ross Davies & Elizabeth Howard, 'The Impact of Regional, Out-of-Town Retail Centres: The Case of the Metro Centre', *Progress in Planning*, Vol. 40. Part 2, 1993.

26 Elizabeth Howard, 'Assessing the impact of shopping-centre development: The Meadowhall case', *Journal of Property Research*, Vol. 10, Issue 2, 1993 pp. 97–119.

27 Jeremy J. Williams, 'Meadowhall: Its Impact on Sheffield City Centre and Rotherham', *International Journal of Retail & Distribution Management*, Vol. 19, No. 1, 1991.

28 Ibid., Ref. 22.

29 Roger Tym & Partners, *Merry Hill Impact Study*, HMSO, London, 1993.

30 Department of the Environment and Welsh Office, *Planning Policy Guidance 6: Town Centres and Retail Developments*, HMSO, London, 1993.

31 URBED, *Vital and Viable Town Centres: Meeting the Challenge*, HMSO, London, 1994.

32 House of Commons Environment Committee, *Fourth Report: Shopping Centres and their Future*, HMSO, London, 1994.

33 Alex Morton & Gerard Dericks, *21st Century Retail Policy: Quality, Choice, Experience and Convenience*, Policy Exchange, London, 2013.

Chapter 4: From Boom to Bust

1 James Kingston, Stockport Council, [interviewed by author], 14 February 2022.

2 Daniel Thomas, 'What went wrong at Debenhams?', *BBC News*, 1 Dec. 2020, <https://www.bbc.co.uk/news/business-55144922>, (accessed 9 January 2023).

3 Tony Coleman, former Director at Burtons, Labour MP & Minister, [interviewed by author], 5 January 2021.

4 Zoe Wood, 'Debenhams 'never recovered from private equity ownership', *The Guardian*, 1 Dec. 2020, <https://www.theguardian.com/

business/2020/dec/01/debenhams-never-recovered-from-private-equity-ownership>, (accessed 9 January 2023).

5   Ibid., Ref. 4.
6   Rebecca Toop, 'Place Test: Liverpool One', *The Developer*, No. 03, 2020.
7   The Academy of Urbanism, 'Princesshay, Exeter: The Great Place Award 2011', *The Academy of Urbanism*, <https://www.academyofurbanism.org.uk/princesshay/>, 2010, (accessed 10 January 2023).
8   Peter Hall, Stephen Marshall & Michelle Lowe, *The Changing Urban Hierarchy in England and Wales, 1913–1998*, Regional Studies, Vol. 35, Issue 9, 2001.
9   Will Kilner, 'Westfield told to get on with it', Telegraph & Argus, 30 Oct. 2007, <https://www.thetelegraphandargus.co.uk/news/1794976.westfield-told-to-get-on-with-it/>, (accessed 9 January 2023).
10 Bradford's Independent Quarter, 'About', *Bradford's Independent Quarter*, <https://indiequarterbradford.wordpress.com/about/>, (accessed 10 January 2023).
11 New Economics Foundation, *Clone Town Britain: The Survey Results on the Bland State of the Nation*, New Economics Foundation, 2004.
12 Andrew Rowell, 'The Wal-Martians Have Landed' in *The Case Against the Global Economy*, eds., Edward Goldsmith & Jerry Mander, Routledge, London, 2001.
13 See Portland Leonard Curtis, 'The business failure of Woolworths', *Portland Leonard Curtis*, <https://www.portbfs.co.uk/in-the-press/the-business-failure-of-woolworths/>, (accessed 10 January 2023).
14 Noella Pio Kivlehan, '10 years after Woolworths' collapse, what can retailers learn?', *Retail Gazette*, 4 Dec. 2018, <https://www.retailgazette.co.uk/blog/2018/12/woolworths-collapse-10-years-ago-first-domino-physical-retail-armageddon/>, (accessed 9 January 2023).
15 Mary Portas, 'The Portas Review: An independent review into the future of our high streets', *Department for Business, Innovation and Skills*, <https://www.gov.uk/government/publications/the-portas-review-the-future-of-our-high-streets>, 2011, (accessed 9 January 2023).
16 Ministry of Housing, Communities & Local Government & The Rt Hon Grant Shapps MP, 'Press Release: Portas Pilots to kick-start high street renaissance', *UK Government*, 26 May 2012, <https://www.gov.uk/government/news/portas-pilots-to-kick-start-high-street-renaissance>, (accessed 10 January 2023).
17 Bill Grimsey et al., *The Grimsey Review: An Alternative Future for the High Street*, The Grimsey Review, 2013.
18 Samantha Fenwick, 'Shopping choices shrink in Portas Pilot towns', *BBC News*, 8 Nov. 2017, <https://www.bbc.co.uk/news/business-41906964>, (accessed 9 January 2023).
19 Ibid., Ref. 17.
20 Bill Grimsey, *Sold Out*, Filament Publishing, London, 2012.
21 Neil Bennett, 'Learning from Elsewhere: Roeselare in Belgium', *Urban Design Journal*, Issue 154, 2020.
22 Georgina Hutton, *Retail Sector in the UK*, The House of Commons, 2018.
23 Centre for Retail Research, 'Who's Gone Bust?', *Centre for Retail Research*, <https://www.retailresearch.org/whos-gone-bust.html>, (accessed 10 January 2023).

24 Peter Brett Associates, *Town Centre Capacity Assessment for Stafford Borough 2019*, Stafford Borough Council, 2019.
25 Experian Goad, *Stafford – Goad town centre reports*, Experian, 2012-2022.
26 Leah Cassady, 'Three shops at Stafford shopping centre close', *In Your Area Newsroom*, 25 May 2021, <https://www.inyourarea.co.uk/news/three-shops-at-stafford-shopping-centre-close/>, (accessed 9 January 2023).
27 Bill Grimsey et al., ed. Siobhán Crozier, *The Grimsey Review 2: It's time to reshape our town centres*, The Grimsey Review, 2018.
28 Treasury Select Committee, *Impact of Business Rates on Business*, The House of Commons, 2019.
29 Zoe Wood, 'Why UK high street retailers want urgent reform of business rates', *The Guardian*, 6 June 2020, <https://www.theguardian.com/business/2020/mar/06/why-uk-high-street-retailers-want-urgent-reform-of-business-rates>, (accessed 9 January 2023).
30 Patrick Collinson, 'M&G suspends £2.5bn property fund blaming retail crisis and Brexit, *The Guardian*, 4 Dec. 2019, <https://www.theguardian.com/money/2019/dec/04/m-and-g-suspends-property-portfolio-fund-retail-downturn-brexit>, (accessed 9 January 2023).
31 See Local Data Company & The British Retail Consortium, 'BRC-LDC Vacancy Monitor, Q1 2022', *Local Data Company*, <https://www.localdatacompany.com/blog/press-release-brc-ldc-vacancy-monitor-q1-2022>, (accessed 10 January 2023).
32 Sarah Townsend, 'Intu forced to abandon £1bn fund raising', *Place North West*, 4 March 2020, <https://www.placenorthwest.co.uk/intu-forced-to-abandon-1bn-fund-raising/>, (accessed 9 January 2023).
33 Ministry of Housing, Communities & Local Government, 'The High Street Report', *UK Government*, <https://www.gov.uk/government/publications/the-high-street-report>, 2018, (accessed 10 January 2023).
34 See High Streets Task Force, 'High Streets Task Force', *High Streets Task Force*, <https://www.highstreetstaskforce.org.uk/>, (accessed 10 January 2023).
35 Centre for Cities, 'High streets recovery tracker', <https://www.centreforcities.org/data/high-streets-recovery-tracker/>, *Centre for Cities* (accessed 10 January 2023).
36 Hugh Radojev, 'Will more retailers ditch Oxford Street?', *Retail Week*, 21 Jan. 2021, <https://www.retail-week.com/stores/will-more-retailers-ditch-oxford-street/7036623.article?authent=1>, (accessed 9 January 2023).
37 Benjamin Roberts-Haslam, 'Lark Lane development branded mind boggling', *Liverpool Echo*, 2 April 2022, <https://www.liverpoolecho.co.uk/news/liverpool-news/lark-lane-development-branded-mind-23576228>, (accessed 9 January 2023).
38 Caoimhe Gordon, 'Data: Shop vacancies 'at highest rate ever recorded' as uncertainty lingers', *Retail Week*, 30 July 2021, <https://www.retail-week.com/stores/data-shop-vacancies-at-highest-rate-ever-recorded-as-uncertainty-lingers/7040364.article>, (accessed 6 January 2023).
39 Ibid., Ref. 32.
40 Tom Whittington, 'How to repurpose retail space', *Savills Impacts*, May 2020, <https://www.savills.com/impacts/social-change/how-to-repurpose-retail-space.html>, (accessed 9 January 2023).
41 Daniela Coppola, 'Internet retail sales as a

percentage of total retail sales in Great Britain from January 2018 to October 2022', *Statista*, <https://www.statista.com/statistics/286384/internet-share-of-retail-sales-monthly-in-the-united-kingdom-uk/>, (accessed 9 January 2023).
42 Ibid., Ref. 37.
43 Jonathan Glancey, 'The death of the US shopping mall', *BBC Culture*, 21 Oct. 2014, <https://www.bbc.com/culture/article/20140411-is-the-shopping-mall-dead>, (accessed 9 January 2023).

Chapter 5: Independent and Creative
1   Quoted in David Rudlin, 'The 1970s: London and the Three-day week', Climax City, 1 Dec. 2014, <https://climax.city/2014/01/12/the-1970s-london-and-the-three-day-week/>, (accessed 10 January 2023).
2   Walt Whitman, *Song of Myself*, pt. 51, poem, 1982.
3   John Burton, *It's About Control (Spitalfields/Camden Market)*, conference presentation at The Academy of Urbanism, 27 Jan. 2022.
4   Quotes from interviews with traders. See David Rudlin, Lucy Montague & Vicky Payne, 'Tales of the High Street', *Tales of the High Street*, <http://talesofthehighstreet.com/>, (accessed 10 January 2023).
5   Maya Yarowsky, 'Teddy Sagi's London Take-Over: Israeli Billionaire Buys Up More Of Camden Market', *No Camels*, 13 Oct. 2014, <https://nocamels.com/2014/10/teddy-sagis-london-take-over-israeli-billionaire-buys-up-more-of-camden-markets/>, (accessed 10 January 2023).
6   George Hammond, 'London's Camden Market owner sets out stall for £1.5bn sale', *Financial Times*, 2 June 2022, <https://www.ft.com/content/b4b9b680-c0e2-4544-8ee3-fde732058506>, (accessed 31 January 2023).
7   Demos, *The Boho Britain Creativity Index*, London, 2003.
8   Helen Cater, 'Gritty city wins the boho crown', *The Guardian*, 26 May 2003, <https://www.theguardian.com/2003/may/26/communities.arts>, (accessed 10 January 2023).
9   David Rudlin, Rob Thompson & Sarah Jarvis, *Urbanism*, Routledge, London, 2016.
10 See Chris Ratcliff, ed., 'HebWeb', *Hebden Bridge Web*, <https://www.hebdenbridge.co.uk/>, (accessed 10 January 2023).
11 New Economics Foundation, Clone Town Britain: *The Survey Results on the Bland State of the Nation*, New Economics Foundation, 2004.
12 The Newsroom, 'The village that discovered the value of co-operation', *The Yorkshire Post*, 29 Jan. 2010, <https://www.yorkshirepost.co.uk/news/village-discovered-value-co-operation-1989982>, (accessed 29 January 2023).
13 Association of Convenience Stores, 'The Local Shop Report 2021', *Association of Convenience Stores*, <https://www.acs.org.uk/research/local-shop-report>, 2021, (accessed 10 January 2023).
14 'High Street Revival', *You and Yours*, radio programme, BBC Radio 4, London, broadcast 3 Jan. 2022.
15 British Independent Retailers Association (BIRA), 'Increase in the number of independent openings subdued by a rise in closures across GB', *BIRA*, <https://bira.co.uk/resources/increase-independents-rise-closures-uk-2018>, 2018, (accessed 9 January 2023).
16 Centre for Retail Research, 'The Crisis in Retailing: Closures and Job Losses', *Centre for Retail Research*, <https://www.retailresearch.org/retail-crisis.html>, (accessed 9 January 2023).

17 Bill Grimsey et al., *The Grimsey Review: Against All Odds: How independent Retail, Hospitality, and Services Businesses have adapted to survive the pandemic*, The Grimsey Review, 2021.

18 James Kingston, Stockport Council, [interviewed by author], 14 February 2022.

19 See Shearer Property Regen Limited, 'Vision', *Coventry City Centre South*, <https://www.coventrycitycentresouth.co.uk/vision/>, (accessed 10 January 2023).

20 Sarah Butler & Stephen Morris, 'Retail has changed so much: local makers lead the rebirth of the department store', *The Guardian*, 8 Sept. 2021, <https://www.theguardian.com/lifeandstyle/2021/sep/08/retail-has-changed-so-much-local-makers-lead-the-rebirth-of-the-department-store>, (accessed 29 January 2023).

21 Jane Jacobs, *The Death and Life of Great American Cities*, Vintage Books, New York, 1961.

Chapter 6: Grocers and Purveyors of Fine Food

1 Simon Bland, 'New opening: Weezy brings you locally sourced groceries in minutes PLUS get £10 off your first order', *Manchester Wire*, 16 April 2021, <https://manchesterwire.co.uk/new-opening-weezy-brings-you-locally-sourced-groceries-in-minutes/>, (accessed 10 January 2023).

2 George Iddenden, 'Delivery Wars: The Rise of Ultra-Fast Delivery in the UK', *Charged*, 23 July 2021, <https://www.chargedretail.co.uk/2021/07/23/delivery-wars-the-rise-of-ultra-fast-delivery-in-the-uk/>, (accessed 10 January 2023).

3 Arielle Pardes, 'The Speedy Downfall of Rapid Delivery Startups', *Wired*, 15 July 2022, <https://www.wired.com/story/the-speedy-downfall-of-rapid-delivery/>, (accessed 10 January 2023).

4 Joanna Partridge, 'Rapid delivery service Getir to buy UK rival Weezy', *The Guardian*, 23 Nov. 2021, <https://www.theguardian.com/business/2021/nov/23/rapid-delivery-service-getir-to-buy-uk-rival-weezy>, (accessed 10 January 2023).

5 McKinsey & Company, *Navigating the market headwinds: The state of grocery retail 2022*, McKinsey & Company, 2022.

6 Tim Bradshaw & Attracta Mooney, 'Disaster strikes as Deliveroo becomes worst IPO in London's history', *Financial Times*, 31 March 2021, <https://www.ft.com/content/bdf6ac6b-46b5-4f7a-90db-291d7fd2898d>, (accessed 10 January 2023).

7 Judith Fischer, 'Appetite for rapid grocery delivery is growing around Europe', *Knight Frank*, 28 April 2022, <https://www.knightfrank.com/research/article/2022-04-28-appetite-for-rapid-grocery-delivery-is-growing-around-europe>, (accessed 10 January 2023).

8 George Nott, 'Rapid grocery dark stores in UK set to number 1,500 by 2030', *The Grocer*, 24 Feb. 2022, <https://www.thegrocer.co.uk/technology-and-supply-chain/rapid-grocery-dark-stores-in-uk-set-to-number-1500-by-2030/664831.article>, (accessed 10 January 2023).

9 PYMNTS, 'Ocado Reels in Delivery Expansion as UK Shoppers Head to Stores', *PYMNTS*, 21 July 2022, <https://www.pymnts.com/news/ecommerce/2022/ocado-reels-in-delivery-expansion-as-uk-shoppers-head-to-stores/>, (accessed 10 January 2023).

10 Emma Simpson, 'Almost 50 shops a day disappear from High Streets', *BBC News*, 5 Sept. 2021, <https://www.bbc.co.uk/news/business-58433461>, (accessed 10 January 2023).

11 IBISWorld, 'Food Markets in the UK – Number of Businesses 2011–2029', *IBISWorld: Industry Statistics*, <https://www.ibisworld.com/united-kingdom/number-of-businesses/food-markets/14647/>, (accessed 10 January 2023).

12 Quoted in Mary Portas, 'The Portas Review: An independent review into the future of our high streets', *Department for Business, Innovation and Skills*, <https://www.gov.uk/government/publications/the-portas-review-the-future-of-our-high-streets>, 2011, (accessed 9 January 2023).

13 Babita Sharma, *The Corner Shop: Shopkeepers, the Sharmas and the Making of Modern Britain*, John Murray Press, London, 2020.

14 Minority Rights Group International, 'World Directory of Minorities and Indigenous Peoples: United Kingdom, South Asians', *Minority Rights Group International*, <https://minorityrights.org/minorities/south-asians/>, (accessed 9 January 2023).

15 David Visick, 'Forget CTN, fresh food is the future', *Convenience Store*, 11 Dec. 2009, <https://www.conveniencestore.co.uk/news/forget-ctn-fresh-food-is-the-future/205858.article>, (accessed 29 January 2023).

16 Babita Sharma, 'Counter culture: my life growing up in a corner shop', *The Guardian*, 19 May 2019, <https://www.theguardian.com/society/2019/may/19/counter-culture-my-life-growing-up-in-a-corner-shop-babita-sharma>, (accessed 9 January 2023).

17 Neil Wrigley & Erin Brookes, eds., *Evolving High Streets: Resilience and Reinvention Perspectives from Social Science*, University of Southampton, Southampton, 2014.

18 Robin Mannering, 'UK convenience market to grow 17.6% by 2023, says IGD', *Convenience Store*, 05 June 2018, <https://www.conveniencestore.co.uk/news/uk-convenience-market-to-grow-176-by-2023-says-igd-/567810.article>, (accessed 10 January 2023).

19 Sana Noor Haq, 'How South Asian corner shop culture helped the UK survive Covid-19', *gal-dem*, 2 Aug. 2020, <https://gal-dem.com/how-south-asian-corner-shop-culture-helped-the-uk-survive-covid-19/>, (accessed 10 January 2023).

20 Maggie Tillman, 'Amazon Go and Amazon Fresh: How the just walk out tech works', *Pocket-lint*, 11 March 2022, <https://www.pocket-lint.com/gadgets/news/amazon/139650-what-is-amazon-go-where-is-it-and-how-does-it-work/>, (accessed 10 January 2023).

Chapter 7: Food and Beverage

1 'Nick Johnson: Why My Food Markets Matter', *Commercial Real Estate Developer Interviews*, podcast, Floorplate, released 11 May 2021.

2 Dunns Food and Drinks, 'New Street Food Trend Report', *Dunns Food and Drinks*, <https://www.dunnsfoodanddrinks.co.uk/inspiration/new-street-food-trend-report/>, 2019, (accessed 10 January 2023).

3 Tom Pegden, 'Devastating numbers of pub closures as costs spiral', *Business Live*, 4 July 2022, <https://www.business-live.co.uk/retail-consumer/devastating-numbers-pub-closures-costs-24389357>, (accessed 10 January 2023).

4 See Wikipedia, 'List of casual dining restaurant chains', *Wikipedia*, <https://en.wikipedia.org/wiki/List_of_casual_dining_restaurant_chains>, (accessed 10 January 2023).

5 Statista Research Department, 'Number of international and U.S.-based Starbucks stores from 2005 to 2022', *Statista*, <https://www.statista.com/statistics/218366/number-of-international-and-us-starbucks-stores/>, 2022, (accessed 10 January 2023).

6 Trefis Team, 'Why Is Coca-Cola Paying A Hefty Premium For Costa Coffee?', *Forbes*, 4 Sept. 2018, <https://www.forbes.com/sites/greatspeculations/2018/09/04/why-is-coca-cola-paying-a-hefty-premium-for-costa-coffee/?sh=6444c7641643>, (accessed 10 January 2023).

7 Madalena Cardoso, 'Coffee shop industry UK: overview, stats & trends', *Hubl*, 24 May 2022, <https://www.hublapp.co.uk/post/coffee-shop-industry-uk-overview-stats-trends>, (accessed 10 January 2023).

8 Footprint, 'Coffee shop sales fall 40% but big chains expand', *Footprint*, 18 Feb. 2021, <https://www.foodservicefootprint.com/coffee-shop-sales-fall-40-but-big-chains-expand/>, (accessed 10 January 2023).

9 Mario Aksiyote, 'The Next Wave: Predicting the future of coffee in New York City', *Topos*, 7 Sept. 2017, <https://medium.com/topos-ai/the-next-wave-predicting-the-future-of-coffee-in-new-york-city-23a0c5d62000>, (accessed 10 January 2023).

10 Drew Austin, 'More songs about buildings and food', *Kneeling Bus*, 13 Aug. 2021, <https://kneelingbus.substack.com/p/188-more-songs-about-buildings-and>, (accessed 10 January 2023).

11 Jonathan Nunn, 'Sohofication is strangling our city centres', *Dezeen*, 27 Sept. 2022, <https://www.dezeen.com/2022/09/27/sohofication-strangling-city-centres-jonathan-nunn-opinion/>, (accessed 10 January 2023).

12 Jon Henley, 'The aggressive, outrageous, infuriating (and ingenious) rise of BrewDog, *The Guardian*, 24 March 2016, <https://www.theguardian.com/lifeandstyle/2016/mar/24/the-aggressive-outrageous-infuriating-and-ingenious-rise-of-brewdog>, (accessed 10 January 2023).

13 IBISWorld, 'Takeaway & Fast-Food Restaurants in the UK – Market Research Report', *IBISWorld*, <https://www.ibisworld.com/united-kingdom/market-research-reports/takeaway-fast-food-restaurants-industry/>, 2022, (accessed 10 January 2023).

14 The Comptroller and Auditor General, *Childhood obesity*, Department of Health & Social Care, National Audit Office, 2020.

15 Gehl Architects, *Understanding Southwark's Food Experience*, Guy's and St. Thomas Charity, 2019.

16 Jack Shenker, 'They're stealing our customers and we've had enough': is Deliveroo killing restaurant culture?', *The Guardian*, 25 April 2021, <https://www.theguardian.com/global-development/2021/apr/25/deliveroo-tech-delivery-restaurant-service-dark-kitchens>, (accessed 10 January 2023).

17 Anna Wiener, 'Our Ghost-Kitchen Future', *The New Yorker*, 28 June 2020, <https://www.newyorker.com/news/letter-from-silicon-valley/our-ghost-kitchen-future>, (accessed 10 January 2023).

18 Josh Barro, 'If Uber's Food-Delivery Business Isn't Profitable Now, When Can It Be?', *Intelligencer*, 10 Aug. 2020, <https://nymag.com/intelligencer/2020/08/if-uber-eats-isnt-profitable-now-when-can-it-be.html>, (accessed 10 January 2023).

Chapter 8: Online and E-Commerce

1   Lorraine Hahn, 'Interview with Jack Ma', *CNN International*, 25 April 2008.
2   Duncan Clark, *Alibaba: The House that Jack Ma Built*, Harper Colins, New York, 2016.
3   James Kynge, 'Alibaba steps up competition with Amazon in global ecommerce market', *Financial Times*, 07 May 2019, <https://www.ft.com/content/3d25007c-713d-11e9-bbfb-5c68069fbd15>, (accessed 10 January 2023).
4   Paul Mozur & Esther Fung, 'Alibaba to Pay $692 Million for Stake in Intime Retail', *The Wall Street Journal*, 31 March 2014, <https://www.wsj.com/articles/alibaba-to-pay-692-million-for-35-stake-in-intime-retail-1396234141>, (accessed 10 January 2023).
5   Lingling Wei & Jing Yang, 'Ant Founder Jack Ma Faces Backlash From Regulators', *The Wall Street Journal*, 3 Nov. 2020, <https://www.wsj.com/articles/ant-founder-jack-ma-faces-backlash-from-regulators-11604442018>, (accessed 10 January 2023).
6   Lily Kuo, 'Jack Ma is tamed: How Beijing showed tech entrepreneur who is boss', *The Guardian*, 4 Nov. 2020, <https://www.theguardian.com/business/2020/nov/04/jack-ma-ant-group-is-tamed-social-media-reacts-after-china-blocks-ipo>, (accessed 10 January 2023).
7   Genecon & Partners, *Understanding High Street Performance*, Department for Business, Innovation & Skills, 2011.
8   Paul Tostevin, 'Leaders and laggards: the rise of online retail', *Savills Impacts*, Sept. 2019, <https://www.savills.com/impacts/technology/leaders-and-laggards-the-rise-of-online-retail.html>, (accessed 10 January 2023).
9   Centre for Retail Research, 'Who's Gone Bust?', *Centre for Retail Research*, <https://www.retailresearch.org/whos-gone-bust.html>, (accessed 10 January 2023).
10 Aaryaman Aashind, 'UK Online Shopping Statistics', *Cybercrew*, <https://cybercrew.uk/blog/uk-online-shopping-statistics/#:~:text=The%20total%20value%20of%20monthly,British%20Pounds%20in%20January%202022>, 2022, (accessed 10 January 2023).
11 I-AM Shift, 'The Convergence Continuum: Retail Sector Trend Report', *I-AM Shift*, <https://www.i-amshift.com/archive/>, (accessed 10 January 2023).
12 Lisa Hooker, 'Younger people – your future consumers – now as likely to enjoy shopping in-store as online', *Retail Week*, 5 May 2022, <https://www.retail-week.com/customer/younger-people-your-future-consumers-now-as-likely-to-enjoy-shopping-in-store-as-online/7041734.article?authent=1>, (accessed 10 January 2023).
13 Lukas Peters, 'Top online stores in the United Kingdom in 2021, by e-commerce net sales', *Statista*, <https://www.statista.com/forecasts/870307/united-kingdom-top-online-stores-united-kingdom-ecommercedb>, 2022, (accessed 9 January 2023).
14 Daniel Slater, 'Elements of Amazon's Day 1 Culture', *Amazon*, <https://aws.amazon.com/executive-insights/content/how-amazon-defines-and-operationalizes-a-day-1-culture/>, 2016, (accessed 11 January 2023).
15 Brian Dumaine, *Bezonomics: How Amazon Is Changing Our Lives, and What the World's Best Companies Are Learning from It*, Simon and Schuster UK, London, 2021.
16 Ljubica Gjorgievska, '33+ Amazon UK Statistics to Get You in the Shopping Mood', *Don't Disappoint Me*, 1 Aug. 2022, <https://dontdisappoint.me.uk/resources/technology/amazon-statistics-uk/>, (accessed 11 January 2023).
17 Stephanie Chevalier, 'Number of active Amazon marketplace sellers in 2019, by country', *Statista*, <https://www.statista.com/statistics/1086664/amazon-3p-seller-by-country/>, 2022, (accessed 11 January 2023).
18 Adam Cohen, *The Perfect Store*, Back Bay Books, New York, 2003.
19 Elen Lewis, *The eBay Phenomenon*, Marshall Cavendish, London, 2008.
20 Mike Isaac, 'Growth Dip in Auctions Cuts Results for eBay', *The New York Times*, 16 Oct. 2014, <https://www.nytimes.com/2014/10/16/technology/growth-dip-in-auctions-cuts-results-for-ebay.html>, (accessed 10 January 2023).
21 Dave Chaffey, 'eBay Marketing Strategy Case Study', *Smart Insights*, 11 May 2021, <https://www.smartinsights.com/ecommerce/ecommerce-strategy/ebay-case-study-2/>, (accessed 10 January 2023).
22 Michael Goul, 'EBay Study: How to build trust and improve the shopping experience', *Arizona State University*, 8 May 2021, <https://news.wpcarey.asu.edu/20120508-ebay-study-how-build-trust-and-improve-shopping-experience>, (accessed 10 January 2023).
23 Gordon Fletcher et al., 'The Social Supply Chain and the Future High Street', *The University of Manchester*, 2016.
24 Centre for Retail Research, 'Mobile Retailing', *Centre for Retail Research*, <https://www.retailresearch.org/mobile-retailing.html>, (accessed 10 January 2023).
25 ICSC, 'The Halo Effect II: Quantifying the Impact of Omnichannel', ISCU, <https://www.icsc.com/thehaloeffectii>, 2018, (accessed 10 January 2023).
26 Blaire Erskine, 'The Untold Truth Of Etsy', *The List*, 23 Jan. 2023, <https://www.thelist.com/197941/the-untold-truth-of-etsy/>, (accessed 29 Jan 2023).
27 Max Chafkin, 'Can Rob Kalin Scale Etsy?', *Inc.*, 1 April 2011, <https://www.inc.com/magazine/20110401/can-rob-kalin-scale-etsy.html>, (accessed 29 January 2023).
28 Josh Silverman, 'Etsy's CEO on Q2 2017 Results – Earnings Call Transcript', *Seeking Alpha*, <https://seekingalpha.com/article/4094702-etsys-etsy-ceo-josh-silverman-on-q2-2017-results-earnings-call-transcript>, (accessed 29 January 2023).
29 Benjamin Snyder, 'A huge percentage of Etsy sellers are women', *Fortune*, 23 July 2015, <https://fortune.com/2015/07/23/etsy-sellers-women/>, (accessed 29 January 2023).
30 Kathleen Davis, 'The Etsy Economy and Changing the Way We Shop', *Entrepreneur*, 22 March 2013, <https://www.entrepreneur.com/starting-a-business/the-etsy-economy-and-changing-the-way-we-shop/226180>, (accessed 29 January 2023).

Chapter 9: Sound and Vision

1   Charlotte Krol, 'UK vinyl spending set to overtake CDs for first time since 1980s', *NME*, 23 March 2021, <https://www.nme.com/news/music/uk-vinyl-spending-set-to-overtake-cds-for-first-time-since-1980s-2906449>, (accessed 11 January 2023).
2   Ellen Peirson-Hagger, 'It's unmanageable: How the vinyl industry reached breaking point', *The New Statesman*, 16 Sept. 2021, <https://www.newstatesman.com/culture/music/2021/09/its-unmanageable-how-the-vinyl-industry-reached-breaking-point>, (accessed 11 January 2023).
3   Mitch Betts, 'Internet Webcasts Become Corporate Bandwidth Hogs', *Computerworld*, 22 May 2000, <https://www.computerworld.com/article/2595196/internet-webcasts-become--corporate-bandwidth-hogs.html>, (accessed 11 January 2023).
4   Tim Ingham, 'A New Report Says Independent Artists Could Generate More Than $2 Billion in 2020', *Rolling Stone*, 16 March 2020, <https://www.rollingstone.com/pro/features/raine-group-independent-artists-2-billion-in-2020-967138/>, (accessed 11 January 2023).
5   Rowan Moore, 'Tŷ Pawb review – an art gallery that truly is everybody's house', *The Guardian*, 1 Sept. 2018, <https://www.theguardian.com/artanddesign/2018/sep/01/ty-pawb-review-art-gallery-everybodys-house-wrexham-market>, (accessed 11 January 2023).
6   Holliss Vincent, *Sunderland Retail Needs Assessment*, Sunderland City Council, 2016.
7   Sarah Butler, 'From a Debenhams to a creative hub: closed stores get new lease in community life', *The Guardian*, 1 Dec. 2021, <https://www.theguardian.com/business/2021/dec/01/doors-open-for-uk-community-projects-as-retail-chains-fold>, (accessed 11 January 2023).
8   BBC News, 'HMV calls in administrators for second time in six years', *BBC News*, 28 Dec. 2018, <https://www.bbc.co.uk/news/business-46699290>, (accessed 11 January 2023).
9   Caoimhe Gordon, 'Interview: HMV's Doug Putman on stores, streaming and centenary celebrations', *Retail Week*, 8 Sept. 2021, <https://www.retail-week.com/entertainment/interview-hmvs-doug-putman-on-stores-streaming-and-centenary-celebrations/7040542.article>, (accessed 11 January 2023).
10 Andy Ash, 'The rise and fall of Blockbuster and how it's surviving with just one store left', *Insider*, 12 Aug. 2020, <https://www.businessinsider.com/the-rise-and-fall-of-blockbuster-video-streaming-2020-1?r=US&IR=T>, (accessed 11 January 2023).
11 Ibid., Ref. 10.
12 Katie Grant, 'Nostalgia can be very healing: How the last UK video shop became a mecca for tape heads around the world', *iNews*, 28 Aug. 2021, <https://inews.co.uk/news/consumer/last-uk-video-shop-liverpool-video-videodyssey-nostalgia-mecca-tape-heads-world-1171705>, (accessed 11 January 2023).

Chapter 10: Home and Garden

1   Jill Treanor, 'MFI sold for £1 and repackaged as Galiform', *The Guardian*, 23 Sept. 2006, <https://www.theguardian.com/business/2006/sep/23/privateequity>, (accessed 11 January 2023).
2   Mark Sweney, 'Made.com plans to cut third of staff as it seeks emergency investment or buyer', *The Guardian*, 23 Sept. 2022, <https://www.theguardian.com/business/2022/sep/23/madecom-plans-to-cut-a-third-of-staff-as-it-seeks-buyer-or-investment>, (accessed 11 January 2023).
3   Julia Kollewe, 'B&Q owner Kingfisher's profits fall 30% amid cost of living crisis', *The Guardian*, 20 Sept. 2022, <https://www.theguardian.com/business/2022/sep/20/bq-kingfisher-profits-cost-of-living-crisis-mini-budget>, (accessed 11 January 2023).
4   Cassie Barton et al., 'Extending home ownership: Government Initiatives', *House of Commons Library*, <https://commonslibrary.parliament.uk/research-briefings/sn03668/>, 2021, (accessed 11 January 2023).

5   Sarah Butler, 'Ikea replaces Topshop as furnishings become high street fashion', *The Guardian*, 30 Oct. 2021, <https://www.theguardian.com/business/2021/oct/30/ikea-topshop-oxford-street-london-store-retail>, (accessed 11 January 2023).

6   Daphne Howland, 'Wayfair back in the red in Q2 as customers quit', *Retail Dive*, 4 Aug. 2022, <https://www.retaildive.com/news/wayfair-in-red-q2-earnings-results/628871/>, (accessed 11 January 2023).

Chapter 11: Fashion and Beauty

1   Euromonitor International, 'Retailing Global Industry Overview', *Euromonitor International*, <https://www.euromonitor.com/retailing-global-industry-overview/report>, 2020, (accessed 11 January 2023).

2   Tony Coleman, former Director at Burtons, Labour MP & Minister, [interviewed by author], 5 January 2021.

3   Georgia Aspinall, 'Why Did We All Stop Shopping At Topshop? Seven Shoppers Tell Us Their Reasons', *Grazia*, 20 Jan. 2021, <https://graziadaily.co.uk/life/in-the-news/is-topshop-closing-down-going-bust-collapse/>, (accessed 11 January 2023).

4   Retail Economics, 'UK Retail Trends for 2021 Report', *Retail Economics*, <https://www.retaileconomics.co.uk/outlook-for-the-uk-retail-industry-2021>, 2021, (accessed 11 January 2023).

5   Elliott Clayton, 'PrettyLittleThing Doubled Down on Personalized Media; Its Revenue Jumped 38%', *Adweek*, Feb. 2020, <https://www.adweek.com/partner-articles/prettylittlething-doubled-down-on-personalized-media-its-revenue-jumped-38/>, (accessed 11 January 2023).

6   Joanna Partridge, 'Boohoo profits soar as Covid turns customer focus to loungewear', *The Guardian*, 5 May 2021, <https://www.theguardian.com/business/2021/may/05/boohoo-profits-soar-as-covid-turns-customer-focus-to-loungewear>, (accessed 11 January 2023)

7   Zoe Wood & Sarah Butler, 'After Topshop owner Arcadia's demise, what now for UK clothes shopping?', *The Guardian*, 13 Feb. 2021, <https://www.theguardian.com/business/2021/feb/13/after-topshop-owner-arcadia-demise-what-now-for-uk-clothes-shopping>, (accessed 11 January 2023).

8   Nils Pratley, 'Boohoo tumbles as reality of online clothes shopping hits home', *The Guardian*, 4 May 2022, <https://www.theguardian.com/business/nils-pratley-on-finance/2022/may/04/boohoo-tumbles-as-reality-of-online-clothes-shopping-hits-home>, (accessed 11 January 2023).

9   Sarah O'Connor, 'Fast-fashion retailers called before parliament', *Financial Times*, 9 Nov. 2018, <https://www.ft.com/content/2471938e-e37a-11e8-8e70-5e22a430c1ad>, (accessed 11 January 2023).

10 Caroline Wheeler et al., 'Boohoo: fashion giant faces slavery investigation', *The Sunday Times*, 5 July 2020, <https://www.thetimes.co.uk/article/boohoo-fashion-giant-faces-slavery-investigation-57s3hxcth>, (accessed 11 January 2023).

11 Sarah Butler & Rob Davies, 'Boohoo shareholders demand answers after shares plunge by a third', *The Guardian*, 7 July 2020, <https://www.theguardian.com/business/2020/jul/07/boohoo-shares-concern-factory-conditions>, (accessed 11 January 2023).

12 Sarah Butler, 'Incredible Boohoo denying knowledge of factory allegations, says MP', *The Guardian*, 16 July 2020, <https://www.theguardian.com/business/2020/jul/16/incredible-boohoo-denying-knowledge-of-factory-allegations-says-mp>, (accessed 11 January 2023).

13 Tom Vanderbilt, 'Long Live the Industrial City', *Wilson Quarterly*, 6 April 2011, <https://longreads.com/2011/04/06/long-live-the-industrial-city/>, (accessed 11 January 2023).

14 Ethical Trading Initiative, 'Working conditions in the Leicester garment industry', *Ethical Trading Initiative*, <https://www.ethicaltrade.org/issues/company-purchasing-practices/working-conditions-leicester-garment-industry>, (accessed 11 January 2023).

15 Archie Bland & Annie Kelly, 'Boohoo booms as Leicester garment factories are linked to lockdown', *The Guardian*, 4 July 2020, <https://www.theguardian.com/uk-news/2020/jul/04/boohoo-booms-leicester-garment-factories-linked-lockdown>, (accessed 11 January 2023).

16 Sarah O'Connor, 'Dark factories: labour exploitation in Britain's garment industry', *Financial Times*, 17 May 2018, <https://www.ft.com/content/e427327e-5892-11e8-b8b2-d6ceb45fa9d0>, (accessed 11 January 2023).

17 Helle Abelvik-Lawson, 'The UK's fast fashion habit is getting worse – and it's destroying the planet', *Greenpeace*, 23 Nov. 2020, <https://www.greenpeace.org.uk/news/the-uks-fast-fashion-habit-is-getting-worse-and-its-destroying-the-planet/>, (accessed 11 January 2023).

18 Ashley Armstrong & Elizabeth Burden, 'Boohoo's £90m marketing spend pays off', *The Times*, 26 Sept. 2019, <https://www.thetimes.co.uk/article/boohoo-s-90m-marketing-spend-pays-off-kzpg9v9rm>, (accessed 11 January 2023).

19 Jill Foster, 'Would you go out with your hair in Curlers? It's all the rage in Liverpool – so will the rest of Britain follow suit?', *The Daily Mail*, 30 July 2015, <https://www.dailymail.co.uk/femail/article-3179061/Would-hair-curlers-s-rage-Liverpool-rest-Britain-follow-suit.html>, (accessed 11 January 2023).

20 Rebecca Toop, 'Place Test: Liverpool One', *The Developer*, No. 03, 2020.

21 L'Oreal, 'L'Oreal 2020 Annual Report', *L'Oreal*, <https://www.loreal-finance.com/en/annual-report-2020/>, 2020, (accessed 11 January 2023).

22 Seb James, 'Coronavirus – A message from Seb James, Managing Director, Boots UK and ROI', *Boots*, 17 March2020, <https://www.boots-uk.com/newsroom/features/coronavirus-a-message-from-seb-james-managing-director-boots-uk-and-roi/>, (accessed 11 January 2023).

23 Zoe Wood, 'Next to create new chain of upmarket beauty halls', *The Guardian*, 7 May 2020, <https://www.theguardian.com/business/2020/may/07/next-to-create-new-chain-of-upmarket-beauty-halls>, (accessed 11 January 2023).

24 Sarah Butler, 'Debenhams returns to high street with Manchester beauty store', *The Guardian*, 3 Dec. 2021, <https://www.theguardian.com/business/2021/dec/03/debenhams-returns-to-high-street-with-manchester-beauty-store>, (accessed 11 January 2023).

25 Jack Stratten, 'Top 45 Online Retailers who went Offline', *Insider Trends*, 29 June 2018, <https://www.insider-trends.com/top-45-online-retailers-who-went-offline/>, (accessed 11 January 2023).

26 Unibail-Rodamco-Westfield, Westfield How We Shop: The Next Decade', *Unibail-Rodamco-Westfield*, https://www.unibail-rodamco-westfield.de/en/westfield-how-we-shop-a-new-decade-of-experience-retail-dawns-europe>, 2020, (accessed 11 January 2023).

27 George Davies, 'Return of the fashion maverick', *The Independent*, 14 Oct. 1995, <https://www.independent.co.uk/news/business/return-of-the-fashion-maverick-1577671.html>, (accessed January 2023).

Chapter 12: The City

1   Brendan O'Flaherty, *City Economics*, Harvard University Press, USA, 2009

2   Centre for Cities, 'High streets recovery tracker', <https://www.centreforcities.org/data/high-streets-recovery-tracker/>, *Centre for Cities* (accessed 10 January 2023).

3   Kathrin Enenkel, 'Why cities will be our main job creators post-Covid', *Centre for Cities*, 31 March 2021, <https://www.centreforcities.org/blog/why-cities-will-be-our-main-job-creators-post-covid/> (accessed 10 January 2023).

4   Paul Whysall, 'Retail planning and retail change in Central Nottingham since the 1970s', *The Town Planning Review*, Vol. 84, No. 6, 2013.

5   Rima Sabina Aouf, 'Heatherwick proposal for Nottingham development incorporates ruins of shopping centre', *Dezeen*, 10 Dec. 2021, <https://www.dezeen.com/2021/12/10/heatherwick-proposal-nottingham-shopping-centre-architecture-news/>, (accessed 11 January 2023).

6   Nottingham City Council GIS Team, 'Broadmarsh, Nottingham – The Big Conversation', *Nottingham City Council*, <https://storymaps.arcgis.com/stories/21c59c2e9c52410b9278230ea7828acc>, 2022, (accessed 11 January 2023).

7   Ibid., Ref. 4.

8   Paul Wythsall, 'The Changing Retail Structure of Central Nottingham, 1974-84' in *Retail Planning and Development: What next – Where?*, Planning, Transport Research and Computation annual meeting, London, 1985.

9   Geoffrey C. Smith & N. K. Dolman, 'Consumer responses to alternative retail environments in Nottingham's central area', *East Midlands Geographer*, Vol. 7, 1981.

10 Nadia Elghamry, 'Ugly Sister Gets a Face Lift', *Estates Gazette*, 9 Nov. 2002.

11 Lynsey Hanley, 'Shopping, how it became our national disease', *New Statesman*, No. 135, 2006.

12 Competition and Markets Authority, 'Capital Shopping Centres / Broadmarsh Retail Ltd Partnership', *UK Government*, <https://www.gov.uk/cma-cases/capital-shopping-centres-broadmarsh-retail-ltd-partnership>, 2012, (accessed 11 January 2023).

13 BBC News, 'Nottingham's Broadmarsh shopping centre risk', *BBC News*, 3 March 2013, <https://www.bbc.co.uk/news/uk-england-nottinghamshire-21633311>, (accessed 11 January 2023).

14 Joseph Locker, 'Nottingham Broad Marsh vision hailed as extraordinary as new plans unveiled for the first time', *Nottinghamshire Live*, 7 Dec. 2021, <https://www.nottinghampost.com/news/local-news/nottingham-broad-marsh-vision-hailed-6310744>, (accessed 11 January 2023).

15 Anjli Raval & Andrew Edgecliffe-Johnson, 'Summer is over. Will everyone now go back to the office?', *Financial Times*, 2 Sept. 2022, <https://www.ft.com/content/1709fb0d-48b6-493a-b649-4c0c6d5ece38>, (accessed 11 January 2023).

16 Elena Magrini, 'How will Coronavirus affect jobs in different parts of the country?', *Centre for Cities*, 17 March 2020, <https://www.centreforcities.org/

blog/how-will-coronavirus-affect-jobs-in-different-parts-of-the-country/>, (accessed 10 January 2023).

17 Price Waterhouse Coopers, 'The Economic Impact of Returning to the Office', *Price Waterhouse Coopers*, <https://www.pwc.co.uk/services/economics/insights/the-economic-impact-of-returning-to-the-office.html>, (accessed 10 January 2023).

18 Department for Levelling Up, Housing and Communities, 'Levelling Up the United Kingdom', *UK Government*, <https://www.gov.uk/government/publications/levelling-up-the-united-kingdom>, (accessed 11 January 2023).

19 Will Dunn, 'Why energy prices could kill working from home', *The New Statesman*, 26 Aug. 2022, <https://www.newstatesman.com/business/work/2022/08/why-energy-prices-will-kill-working-from-home>, (accessed 10 January 2023).

20 Price Waterhouse Coopers, 'Employers set to reduce office space by up to 9m sq ft – the equivalent of 14 skyscrapers', *Price Waterhouse Coopers*, <https://www.pwc.co.uk/press-room/press-releases/employers-set-to-reduce-office-space-by-up-to-9m-sq-ft---the-equ.html>, (accessed 11 January 2023).

21 Carsten Foertsch, 'Quick Facts about the UK's Coworking Spaces', *Deskmag*, 1 Oct. 2018, <https://www.deskmag.com/en/coworking-city-country-profiles/quick-facts-about-the-uk-coworking-spaces-market-report-study-britain-london-1013>, (accessed 10 January 2023).

22 Michael O'Connor & Jonathan Portes, 'Estimating the UK population during the pandemic', *Economic Statistics Centre of Excellence*, 14 Jan. 2021, <https://www.escoe.ac.uk/estimating-the-uk-population-during-the-pandemic/>, (accessed 10 January 2023).

23 Harris MacLeod, '52% of Londoners want to leave', *YouGov*, 27 Nov. 2021, <https://yougov.co.uk/topics/politics/articles-reports/2012/11/27/52-londoners-want-leave>, (accessed 10 January 2023).

24 'City Living, Covid Vaccine Scams, Side Hustle Advice', *You and Yours,* radio programme, BBC Radio 4, London, broadcast 29 July 2021.

25 Ibid., Ref. 2.

26 Hugh Radojev, 'Will more retailers ditch Oxford Street?', *Retail Week*, 21 Jan. 2021, <https://www.retail-week.com/stores/will-more-retailers-ditch-oxford-street/7036623.article?authent=1>, (accessed 9 January 2023).

27 See Local Data Company & The British Retail Consortium, 'BRC-LDC Vacancy Monitor', *Local Data Company*, <https://www.localdatacompany.com/blog/brc-vacancy-monitor>, (accessed 10 January 2023).

28 Ibid., Ref. 26.

29 Jess Clark, 'Concerns over Oxford Street being overrun with US candy stores', *The Guardian*, 17 June 2022, <https://www.theguardian.com/uk-news/2022/jun/17/oxford-street-us-candy-stores>, (accessed 10 January 2023).

30 Sahar Nazir, 'London's West End warns business rates will push retailers to quit area', *Retail Gazette*, 11 Aug. 2020, <https://www.retailgazette.co.uk/blog/2020/08/londons-west-end-warns-business-rates-will-push-retailers-to-quit-area/>, (accessed 10 January 2023).

31 Jem Bartholomew, 'London's Marble Arch Mound attraction to close this weekend', *The Guardian*, 7 Jan. 2022, <https://www.theguardian.com/uk-news/2022/jan/07/londons-marble-arch-mound-attraction-to-close-this-weekend>, (accessed 10 January 2023).

32 Andrew Saint ed., 'Survey of London, Volume 53: Oxford Street', *The London Journal*, Vol. 45, Issue 3, 2020.

33 Simon Jenkins, 'Top of the shops: how has Oxford Street survived the slow death of the high street?', *The Guardian*, 5 March 2020, <https://www.theguardian.com/lifeandstyle/2020/mar/05/top-pf-the-shops-oxford-street-survived-death-high-street>, (accessed 11 January 2023).

34 Ibid., Ref. 26.

Chapter 13: The Mall

1 Caoimhe Gordon, 'Data: Shop vacancies 'at highest rate ever recorded' as uncertainty lingers', *Retail Week*, 30 July 2021, < https://www.retail-week.com/stores/data-shop-vacancies-at-highest-rate-ever-recorded-as-uncertainty-lingers/7040364.article>, (accessed 6 January 2023).

2 New Economics Foundation, Clone Town Britain: The Survey Results on the Bland State of the Nation, New Economics Foundation, 2004.

3 David Rudlin, Rob Thompson & Sarah Jarvis, *Urbanism*, Routledge, London, 2016.

4 The Academy of Urbanism, 'Princesshay, Exeter: The Great Place Award 2011', *The Academy of Urbanism*, <https://www.academyofurbanism.org.uk/princesshay/>, 2010, (accessed 10 January 2023).

5 Daily Telegraph, 'Big Brother technology tracks shoppers' mobile phones', *Daily Telegraph*, 5 Jan. 2012, <https://www.telegraph.co.uk/finance/newsbysector/retailandconsumer/8993620/Big-Brother-technology-tracks-shoppers-mobile-phones.html>, (accessed 11 January 2023).

6 Chris Isidore, 'Malls are doomed: 25% will be gone in 5 years', *CNN Money*, 2 June 2017, <https://money.cnn.com/2017/06/02/news/economy/doomed-malls/index.html>, (accessed 11 January 2023).

7 IBIS World, 'Department Stores in the US – Market Size 2005–2028', *IBISWorld: Industry Statistics*, <https://www.ibisworld.com/industry-statistics/market-size/department-stores-united-states/>, (accessed 29 January 2023).

8 Ellen Dunham Jones & June Williamson, 'Dead and Dying Shopping Malls, Re-Inhabited', *Architectural Design*, Vol. 87, Issue 5, 2017.

9 Sahar Nazir, '70 UK shopping centres at threat of permanent closure', *Retail Gazette*, 7 June 2021, <https://www.retailgazette.co.uk/blog/2021/06/70-uk-shopping-centres-at-threat-of-permanent-closure/>, (accessed 11 January 2023).

10 Sarah Butler, 'Up to 70 UK shopping centres could close amid Covid crisis', *The Guardian*, 5 June 2021, <https://www.theguardian.com/business/2021/jun/05/up-to-70-uk-shopping-centres-could-close-amid-covid-crisis>, (accessed 11 January 2023). `

11 Unibail-Rodamco-Westfield, 'Westfield How We Shop: The Next Decade', *Unibail-Rodamco-Westfield*, https://www.unibail-rodamco-westfield.de/en/westfield-how-we-shop-a-new-decade-of-experience-retail-dawns-europe>, 2020, (accessed 11 January 2023).

12 Tom Shearsmith, 'The Interview: Harita Shah, Westfield Director of Brand, Creative, Media, Comms & Events', *The Industry.Fashion*, 29 Oct. 2021, <https://www.theindustry.fashion/the-interview-harita-shah-westfield-director-of-brand-creative-media-comms-events/>, (accessed 11 January 2023).

13 Interview with Rob Monaghan Director of development Cheshire West and Chester Council, 9 June 2021.

Chapter 14: The Town

1 Dave Kennedy, former Director of Development at Barnsley Council, [interviewed by author], 18 May 2020.

2 Alan Simpson & Brian Lewis, *Urban Renaissance Towns (Barnsley, Doncaster, Huddersfield, Grimsby, Scarborough and Wakefield)*, Pontefract Press, UK, 2002.

3 Will Alsop, *Remaking Barnsley Strategic Development Framework 2003-2033*, Barnsley MDC & Yorkshire Forward, 2003.

4 Tom Whittington, 'How to repurpose retail space', *Savills Impacts*, May 2020, <https://www.savills.com/impacts/social-change/how-to-repurpose-retail-space.html>, (accessed 9 January 2023).

5 Mary Portas, 'The Portas Review: An independent review into the future of our high streets', *Department for Business, Innovation and Skills*, <https://www.gov.uk/government/publications/the-portas-review-the-future-of-our-high-streets>, 2011, (accessed 9 January 2023).

6 Bláthnaid Duffy, Director of Planning, Development & Regeneration at Lambert Smith Hanson, [interviewed by author], 21 July 2020.

7 Andrew Napier, 'Investigation highlights culture of adversity at Winchester Council', *Hampshire Chronicle*, 24 Sept. 2020, <https://www.hampshirechronicle.co.uk/news/18743084.investigation-highlights-culture-adversity-winchester-council/>, (accessed 11 January 2023).

8 Ian Charie, [interviewed by author], 30 June 2020.

9 JTP Architects, 'Central Winchester Regeneration', *Winchester City Council*, community planning event, 20 June 2018.

10 Winchester City Council, 'Central Winchester Regeneration Supplementary Planning Document (SPD)', *Winchester City Council*, <https://www.jtp.co.uk/projects/community-planning/central-winchester-community-planning-weekend>, 2018, (accessed 12 January 2023).

11 Andrew Napier, 'Kim Gottlieb calls for city council chief executive to be replaced', *Hampshire Chronicle*, 1 Dec. 2020, <https://www.hampshirechronicle.co.uk/news/18897596.kim-gottlieb-calls-city-council-chief-executive-replaced/>, (accessed 11 January 2023).

12 Nick Edmondson, 'Guildford named luxury shopping capital of the UK', *Surrey Live*, 23 Aug. 2013, <https://www.getsurrey.co.uk/news/local-news/guildford-named-luxury-shopping-capital-5773589/>, (accessed 11 January 2023).

13 Graham Ruddick, 'Guildford is luxury shopping capital of the UK', *The Telegraph*, 18 Aug. 2013, <https://www.telegraph.co.uk/finance/newsbysector/retailandconsumer/10250830/Guildford-is-luxury-shopping-capital-of-the-UK.html>, (accessed 11 January 2023).

14 Guildford Borough Council, 'Shaping Guildford's Future', *Shaping Guildford*, <https://shapingguildford.co.uk/>, (accessed 11 January 2023).

15 Guildford Society, 'Where is the Centre of the Town?', *Guildford Society*, 17 March 2021, <https://www.guildfordsociety.org.uk/TCCentre.html>, (accessed 12 January 2023).

16 JTP Architects & St Edward, 'April 2022 Scheme

Summary', *North Street Regeneration*, <https://www.northstreetregeneration.co.uk/latest-scheme-summary.html>, (accessed 12 January 2023).

17 Ibid., Ref. 12.

18 BBC News, 'Preston Tithebarn development public inquiry begins', *BBC News*, 18 May 2010, <http://news.bbc.co.uk/1/hi/england/lancashire/8688941.stm>, (accessed 11 January 2023).

19 Richard Waite, 'BDP's £700m Tithebarn scheme canned as John Lewis pulls out', *Architects' Journal*, 3 Nov. 2011, <https://www.architectsjournal.co.uk/archive/bdps-700m-tithebarn-scheme-canned-as-john-lewis-pulls-out>, (accessed 11 January 2023).

20 Ben Willis, 'Barnsley makeover plan flounders', *The Guardian*, 22 April 2005, <https://www.theguardian.com/society/2005/apr/22/urbandesign.architecture>, (accessed 12 January 2023).

21 Ibid., Ref. 1.

22 David Shepherd, [interviewed by author], May 2020.

23 See *Doncopolitan*, Issue 05, 2014, <https://issuu.com/warrendraper/docs/doncopolitan_boyo_issuu_issue>, (accessed 30 January 2023).

24 John Harris, 'How Doncaster is giving power back to the people', *Idler Magazine*, 4 March 2019, <https://www.idler.co.uk/article/how-doncaster-is-giving-power-back-to-the-people/>, (accessed 12 January 2023).

25 John Harris, 'Amazon v the high street – how Doncaster is fighting back', *The Guardian*, 11 Oct. 2018, <https://www.theguardian.com/uk-news/2018/oct/11/amazon-v-the-high-street-how-doncaster-is-fighting-back>, (accessed 11 January 2023).

26 Doncaster Council, *Retail Strategy: Local Plan Evidence Base*, Doncaster Council, 2019.

27 Cushman & Wakefield, *Retail and Town Centre Study 2016*, Colchester Borough Council, 2016.

28 Katherine Palmer, 'South Lanes leading the way for future of Colchester town centre', *Daily Gazette & Essex County Standard*, 11 Jan. 2020, <https://www.gazette-news.co.uk/news/18143700.south-lanes-leading-way-future-colchester-town-centre/>, (accessed 10 January 2023).

29 The Great British High Street, 'Sir Issacs Walk & Eld Lane: Colchester', *The Great British High Street, 2019*, <https://thegreatbritishhighstreet.co.uk/high-street-of-the-year-awards/rising-star-colchester>, (accessed 10 January 2023).

30 Ibid., Ref. 28.

31 CPW Planning, *Retail and Town Centre: Study Update 2020*, Colchester Borough Council, 2020.

32 Frome Admin, 'Regeneration of Frome', *Frome Shops*, 27 July 2015, <https://fromeshops.wordpress.com/2015/07/27/regeneration-of-frome/>, (accessed 10 January 2023).

33 John Peverley, 'The Regeneration of Frome', *Urban Design Journal*, Issue 83, 2001.

34 Peter Macfadyen, *Flatpack Democracy: A DIY Guide to Creating Independent Politics*, Eco-logic Books, Bath, 2014.

35 See The Frome Independent, 'The Frome Independent: More Than a Market', *The Frome*

Independent, <https://thefromeindependent.org.uk>, (accessed 10 January 2023).

Chapter 15: The High Street

1 Karan Modha, [interviewed by author], 28 November 2019.

2 BBC News, 'Ugandan Asians advert foolish, says Leicester councillor', *BBC News*, 8 Aug. 2012, <https://www.bbc.co.uk/news/uk-england-leicestershire-19165216>, (accessed 12 January 2023).

3 Vicky Frost, 'Sugar and Spice', *The Guardian*, 31 Oct. 2007, <https://www.theguardian.com/lifeandstyle/2007/oct/31/foodanddrink.foodfestivals>, (accessed 12 January 2023).

4 Phil Jones Associates, 'Belgrave Road, Leicester', *Phil Jones Associates*, <https://pja.co.uk/project/belgrave-road-leicester/>, (accessed 12 January 2023).

5 Andy Munro, *Going for a Balti: The Story of Birmingham's Signature Dish*, Brewin Books, Redditch, 2015.

6 Alex Nelson, 'Goodness Gracious Me at 20: the genius of Going for an English', *The i*, 18 Jan. 2018, <https://inews.co.uk/culture/television/goodness-gracious-me-going-for-an-english-117853>, (accessed 12 January 2023).

7 Sanjeeta Bains, 'How the Balti Triangle has changed – has it fallen out of favour with Brummies?', *Birmingham Live*, 3 Nov. 2018, <https://www.birminghammail.co.uk/whats-on/food-drink-news/how-balti-triangle-struggling-customers-15353756>, (accessed 12 January 2023).

8 Friedrich Engels, *The Condition of the Working Class in England*, Oxford University Press, Oxford, 2009.

9 John Cooper-Clarke, *I Wanna be Yours*, Pan MacMillan, London, 2020.

10 Bill Hillier, 'Cities as Movement Economies', *Urban Design International*, Vol. 1, Issue 1, 1996.

11 Matthew Carmona, 'The existential crisis of traditional shopping streets: the sun model and the place attraction paradigm', *Journal of Urban Design*, Vol. 27, Issue 1, 2021.

12 Hayley Holgate, 'High streets in Great Britain: March, 2020', *Office for National Statistics*, <https://www.ons.gov.uk/peoplepopulationandcommunity/populationandmigration/populationestimates/articles/highstreetsingreatbritain/march2020>, 2020, (accessed 12 January 2023).

13 Linda Piper, 'Tesco and Co-op closures put Welling traders under pressure, *News Shopper*, 22 Oct. 2008, <https://www.newsshopper.co.uk/news/3780615.tesco-and-co-op-closures-put-welling-traders-under-pressure/>, (accessed 12 January 2023).

14 Mark Davey, 'Fixing the Intangibles – Identity, Brand and USP', *Urban Design Journal*, Issue 154, 2020.

15 Neil Kirby, [interviewed by author], 3 June 2021.

16 News Desk, 'Peckham Levels is well on its way after Make Shift sign lease with Southwark Council', *Southwark News*, 8 Dec. 2016, <https://southwarknews.co.uk/news/regeneration/

peckham-levels-well-way-makeshift-sign-lease-southwark-council/>, (accessed 12 January 2023).

17 See Peckham Levels, 'The Culture of Enterprise: Make, Shift, Create', Peckham Levels, <https://peckhamlevels.org/the-culture-of-enterprise-make-shift-create/>, (accessed 12 January 2023).

18 Lucy Lovell, 'We're calling it: Peckham is still London's coolest neighbourhood', *Time Out*, 17 Sept. 2019, <https://www.timeout.com/london/news/were-calling-it-peckham-is-still-londons-coolest-neighbourhood-091719>, (accessed 12 January 2023).

19 Rob Monaghan, [interviewed by author], June 2021.

20 Catherine Jones, 'Cultural revolution arrives in Garston', *Liverpool Echo*, 30 May 2008, <https://www.liverpoolecho.co.uk/news/liverpool-news/cultural-revolution-arrives-in-garston-3487415>, (accessed 12 January 2023).

Chapter 16: Conclusions: New Life for Town Centres

1 Hugh Radojev, 'Data: Store closures slow in remarkable post-pandemic retail recovery', *Retail Week*, 22 Sept. 2022, <https://www.retail-week.com/stores/data-store-closures-slow-in-remarkable-post-pandemic-retail-recovery/7042400.article?authent=1>, (accessed 11 January 2023).

2 David Rudlin & Shruti Hemani, *Climax City: Masterplanning and the Complexity of Urban Growth*, RIBA Publishing, London, 2019.

3 Colin Amery & Dan Cruickshank, *The Rape of Britain*, Harper Collins, UK, 1975.

4 URBED, *Vital and Viable Town Centres: Meeting the Challenge*, HMSO, London, 1994.

5 Alex Morton & Gerard Dericks, *21st Century Retail Policy: Quality, Choice, Experience and Convenience*, Policy Exchange, London, 2013.

6 Tom Whittington, 'How to repurpose retail space', *Savills Impacts*, May 2020, <https://www.savills.com/impacts/social-change/how-to-repurpose-retail-space.html>, (accessed 9 January 2023).

7 Statista Research Department, 'Retail space per capita in selected countries worldwide in 2018', *Statista*, <https://www.statista.com/statistics/1058852/retail-space-per-capita-selected-countries-worldwide/>, 2022, (accessed 9 January 2023).

8 Philip Woolner, 'Class E town centre-to-residential permitted development right to come into effect in August, *Cheffins*, 1 April 2021, <https://www.cheffins.co.uk/about/news/view.class-e-town-centretoresidential-permitted-development-right-to-come-into-e_691.htm>, (accessed 12 January 2023).

9 Zoe Wood, 'Beales to close 12 of its 23 department stores', *The Guardian*, 7 Feb. 2020, <https://www.theguardian.com/business/2020/feb/07/beales-to-close-12-of-its-23-department-stores>, (accessed 11 January 2023).

10 Peter Brett Associates, *Town Centre Investment Zones: Getting investment back into the high street*, British Property Federation, 2016.

11 KPMG, *Hope for the High Street: A new model for delivering change*, KPMG, 2016.

INDEX

Note: page numbers in italics refer to illustrations.

IMAGE CREDITS